Rural and Tribal Communities in India

RURAL AND TRIBAL COMMUNITIES IN INDIA

K. Narendra Mohan

CENTRUM PRESS
NEW DELHI-110002 (INDIA)

CENTRUM PRESS
H.O.: 4360/4, Ansari Road, Daryaganj,
New Delhi-110002 (India)
Tel: 23278000, 23261597, 23255577, 23286875
B.O.: No. 1015, Ist Main Road, BSK IIIrd Stage,
IIIrd Phase, IIIrd Block, Bengaluru-560085 (INDIA)
Tel: 080-41723429
Email: centrumpress@gmail.com
Visit us at: www.centrumpress.com

Rural and Tribal Communities in India

First Edition, 2012

ISBN 978-93-81293-60-7

PRINTED IN INDIA

Printed at Tarun Offset, Delhi

Contents

Preface

The tribes of India are mainly concentrated in the rural areas or near the forested areas in the country. The tribes were initially very illiterate and backward and were one of the neglected sections in the country. However, the Government of India has made concerted efforts to enhance the standard of living and the overall condition of these tribes. The government is trying to educate these tribes without destroying their culture or traditions. Though, the tribal culture seems very backward and strange, some of the tribal traditions are based on scientific rules and modern principles. The tribes of India continue to be an interesting facet that attracts art lovers and researchers from far off nations. The leading tribes include the Bhils, the Gonds, Khasi, Mishing, Santal, Thakar, Nagas, Mizo and such other numerous tribes. The Bhils are one of the largest tribes in India and are spread over an extensive area in the country. The Bhils mainly inhabit central and western India, Gujarat, Maharashtra, Madhya Pradesh and Rajasthan. However, the tribe is also found to some extent in the northeastern state of Tripura. During the medieval and the British ages, the Bhils were a part of the royal armies and were well known for their bravery and fighting spirit. Apart from the Bhils, yet another important tribe in India is the Gond tribe. The Gonds are also spread extensively over central India. The areas dominated by the Gonds include Madhya Pradesh, eastern Maharashtra, Chhattisgarh and northern Andhra Pradesh. The Gonds are pre-dominantly agriculturists and mainly practice shifting cultivation. The Gonds mainly speak dialects based on the Dravidian languages.

Tribals underwent a change not only in their relationship with land but also in their relationship with forests. Tribes were greatly dependent on forest for their day-to-day needs, including food, shelter, instruments, medicine, and in some cases even clothes. As long as the tribes were in control of forest and unrestricted use of its produce, they had no difficulty meeting these needs. In turn they preserved the forest as it was their life support system. As said before, it was the entry of British that drastically altered this relationship. To British, the forest were an important source of revenue and profit, hence their forest policy in traduced state control over forest resources and imposed the curtailment of rights and privileges over them. This policy was continued in post-Independence era of economic development with even stricter regulation and enforcement.

A majority of the rural population in India lives on agriculture and linked occupations in the rural areas. Though, agriculture has been the primary occupation of rural people in India since the ancient period, the scenario is changing day by day. Many Indian villagers have engaged themselves in various non-agricultural occupations in the recent years. There is also a common trend among the Indian villagers to migrate to the urban areas to work as labourers or get into alternate professions. The literacy rate among the rural population in India has also increased significantly in the recent years. The current literacy rate in the Indian rural areas is as high as 65%, which is quite impressive. The rural population in India provides the real picture of the Indian society. However, the Indian villagers face a lot of difficulties like poverty in their daily life. The authorities have taken many initiatives to improve the quality of life of the rural population in India, in the recent years.

This book elaborately discusses all relevant issues in comprehensive way of Rural and Tribal Communities and the subject matter in a concise and an intelligible form, keeping in view the needs of the average student, researcher and teacher. This book will be of interest to all those who work in development and who have a particular concern for minorities, indigenous peoples and culturally marginalised groups.

—*Editor*

1

The Tribal of India

Many anthropologists have tried to define a tribe but with little success. The term tribe has not been defined in the constitution of India. The term tribe does not mean a backward or uncivilized people of India. And they are not backward Hindus because their religion is different from Hinduism but they are integral part of the Indian civilization. The best way to understand the term tribe is to know the socio-cultural and religious significance of the tribal people.

Definitions of the Term Tribes

According to Sachchidananda, an eminent anthropologist defines a tribal, "it has been generally held that geographical isolation, economic backwardness, a distinctive language and religion are the main distinguishing characteristics of Indian tribe". Henry H. Presler, a missionary in India working for several years, did good research on tribal people and wrote a book that entitled Primitive Religions of India. To him, Tribe means a state of mind and society, characterized by isolation, homogeneity, sacredness, illiteracy and simplicity.

The tribal in India are called different names in different places. Some of popular name are Vanya-jati {castes of forest} Vanvasi {inhabitants of forest} Pahari {hill dwellers} Adim-jati{ original communities} Jan-jati { folk people} Adimijati { original castes} But it is very important to note that most of these names are Hindi language and given by non-tribals. However, each tribe is identified by its own name, such as the santals, Bhils and Mundas etc.

A tribe is not necessarily a people who are uncivilized backward, illiterate, primitive, or with territorial interest. But a tribe is;

1. An indigenous and homogenous unit and a people who claims a common ancestry.
2. A tribe is a people group which follow a indigenous (ethnic) religion, unaffected by organized religions, particularly of Hinduism.
3. A social group with territorial affiliation, people live in a particular geographical area.
4. A people who are united by a common language.
5. A people who follow their traditions and customs which they consider as sacred.
6. A people who have simplicity of mind and life.
7. A people who follow oral traditions
8. A people with simple social and political organization.
9. A people whose society is characterized by a strong group consciousness and communal solidarity.

The Basic Characteristics of the Tribals;

1. They are simple and truthful
2. They are hard working and industrious
3. They are community conscious.
4. They are self-reliant-they help themselves
5. They identified themselves with their land
6. They are conservative in regard to change.

The tribes in India can be classified into two kinds. First, Normal Tribes whose occupations did not consist of criminal activities though they occasionally did commit crime. These are called scheduled tribes under the India constitution. Second, Criminal tribes are ethnic groups said to have been living by criminal means though they occasionally abstain from committing criminal activities.

These criminal tribe are classified into two groups. Those that wander about like gypsies and those settled in villages. Some six million (60 Lakhs) people of this kind are found in the Indian sub-continent.

TRIBAL CONCENTRATION

The tribal people in India are identified with their geographical concentration. Therefore land is the key to tribal identity.

The tribal can not be separated from their homeland. To understand the tribal identity we have to study their geographical concentration. The tribal in India are concentrated in five main natural groups which are based on ecological, social, economic, administrative, ethnic and racial factors.

Himalayan Region

Several tribal groups are living in Northern and North-Eastern India which consists 12 % of the total tribal population. The tribes include the Nagas, Khasis, Garos, Mishmis, Limbus, Lepchas, daflas, abors, Mikirs, and kukiLushais.

Central India Region

This includes the plateaus and mountain belts, north of the krishna river and south of Indo-Gangetic basin. This is the largest tribal region which cover several states such as Madhya Pradesh, Orissia, Bihar, West Bengal and some part of Maharashtra. The main tribes are Juangs, Kharias, Hos, Santals, Gonds, Mundas, Oraons, Birhors, Bhuiyas, Saoras, Baigas, and Kols. Over 50 % of total tribe population is represented by this region.

Southern Region

This region covers South Western India, in the hills and the converging lines of the Ghats, south of Krishna river. This region covers all the four southern states. Kerala, Tamil Nadu, Karnataka, and Andhra Pradesh. The tribes who live in this region are Todas, Paniyans, Kurumbas, Kotas, Sholigas, Kadars, Kanikkars, Muthuvans, Mannans, Uralis, Malapantarams, Koyas, Yenadis, Chenchus, Irulas, etc... and about 6 % of the tribal population live in this region.

Western India region

This region covers the Aravlli hills and kandesh region, stretching from south Rajasthan to Gujarat, Madhya Pradesh to western Maharashtra. The tribes such as Kukana, dhodia,

Varli, Vassavi and Choudhri found in this region. It consists about 26 % of the tribal population of the India.

Islands Region

This region includes the Andaman & Nicobar and Lakshaweep Islands. The majority of people in this region are tribal.

The Religion of Indian Tribals

Indigenous and close to the Christan faith. Most of the tribal in India have their own religion. It is part of their tribal life and is identified with their religion, such as Santal religion, Kukna religion, etc. The tribal religion is defined as animism. It means belief in spirit world. It can not be defined as Hindusim. Some tribal have been converted into Hinduism and this process of conversion is called sanskritization. In spite of this, most of the tribal still practice their traditional faiths.

Tribal Religion Definitions

Tribal religion is known by various names. The common name by which it is known is Animism. Edward Tylor who first introduced the term animism". It defines " belief in supernatural beings and powers. It is the deep lying doctrine of spiritual beings, which embodies the very essence of spiritualistic as opposed to materialistic. Another name used is "animatism" that is belief in impersonal power. There are also other names such as spirit ism, ancestor worship and fetishism used to explain the tribal religions.

The Tribal Religion Focus

First, focused towards GOD-the Supreme Being. All ritual sacrifices and festivals are observed to direct their piety towards the unknown supreme GOD in whose existence they have firm belief. Second, focused towards the tribe-the people. They believe in the institution of tribe and hence they would do anything to preserve and protect the unity and integrity of the tribe. Third, focused towards the ancestors-the spirit. Tribal believe in the existence of the spirit of their ancestors. These spirit stay at home, in the houses of their descendants, and supervise their welfare.

The Beliefs of Tribal Religions

1. Belief in Supreme Being
2. Belief in spirit world
3. Belief in supernatural power
4. Belief in magic and witchcraft
5. Belief in blood sacrifice.

Belief In A Supreme God and in his Creation

Apart form their own gods and goddesses the tribal also have faith in a supreme being-the GOD who is above all gods and goddess whom they consider as the God who created the world. For example, the" singh bonga"(meaning great spirit) is the supreme, benevolent, perfect, transcendent creator of Munda Dharma, the religion of Munda triabal.

The Kui dharma of Orissa (religion of Kui tribal) has the supreme creator, Tana Penu..The saoras, a triabl group in Orissia, India, believe that Kittun is the creator of the earth and man. The tribal believe that the supreme God created the world and that human beings are fallen in sin. Even though the salvation aspect is not clear they believe that the creator God has made some provisions which they have to appropriate by worship or sacrifices. Some these beliefs are very similar to biblical record.

Belief in the Spirit World

The spirit world is real for the tribe. They believe in a variety of spirits which inhabit their houses, villages as well as stones, trees and mountains. They believe in four kinds of spirits and each other is different from other. First, the great spirit or pure spirit. He is the creator God and he is worshipped by sacrifices. His character is similar to the GOD of the bible. The Sarma Dharma, tribal religion, express the concept when addressing him in sacrifice " you do not crave for our food or thirst for our drink"

Second, the spirit of the ancestors. Tribal believe that their ancestors still living among them in spirits and that they are interest in their daily life and welfare. Therefore they are worshipped at the time of special day and festivals. Some of them are trouble-making spirit and therefore they have to be contended and appeased by rites and rituals.

Third, the spirits of those who have died outside the tribe. They are the people who have missed their destiny and therefore they roam around in the wild, trying to harase people. These spirit have to be dealt with by ritual, magic and witchcraft.

Four, the spirit of those who are out sides and intruders. They are the enemies of the tribe. They are the Dikus (means out siders) These spirit have to be cast out from the village.

Belief in Supernatural Power

The tribal people believe in the prevalence of spiritual and supernatural power, known as mana, which means spiritual power, that inhabits stones, plants, trees, and animals. This spiritual power is an impersonal, mysterious life force which pervades every thing and transcends all the known forces of nature. This power can be controlled by means of magic. To them mana can be gained by rituals, rites, divination or blood sacrifice.

Belief in Witchcraft and Magic

Belief in the spirit world leads the tribal to believing witchcraft, magic, sorcery, etc. The Shaman, Bhagat or the Witch Doctor is an important and powerful person in any tribal society. He is a religious expert, a native medical doctor as well as a magican. He practices both white magic to help and heal the people and black magic to harm and kill them. People are afraid of witches and witch doctors but people need particularly the shaman. The religious life of the entire tribal society is dependent upon the shaman.

Tribes in India have their religions. Their religions part of their life. As the people are indigenous their religion also in indigenous. In spite of the influence of other religions, the tribals in India still adhere to their own faiths. The beliefs and practices of tribal religions are very close to the Christian faith. Particularly, their view of a supreme being is very similar to the teaching of the Bible on GOD. For these reason, in the past, several thousands of them have identified themselves with the Christian faith. Also today tribals of India are most responsive people to the gospel. Hence, they must be reached without delay.

IMPACT OF INDUSTRIALIZATION ON TRIBALS IN INDIA

The Constitution of India does not define Scheduled Tribes as such. According to Article 342 of the Constitution, the Scheduled Tribes are the tribes or tribal communities or part of or groups within these tribes and tribal communities which have been declared as such by the President through a public notification. As per the 1991 Census, the Scheduled Tribes account for 67.76 million representing 8.08 percent of the country's population. Scheduled Tribes are spread across the country mainly in forest and hilly regions.

The essential characteristics of these communities are:-

1. Primitive Traits
2. Geographical isolation
3. Distinct culture
4. Shy of contact with community at large
5. Economically backward.

Tribals in India are economically and socially very backward. More than 3/4th of Scheduled Tribes women are illiterate. They have high dropout rates in formal education, resulting in disproportionately low representation in higher education. They have very low levels of nutrition. The proportion of Scheduled Tribes below the poverty line is substantially higher than the national average. Most of the Tribals are engaged mostly in low-skilled, low-paying jobs, especially in primary sector. The Constitution of India incorporates several special provisions for the promotion of educational and economic interest of Scheduled Tribes and their protection from social injustice and all forms of exploitation.

Pre-independence Features

Subjugation and exploitation of Tribals is something not new, only the scale and rate at which it has taken place in 18th century onwards is unprecedented. Tribals have always lived in a condition of economic autarky, marked by common ownership of land & forest resources. Tribals were always seen as backward and different from mainstream, and who were to be incorporated into mainstream. So, historically, they have either adopted or were subjugated and mainstream cultural, social, political, religious, economic structures and practices imposed upon them. Earlier tribal societies had a hierarchy of clans, lineages or even villages. But, with the incorporation of the tribes and tribal communities in the larger political system, the basis of inequality in forms other than rank (position) and status began in tribal societies. The alien rulers claimed sovereignty over tribal territory and collected revenue from tribal cultivators through tributaries/zamindars who were often outsiders and sometimes included tribal chiefs whose power increased.

Tribal village councils were superseded by the council of the chiefs/rajas that often comprised of the king's followers and friends. Grants of customary rights over villages were made to such followers. Thus the jagirdaari system or the system of service grants was introduced in tribal areas. Privatization of land during British era led to a flow of capital and penetration by market opened the gates for influx of non-Tribals especially moneylenders and traders into tribal areas. This opened up the way for large scale alienation of land from tribes to non tribes, especially after tribal areas came to be linked by roads and railways.

The mechanism through which this was achieved was fraud, deceit, coercion, and most often debt bondage. This reduced tribal cultivators to the position of tenants, landless labourers, and bondsmen. Thus three-tier agrarian categories emerged in tribal areas, namely, feudatory chief's/zamindars, well-to-do peasants that included a section of Tribals especially village headsmen, and a very large section of small and poor cultivators and landless labourers who were mainly Tribals.

Post-Independence period saw the introduction of various land reform measures as well as measures specially meant for the protection and welfare of tribal people. This succeeded in restricting the transfer of land from Tribals to non-Tribals and also promoted a rich stratum of buyers from among Tribals paving the way for differentiation within tribal society.

Consequently Tribals have now been differentiated into categories such as rich, middle and poor besides the landless. Such differentiation has given rise to a type of class relations that was traditionally absent within tribal societies.

Much of the forested land was declared as government land after survey and settlement. Earlier, Tribals only had to part with a portion of their produce and land belonged to them, but once the land was declared as belonging to Government in British era, the Tribals were declared encroachers upon the very land that they had lived on for centuries. In most cases, as tribal land was commonly owned it never had a owner which government can recognise. Claims of tribes over vast tracts of land were dismissed. Trees and Forests became government property who was now free to exploit them.

The dispossession of Tribals from their land and restriction of control over forest and forest produce that occurred during the colonial period pushed tribal people into the wider labour market. They were compelled to find employment as labourers in nearby quarries, coalfields and emerging towns. One of the most important sectors that Tribals moved en masse was the plantation sector that opened up in Bengal and Assam.

They have also been affected by two more sectors of modern economy-industry and mines. Work in these sectors is divided into various types and grades depending upon skill and knowledge required for work. Not used to work other than cultivation and not being in possession of modern skills and knowledge a very large majority could secure only lowest paid jobs. The entry into white collar occupation has been very difficult.

Post-independence

After Independence, it was thought that Tribes are backward due to their isolation from the mainstream and assimilation with mainstream is the only way for their development.

The different measures taken up for their upliftment are usually divided into three categories

1. Protective: include constitutional and legislative rights that safeguard their interests.

2. Mobilizational: reservations extended to Tribals in various fields.
3. Developmental: programmes and activities initiated for promoting their welfare.

These goals were to be pursued under a kind of administration that was infused with principles of Panchsheela i.e. to let people develop along the lines of their own genius and avoid imposing anything on them and to encourage their traditional arts and culture, their lands and forests to be respected, they be allowed to administer themselves and avoid influx of too many outsiders into tribal territory in the name of administration, not too overwhelm them with schemes and work in cooperation with their own social and cultural institutions, to judge the results by actual level of human character developed. Taking lessons from the effects of European civilization on tribal population in other parts of the world especially in America and Africa, where traditional tribal ways of living and their culture was destroyed, it was cautioned that the ' Indian Civilization' should not have any disastrous consequences on its Tribals. The developmental programmes were to be initiated keeping tribunals in mind and they were to have the final say. Also their traditional rights over forests and land and other resources were to be respected.

Tribals V/S Development

Yet the approach adopted toward tribes has been quite the contrary mainly due to imperatives of national development. Measures undertaken for bringing about the rapid national development were seen as an important mechanism for the integration of tribal society into the national polity. The national objective to build productive structures for future growth and resource mobilization for development was given far more importance than issues concerning the welfare of the tribes and interests of the later were invariably sacrificed in the name of former activities such as building infrastructure, setting up industries and constructing dams for irrigation and power projects for electricity and light included extraction and exploitation of mineral and forest resources a substantial part of these projects were initiated in the areas inhabited by Tribals as these areas happen to be rich reservoirs of mineral and forest resources. This led to an inevitable conflict between tribal and national interests.

These developmental policies drastically altered the relationship of tribes with the natural environment and resources lying therein. Earlier these resources were either individually or collectively owned. But due to policies of state, as aforementioned, there has been a steady erosion of control and use of these resources by Tribals. Tribals were most drastically affected by the exploitation of land and forest. But major source of land alienation, post independence, has been the process of development that the Indian state has followed. Large scale industrialization and exploitation of mineral resources and construction of irrigation dams and power projects that the tribal areas have seen during the period have been responsible for uprooting Tribals on a far larger scale than the transfer of land from tribunals to non Tribals on an individual basis.

Social Consequences of Development

Tribals underwent a change not only in their relationship with land but also in their relationship with forests. Tribes were greatly dependent on forest for their day-to-day needs, including food, shelter, instruments, medicine, and in some cases even clothes. As long as the tribes were in control of forest and unrestricted use of its produce, they had no difficulty meeting these needs. In turn they preserved the forest as it was their life support system. As said before, it was the entry of British that drastically altered this relationship. To British, the forest were an important source of revenue and profit, hence their forest policy in traduced state control over forest resources and imposed the curtailment of rights and privileges over them. This policy was continued in post-Independence era of economic development with even stricter regulation and enforcement.

These policies also lead to environmental degradation as total forest cover went down from 40% in 1950's to just 10% in 1980's. Tribal areas in India have also seen an influx of people from outside in search of employment in industry, mines, railways, government, and ancillary activities that followed as corollary to former activities. These activities have given rise to increasing urbanization of tribal areas but also have caused large scale migration of non-Tribals into tribal territory depriving Tribals of fruits of development in tribal areas. In Jharkhand out of total urban population of the region only 17% are SC's and ST's.

This development process has been of little use to the tribal population. Rather, development of tribal areas has had a deleterious effect on Tribals. The industries and other development projects that have come up have not made jobs available to them. The benefits arising out of power and irrigation projects have not reached the Tribals. There are fewer tribal villages that find electrification and the tribal land under irrigation is almost negligible. By March 2001 only 25% of villages in Jharkhand were electrified and only 18% of total area was under irrigation. In, short the fruits of development have not gone to Tribals but to people from outside. They find themselves increasingly subjected to exploitation and oppression. The movement of population from outside threw tribes open to vagaries of greed, exploitation, and even oppression. The result was that the tribes found themselves uprooted from their lands and resources on a scale unprecedented in history and were forced to move out of their homelands for survival.

This phenomenon of 'resource curse' is not unique to India. In most nations of the world a high level of mineral dependence is associated with retarded economic performance. World Bank attributes institutional weakness and political economy as some of the reasons behind the resource curse. Resource rich countries exhibit weaker institutions compared to resource-poor countries. Mineral rich states have weaker property rights and poor enforcement of law and these lead to retarded development outcomes. In India also mineral dependence has led to poorer quality institutions which in turn result in impaired growth and development outcomes. Point resources-resources extracted from a narrow geographical base-weaken institutions and accountability. In the case of a country with all of its wealth concentrated in a few pockets most of the political and administrative power goes into promoting and facilitating extraction of these resources instead of focusing on the development of area.

Resource curse is very much a reality in mineral rich areas of India. Of the 50 major mining districts, 60% figure among the 150 most backward districts of the country. Poverty and lack of development extract a terrible price. And one of them has been the rise of Naxalism. Tribals now see no other option but to embrace Naxalism in the present model of development, where forceful acquisition of land and displacement of thousands by State are order of the day.

Naxalism began as a peasant movement in 1967 in tiny hamlet of Naxalbari in West Bengal. The fundamental demand was a radical land reform-land to tiller-and a violent takeover of power was seen as only means of achieving this. Governments then were completely unwilling (as they are even now) to yield to these demands and the movement was brutally crushed. Naxalism then capitalised on the tribal angst against the development model being followed by the state. Tribals saw this as an opportunity to escape out of the poverty, displacement and deprivement of lands being forced upon them by successive governments.

Militants have used various tactics to oppose industrial investment. This involves destroying government infrastructure, private machinery, roads, bridges, railway tracks, electric lines, and other industrial infrastructure. This is done under the pretext of 'protecting the tribal homeland by cutting it off from the reach of oppressors'. They also resort to kidnapping of government officials and employees of private companies. The rise of Naxalism can be directly linked to a certain crisis of faith. India's marginalised populations including its Tribals can no longer trust their lives and livelihood in the hands of their government.

For them these developmental projects literally pushed down their throats by government have become synonymous with poverty and insecurity. With their backs to the wall, these communities believe they have found their way out in the violent ways of Naxals In a sense, the phenomenon of Naxalism is as much a crisis of political empowerment as it is sheer economic backwardness, as it is sadly one of the rare opportunities still available to marginalised communities to express their aspirations. A prime reason for spread of naxalism has been failure of state to provide remote areas with facilities for health and education, and prospect for dignified employment. People in these areas have had to cope with an administration that is always indifferent, often corrupt and sometimes brutal. Meanwhile economic development has been powered in good part by wood, water and minerals found on these lands and for whose profitable exploitation they have often had to make way-most of the time involuntarily.

Indian government considers Naxalism only as an 'internal security threat'. Naxalism and its supporters need to be stamped out by State's police and army in a decisive manner. It is precisely this myopic vision that is real problem. Poverty, unemployment, starvation, malnutrition, lack of access to basic necessities like health and education, forced eviction of people from their lands for 'development projects', these do not qualify as 'internal security threat', reactions to all these and resistance and protest against them do.

Current Perspectives on Development

Earlier, the failure development programmes was attributed to traditional socio-economic and cultural system of the Tribals. Hence the emphasis has invariably been on introducing values, attitudes, and institutions that would help them take advantage of fruits of developmental projects. Tribes were seen as backward, ignorant, superstitious and unable to overcome their worldview to recognize and exploit the wealth of resources present in there forest and surroundings in which they live. Of late however, it is increasingly being pointed out that development would be more effective if programmes and schemes were to be evolved in consonance with the ecology, social organization, and cultural values of Tribals. Various experience shave proved that vastly different strategy is required if governments are really keen to solve the problem. The first step is unambiguous acceptance that development policies have failed vast majorities in country. Second is an understanding of basic reasons behind the failure of development policies. And third is to institutionalise the alternative policies.

The issue at forefront today is development but without or with minimal cost to ecology and environment. From this perspective now tribes are seen as representing a storehouse of world-views, systems of knowledge, and ways of life which stands separate from and opposed to the ones governing the modern, industrial world. The tribal communities then stand as the other in whom a search for an alternative is postulated. Now the emphasis is being laid increasingly on the need for conservation. There is also an increasing realisation that conservation is not possible without the participation of rural and tribal communities.

THE TRADITIONAL TRIBAL CULTURE OF LAND USE

The traditional tribal systems are based on the concept of nature in general and land in particular as community sustenance that has come down from the ancestors and has to be preserved for posterity. Because of this close link between the identity of their community and land and other natural resources, they have for centuries managed the resources according to their unwritten customary laws that treat them as renewable. The community that was the legitimising factor in their land use and management systems, built a culture and an economy based on their sustainable use. Land, in this system was a resource which is an asset that is meant to be used according need but not destroyed or exploited for profit.

The tribal traditions of land use in India, in the Northeast in particular, were based on a culture that had three main traits. The first is the sustainable or renewable use of their resource composed of forests, land and water sources that were also their sustenance. Basic to them being renewable was CPRs and community ownership. They did not reject individual ownership completely but combined it with community control. In the Northeast, for example, some like the CPR dependent Aka tribe of Arunachal Pradesh lacked the very concept of individual ownership and had only usufruct rights over the CPRs. In the *jhum* season every family cultivated as much land as it required for its sustenance. After the harvest or the three-year cycle that plot reverted to the community. Others like the Angami of Nagaland combined individual with clan and village ownership but all of it was within a community ethos. A family managed its assets according to the tribe's community-based customary law.

In these as well as other tribes, the community included not merely the present but also the past and the future generations. That goes with the second feature of the resource being renewable. That too is linked to the community. The belief that guided the resource management for a renewable sustenance was that it had been handed over to them by their ancestors. They had, therefore, to be used according to present needs and environmental imperatives and preserved for posterity. That belief itself emanated from the basic principle of sharing and intra and inter-generational equity. Within each generation, their customary law ensured that every family had enough to eat according to its need. The Aka custom of land reverting to the community after using it for *jhum* is one of its examples. Such control ensured that the resource was used according to need and preserved for posterity. That was inter-generational equity. The third feature is the relatively high status of tribal women compared to that of women in caste societies. That too is true more of the Northeast than of other regions. However, while attributing a relatively high status to them no tribe treated women as equal to men. The relatively high status too is based on CPR management. As long the resource is community owned, women exercise partial control over it because of the gender-based division of power between the family and social spheres.

In most tribes, the village council, made up of men alone controls the resource and political power. In most tribal traditions, the woman was in charge of the family and controlled its economy and production. The man represented the family in his society. In matrilineal tribes both descent and inheritance are through the woman but their tribe too is patriarchal and man controls society (Nongkynrih fortcoming).

The working of all these principles is visible in the tribal land ownership and management systems, especially in *jhum* cultivation on which some 25 percent of the tribals in India as a whole and 90 percent in the Northeast sustain themselves. Equity is seen in its decision-making process. Traditionally the village council decided which plot to cultivate in a given year, determined the amount of land to be allotted to each family according to the number of mouths to feed and decided which family with an excess of adults would assist which one with a deficit of workers. After it the man of the house chose the plot his family would cultivate and performed religious rites to mark the beginning of *jhum*. At this stage the woman took charge of cultivation and organised work. As a result, the division of work was more gender friendly in *jhum* than in settled agriculture.

The technology used and the spacing of various crops ensured that land was preserved for the future generations. *Jhum* was practised on slopes of up to 20-degree gradient. To ensure soil preservation, no plough was allowed to be used on it. Only a hoe could be used. The crops planted were spaced. Before the rains began they sowed root crops that protected the soil on the slopes. They sowed paddy and other crops after the rains began. Weeding too was graded. Some weeds that could preserve soil were left behind. Because of spacing in sowing crops, food was available from October to March since also harvesting was spaced. After March summer fruits became available.

Individual Ownership and Settled Agriculture

Basic to the "modern" or formal system is individual property. This system is closer to the caste society based settled agriculture of the past than to the tribal *jhum* or other cultivation. The caste society did keep a community dimension but without equity that is basic to the CPR-based tribal sustenance. One caste owned the land in the village and the rest were service castes that rendered services as priests or barbers, agricultural workers and in other forms. In reality the leaders divided land between various families and each service caste family was attached to a family from the land owning caste. After the harvest the land owning family distributed grains to the service caste families, the quantity depending on its social status. There was similar discrimination in water management too. Men from the land owning caste controlled water and ensured equitable distribution among themselves with focus on irrigation for agriculture. So their water management system paid very little attention to subaltern needs or to drinking water that was the woman's domain.

But unlike in the tribal societies that maintain a separation between the family and society, in settled agriculture that is practised by the caste society, the man controls both the family and social spheres. He owns land, takes decisions on what crops to grow and determines the division of work. Men do work like ploughing that is considered difficult and allot to women tasks that involve standing in wet fields and bending for a long time. In that sense its division of work comes nowhere near the tribal shifting cultivation system in which the woman has decision-making power because of her partial control over the CPRs. Because she is in charge of family production division or labour in this system is somewhat gender-friendly.

However, there were some commonalities too and many differences between the caste-based and tribal systems. Both of them belonged to the informal society. But the caste-based system had some written documents particularly when a king gifted land to a community, a temple or an individual. But village land was managed by the caste that owned it, by and large based on the word of mouth. This caste can be called a community in a broad sense but it was not based on equity that governed tribal sustenance. Both the caste and the tribal land management systems accorded the central role of ownership to men but the former added the role of the caste and reflected the supremacy of the king who could gift land as he desired. That too negated equity that the tribes practised. The caste-related system also had some systems of sharing the CPRs such as the water resources and grazing grounds that belonged to many families but this sharing was linked to agriculture, not to equity.

Gender equity is one more difference between these systems. As stated above the tribal woman had a relatively high status. The man was in control of the resource and had social power while the woman was in charge of production. Since she controlled family production the division of work reflected some gender equity. Her control over the family economy turned her into an econømic asset and provided the basis for her relatively high social status. In the caste-based societies, on the contrary, the man was in charge the resource as well as of production and controlled both the family and society. Thus her subordinate status both in the economy and in her society resulted in the caste woman being accorded a lower social status.

These two systems were thus based on two contradictory sets of principles that can also be called their cultures. Both were based on communities. But the tribal system depended on an inclusive and equitable community while the caste community was exclusive and was founded on a caste and gender-based hierarchy. Power was concentrated in the hands of men from one caste while in the tribes it belonged to men of the whole tribe with some share, though not equitable, accorded to women in the form of control over family production. Both organised their land use system around the concept of sustenance. But the tribes perceived land as the sustenance of the whole community while the caste societies arranged it around the power of men from one caste. The remaining castes had to depend on the land-owning caste. In that sense, this system ensured the material sustenance of all the castes without society equality.

TRANSITION TO THE FORMAL SYSTEM

Both the systems made a transition to a formal status in the colonial age but with different power equation. The formal or "modern" legal system is based on individual property and the written word and is founded on the principle of the State's eminent domain. In this view land is only a commodity for cultivation and construction. This ideology of the formal law ignores the view of land as people's sustenance or part of an ecosystem with the local community at its centre and imposes its own outlook on people's communities. This view became prevalent in the 19th century when the colonial regime enacted land laws to suit its need of exploiting the resources of South Asia to the benefit of the British Indus-trial Revolution. Though legitimised in the name of the civilising mission of Europe, the objective of colonialism was to change the economy of the colony and turn it into a supplier of capital and raw material and a captive market for the finished products of the :Industrial Revolution.

Basic to achieving the objective was monopoly over land for schemes like railways, roads, coalmines and plantations. That required laws meant to turn people's livelihood into a commodity and facilitate land transfer to the profit of the capitalist owners. The process began with the *Permanent Settlement 1793* meant to ensure capital flow through land tax, continued in the laws of the 19th century and culminated in the *Land Acquisition Act 1894*. Through these laws the regime took over power to acquire land to suit its needs. These laws that continue to be in force today, authorise the state to acquire individual land without the owner's consent and pay some compensation. It can appropriate the CPRs without recognising them as the sustenance of their dependants. To these laws should be added others on biodiversity and forests that too were for centuries the sustenance of the "ecosystem people". But the laws turned them into state property. Their dependent communities came to be considered encroachers in their own habitat and were deprived of their rights over the resource. That created a disjunction between them and their sustenance.

The principle on which these laws are based is called eminent domain in the USA and *terra nullius* in Australia. White colonisation of native land in Australia, New Zealand, southern Africa and the Americas was based on this principle that land without an individual title belonged to none, so anyone could occupy it. In 1992 the Australian judiciary declared some land takeover under it unconstitutional but India continues to base its laws on its American version. Its first facet is that land without an individual title is state property and the second is that the State alone has the overriding power to define a public purpose and deprive even individuals of their assets in its name.

LAND ALIENATION AND IMPOVERISHMENT

This changeover came without the involvement of the "ecosystem people" and with no preparation to join the formal society. The colonial state imposed the land laws based on this worldview on the traditional communities. This imposition affected the dominant castes as well as the tribal communities. But many of the former had access to education and other modern inputs. So they had some preparation to deal with the changes. Most traditional tribes, on the contrary, lived on mineral and forest rich land that the colonialist required as raw materials. That turned the imposition of the formal system on the informal societies into an unequal encounter. Land alienation from the traditional to "modern" communities was a consequences since the latter were unable to deal with the changes imposed on them.

This unequal encounter continues to be the basis of a disjunction and of conflicts between the two systems because the colonial laws continue to be in force in the country. One of its consequences is environmental degradation. The legal system that recognises only individual ownership is a major cause of land loss and environmental degradation. Since the CPRS are not recognised as their sustenance, the communities depending on them cannot prevent outsiders from encroaching on that land. For example, in Tripura in North Eastern India, the tribal proportion has declined from 58 percent in 1951 to 31 percent in 2001 because immigrants have encroached on 60 percent of their community owned land with the help of individual-based laws. Equally important is loss of forests which catered to many needs of the tribal and other rural poor communities. The state handed many of them over to industry as raw material. They were treated as sources of profit and destroyed with no concern for their dependants or for conservation. That impoverished people.

The third source of land loss is acquisition for development projects. The law that empowers the state to acquire land recognises only individual ownership. More than 25 million hectares have been used in India for such projects 1947-2000, around 14 million of them forest and other CPRs. Their inhabitants, most of them tribal and other rural poor like fish and quarry workers are considered encroachers and are not compensated and often not even counted among the displaced. Often records of the CPRs are not kept since they are considered state property and their inhabitants are encroachers. For example, according to official accounts, in Assam the state used 159,017.37 hectares of land for development projects and displaced 343,262 persons from them 1947–2000. The reality is 1.9 million persons displaced from 567,281.29 hectares. More than 1.5 millions displaced persons and 410,261 hectares were not counted because according to the law these CPRs are state property and their inhabitants are encroachers with no right to live there.

The Vicious Circle

One can mention many other modes of land alienation. The above examples are given only to show the processes that lead to alienation of the people's livelihood. Because of the unequal nature of the encounter, also the reaction of these systems to the problems that the process causes differs. That too is based on their worldview on land and the natural resources all of whose dependants feel the negative impact of the transition from the traditional to the modern economy and new values. But the rural poor, particularly the tribes and other forest dwellers feel its impact more than the remaining groups do because it is an attack on their tradition of judicious use of resources and on the systems they had developed to manage land, forests and CPRs as their renewable sustenance.

Loss of their sustenance begins the vicious circle of impoverishment that forces the dependants of these resources to overexploit them and cause further environmental degradation and more poverty. As the former Brazilian President Fernando Henrique Cardoso (1998) said, the first danger to the environment from people's impoverishment is loss of biodiversity and linked to it, loss of the values through which the communities depending on it had managed the resource as renewable. Studies show that loss of this value system or ideology is basic to the vicious circle that leads to further environmental degradation. But reaction to this process differs according to the class one belongs to and one's ideology or culture. To the urban middle class land alienation and environmental degradation are loss of their recreational spaces while to the rural, particularly tribal, communities it results in loss of their livelihood and consequent impoverishment from which follows further land alienation and destruction of more natural resources. Conflicts are a natural consequence of this contradiction.

The first step of this process is impoverishment of the economic status they are reduced to by the alienation of their sustenance. It begins with landlessness. Then comes joblessness. For example, studies of families displaced by development projects show that in Andhra Pradesh in South India, the proportion of the landless rose from 10.9 per cent before the project to 36.5 per cent after it and in Assam in the Northeast from 15.56 to 24.38 per cent. Even among those who retain land, the average area owned declined, for example in Assam from 1.2 to 0.6 hectares per family. In every state most small and marginal farmers became landless, and medium farmers joined the ranks of small and marginal farmers. They also witnessed a decline in the support mechanisms such as the number of irrigation ponds and wells, poultry, cattle, and draught animals that used to supplement their agricultural income declined.

Joblessness is the next step. The land and other resources that are alienated from them used to provide them work. They lose this resource with no alternative to take its place. Joblessness resulting from it takes two forms. The first is lower access to work and the second is downward occupational mobility. In Andhra Pradesh, for example, 83.72 per cent of the land losers used to work on their land or elsewhere before its loss. After land loss access to work declined to 41.61 per cent. In West Bengal it declined from 91.02 to 53.18 percent and in Assam from 77.27 to 56.41 percent. The second is downward occupational mobility. In most states, more than 50 percent of the land losers who were cultivators before it became landless agricultural labourers or daily wage earners after land loss.

Also displacement can continue as a result of environmental degradation. For example, a new industry often forces people to move out of its neighbourood because after its construction environmental or other consequences such as fly ash and dust generated by the thermal, aluminium, nuclear, cement and other plants destroy the land around it and render it unusable.

Its dependants cannot sustain themselves on it and are forced to move out. Also the noise and dust pollution and constant blasts in the coalmines often force people to leave their homes.

Absorbing a New Culture

The changes do not remain external but enter the community itself through the internalisation of the dominant culture. The major change is the culture the community in general and its elite in particular internalise, of viewing their sustenance as commodity alone. It is seen firstly in the demand the leaders make that individual ownership become the norm in their communities. For example, in the Garo tribe of East Garo in Meghalaya in Northeast India the leaders accepted the culture of individual ownership in the 1980s. A study two decades later shows that 30 percent of the tribal families in this district had become landless since their elite had monopolised much of their land.

These changes also have gender implications. As stated above, even the matrilineal societies are patriarchal. Their leaders absorbs the culture of greater patriarchy and express it in their land relations. That can be seen among the Garo who are a matrilineal tribe but individual ownership is through men. Among the Khasi of Megalaya who too are a matrilineal tribe, the male leaders who control the village council exploit their power to their own advantage and turn community-owned land into their private property. Such change of gender attitudes is seen in other tribes too in the manner in which men interpret their customary law and property relations in their own favour.

Communities thus deprived of their resources absorb the same culture in another form. The first is the vicious circle of viewing their resources as a commodity alone. Once they are deprived of their resource and are impoverished, for sheer survival they overexploit the same resource for an income. For example, studies in all the tribal areas show that once they lose their land, the deprived families fall back on their forests that they had preserved for centuries and cut trees for sale as firewood or timber, and cause more deforestation.

The second to view their own bodies as a commodity. For example, 49 percent of the families displaced by development projects in West Bengal and 56 percent in Assam pulled their children out of school in order to turn them into child labourers. Women began to view their bodies only as a source of income. Because of it prostitution grew enormously among the families that had lost their land. All these instances point to a major change in subaltern culture. These communities lose hope in their future and think only of the present. As a result, children who are an asset for the future become commodities only for the present and are used as a source of income for survival. The same is the view of women's bodies. In other words, women and children become commodities more than men do. This book which is an overview of the changes in land relations, has shown the new culture that grown as their result. It shows that imposition of another culture on a traditional group can result in a culture that is destructive of a community in general and of women in particular. The solution is not either going back to their tradition by opposing modernisation or absolutising the modern system. One cannot prevent all individual ownership either. One has to find an alternative in beginning with the tradition community values and combining them with the traditional community. Tradition has to be modernised and not replaced completely.

2

Characteristics of Indian Tribes

Mandelbaum mentions the following characteristics of Indian tribes:-

- Kinship as an instrument of social bonds.
- A lack of hierarchy among men and groups.
- Absence of strong, complex, formal organization.
- Communitarian basis of land holding.
- Segmentary character.
- Little value on surplus accumulation on the use of capital and on market trading
- Lack of distinction between form and substance of religion
- A distinct psychological bent for enjoying life.

PROBLEMS OF TRIBAL COMMUNITIES

Land Alienation: The history of land alienation among the tribes began during British colonialism in India when the British interfered in the tribal region for the purpose of exploiting the tribal natural resources. Coupled with this tribal lands were occupied by moneylenders, zamindars and traders by advancing them loans etc. Opening of mines in the heart of tribal habitat and even a few factories provided wage labour as well as opportunities for factory employment. But this brought increasing destitution and displacement. After the British came to power, the Forest policy of the British Government was more inclined towards commercial considerations rather than human. Some forests were declared as reserved ones where only authorized contractors were allowed to cut the timber and the forest -dwellers were kept isolated deliberately within their habitat without any effort to ameliorate their economic and educational standards. The expansion of railway in India heavily devastated the forest resources in India. The Government started reserving teak, Sal and deodar forests for the manufacture of railway sleepers. Forest land and its resources provide the best means of livelihood for the tribal people and many tribes including the women engage in agriculture, food gathering and hunting they are heavily dependent on the products of the forest. Therefore when outsiders exploit the tribe's land and its resources the natural life cycle of tribal ecology and tribal life is greatly disturbed.

Poverty and Indebtedness

Majority tribes live under poverty line. The tribes follow many simple occupations based on simple technology. Most of the occupation falls into the primary occupations such as hunting, gathering, and agriculture. The technology they use for these purposes belong to the most primitive kind. There is no profit and surplus making in such economy. Hence there per capita income is very meager much lesser than the Indian average. Most of them live under abject poverty and are in debt in the hands of local moneylenders and Zamindars.In order to repay the debt they often mortgage or sell their land to the moneylenders. Indebtedness is almost inevitable since heavy interest is to be paid to these moneylenders.

Health and Nutrition

In many parts of India tribal population suffers from chronic infections and diseases out of which water borne diseases are life threatening. They also suffer from deficiency diseases. The Himalayan tribes suffer from goiter due to lack of iodine. Leprosy and tuberculosis are also common among them. Infant mortality was found to be very high among some of the tribes. Malnutrition is common and has affected the general health of the tribal children as it lowers the ability to resist infection, leads to chronic illness and sometimes leads to brain impairment. The ecological imbalance like cutting of trees have increased the distances between villages and the forest areas thus forcing tribal women to walk longer distances in search of forest produce and firewood.

Education

Educationally the tribal population is at different levels of development but overall the formal education has made very little impact on tribal groups. Earlier Government had no direct programme for their education. But in the subsequent years the reservation policy has made some changes. There are many reasons for low level of education among the tribal people: Formal education is not considered necessary to discharge their social obligations.

Superstitions and myths play an important role in rejecting education. Most tribes live in abject poverty. It is not easy for them to send their children to schools, as they are considered extra helping hands. The formal schools do not hold any special interest for the children. Most of the tribes are located in interior and remote areas where teachers would not like to go from outside.

Cultural Problems

Due to contact with other cultures, the tribal culture is undergoing a revolutionary change. Due to influence of Christian missionaries the problem of bilingualism has developed which led to indifference towards tribal language. The tribal people are imitating western culture in different aspects of their social life and leaving their own culture. It has led to degeneration of tribal life and tribal arts such as dance, music and different types of craft.

TRIBAL DEVELOPMENT EFFORTS AFTER INDEPENDENCE

The sources of funds made available are

1. State Plan
2. Special Central Assistance
3. Sectoral Programmes of Central Ministries/Departments
4. Institutional Finance.

The State Governments are required to quantify the funds from State Plan for tribal area development in proportion to percentage of tribal population in the states.

CONSTRUCTION OF THE HOSTELS FOR TRIBAL STUDENTS

Construction, Maintenance expense is to be borne by the State Governments/Union Territories. The rates for construction of the hostels are fixed which are different for the plains and the hills. It has been represented by various States that these rates are not workable any more in view of the escalation of prices of building materials and long distance involved particularly for the hilly areas. It is, therefore, proposed to revise the norms and to adopt the State PWD schedule of rates as in the case of construction of Ashram Schools. During 1990-91 to 1992-93, the amount of Rs. 8.64 crores has been released to the States/Union under various stages of completion. The scheme envisages setting up of vocational training institutes in inner tribal areas away from the district headquarters to impart training in various courses relevant to the areas. The tribal youth would be given training in three trades of his or her choice, the course in each trade having duration of four months. The trainee is to be attached at the end of one month training to master craftsman for a period of three months to learn his skills by practical experience. At the end of 15 months, the trainee will emerge as a multi-skilled person who can exploit existing employment potentials to his/her best advantage. This is a Central Sector Scheme where the construction and maintenance costs are fully borne by the Central Government. It is implemented through the State Governments. Proposals are obtained from them along with details of existing infrastructure as well as the employment potentials in the proximity of the proposed location.

Educational complex in low literacy pockets for women in Tribal areas This Scheme provides cent percent financial assistance to NGOs/Organization established by government as autonomous bodies/educational & other institutions like Cooperative Societies, to establish educational complexes in 136 identified districts of erstwhile 11 states (now 13) where tribal female literacy is below 10% as per 1991 census. Educational complex is meant for girls studying from class I to V with strength of 30 students in each class. The grants are provided to meet non-recurring as well as recurring expenses on building (hiring or maintenance) teaching, boarding, lodging and to also for medical and health care of students.

Tribal development Cooperative Corporation

This is a Central Sector Scheme, with 100% grant, available to the state Tribal Development Cooperative Corporation (STDCCs) and other similar corporations of State engaged in collection and trading of minor forest produce (MFP) through tribals Grants under the Scheme are provided to strengthen the Share Capital of Corporations, construction of Warehouses, establishment of processing industries of MFPs etc. to ensure high profitability of the corporation so as to enable them to pay remunerative prices for MFPs to the tribals.

Price Support to Trifed

The Ministry provides Grants-in-aid to its corporation, TRIFED to set off losses on account of fluctuations in prices of MFPs being marketed by it for ensuring remunerative prices to tribal engaged in collection of MFPs either directly or through STDCCs and other such Cooperative Societies. Investment in Share Capital of Trifed The Ministry is the largest shareholder of TRIFED with over 99% contribution in its Share Capital. Under this Scheme, the Ministry provides funds to TRIFED as its contribution in the Share Capital.

Village Grain Banks

This Scheme provides Grants for establishment of Village Grain Banks to prevent deaths of STs specially children in remote and backward tribal villages facing or likely to face starvation and also to improve nutritional standards. The Scheme provides funds for building storage facility, procurement of Weights & Measures and for the purchase of initial stock of one quintal of food grain of local variety for each family. A Committee under Chairmanship of village Headman runs the Grain Bank thus established.

Grant-In-Aid to Voluntary Organizations

As many as 27 types of projects with focus on tribal education, literacy, medical & health care, vocational training in agriculture, horticulture, craftsmanship etc., are being supported by the Ministry under this Scheme through registered Non-Governmental Organizations.

Research and Training

Under the Scheme "Research & Training" the Ministry provides financial assistance under Grants to Tribal Research Institutes on 50:50 sharing basis; for conducting Research & Evaluation Studies, Seminars, and Workshops etc. Award of Research Fellowship to Tribal Students on 100% basis registered in Indian Universities. Supporting projects of All-India or Inter-State nature on 100% basis to NGOs/Universities etc. for conducting research on tribal matters, Travel Grants and for Publication of Books on tribals.

Development of Primitive Tribal Groups

Under this Scheme cent percent assistance is provided to NGOs and other institutions for undertaking projects on development of PTGs on activities mainly focusing on their food security literacy, agriculture technology up gradation, etc.

Post Matric Scholarships, Overseas Scholarships and Book Banks

The post-matric scholarship Scheme provides financial assistance to all ST students for pursuance of post-matric studies in recognized institutions within India. The Scheme provides for 100% assistance from the Ministry to State Governments and UT Administrations implementing the Scheme, over and above their respective committed liabilities. The Ministry also gives financial assistance for setting up Book-Banks in institutions running professional courses like Medicine, Engineering, Law, Agriculture, Veterinary, Chartered Accountancy, Business Management, and Bio-Sciences. Annually, Ministry provides financial assistance to 9 meritorious ST students for Postgraduate, Doctoral and Post-Doctoral studies in foreign universities/institutions of repute.

Up gradation of Merit and Coaching

These Schemes provide 100% central assistance to State/ UT Administrations. The up gradation of merit Scheme is for arranging coaching classes in reputed colleges for developing competence among ST students for their better performance in competitive examinations conducted by various universities institutes for admission to Medical and Engineering courses while the Scheme for coaching is for conducting Pre-Examination Coaching for tribal students for various examinations conducted by UPSC, SSC, Banking Services Recruitment Boards etc.

Tribal Advisory Council (Tac)

Eight states having scheduled areas, namely, Andhra Pradesh, Bihar (now Bihar & Chhattisgarh), Gujarat, Himachal Pradesh, Maharashtra, Madhya Pradesh (now Madhya Pradesh and Chhattisgarh), Orissa & Rajasthan and two non-scheduled area states, namely, Tamil Nadu and West Bengal have constituted tacs. The TAC consists of not more than twenty-five members of whom as many as three-fourth members are scheduled tribe representatives of the state legislative assembly. The governor of the state may refer matters concerning to administration of welfare of tribals to the TAC for recommendations. The ministry issues guidelines for TAC. As per latest guidelines the TAC should meet at least twice a year and discuss the issues concerning tribal interests and making appropriate recommendation for protection of tribal interests.

Point 11(b) of 20-point Programme

The point 11 (b) of 20-point programme is to provide economic assistance to the scheduled tribe families to enable them to rise above poverty line. The ST families are assisted through various schemes implemented by departments of agriculture, rural development, horticulture, animal husbandry, sericulture, forestry, small & cottage industries, etc. The ministry fixes the targets for 22-states/ut s and also monitors the progress of achievements on monthly basis. The officers of the ministry inspected more than 75 projects in the states of Andhra Pradesh, Assam, Manipur, Meghalaya, Orissa, West Bengal, Jharkhand, Maharashtra and Madhya Pradesh.

ADIVASI

Adivasi is an umbrella term for a heterogeneous set of ethnic and tribal groups claimed to be the aboriginal population of India. They comprise a substantial indigenous minority of the population of India.

Adivasi societies are particularly present in the Indian states of Kerala, Orissa, Madhya Pradesh, Chattisgarh, Rajasthan, Gujarat, Maharashtra, Andhra Pradesh, Bihar, Jharkhand, West Bengal, Mizoram and other northeastern states, and the Andaman and Nicobar Islands. Many smaller tribal groups are quite sensitive to ecological degradation caused by modernization.

Both commercial forestry and intensive agriculture have proved destructive to the forests that had endured swidden agriculture for many centuries. Officially recognized by the Indian government as "Scheduled Tribes" in the Fifth Schedule of the Constitution of India, they are often grouped together with scheduled castes in the category "Scheduled Castes and Tribes", which is eligible for certain affirmative action measures.

Connotations of the Word 'Adivasi'

Although terms such as *atavika* (Sanskrit for *forest dwellers*), *vanvasi* or *girijan* (*hill people*) are also used for the tribes of India, *adivasi* carries the specific meaning of being the original and autochthonous inhabitants of a given region, and was specifically coined for that purpose in the 1930s. Over a period of time, unlike the terms "aborigines" or "tribes", the word "*adivasi*" has also developed a connotation of past autonomy which was disrupted during the British colonial period in India and has not been restored.

Opposition to usage of the term is varied, and it has been argued that the "original inhabitant" contention is based on dubious claims and that the adivasi - non adivasi divide that is created is artificial. It should also be noted that in Northeast India, the term Adivasi applies only to the Tea-tribes imported from Central India during colonial times, while all tribal groups refer collectively to themselves by using the English word "tribes".

Scheduled Tribes

The Constitution of India, Article 366 (25) defines Scheduled Tribes as "such tribes or tribal communities or part of or groups within such tribes or tribal communities as are deemed under Article 342 to the scheduled Tribes (STs) for the purposes of this Constitution". In Article 342, the procedure to be followed for specification of a scheduled tribe is prescribed. However, it does not contain the criterion for the specification of any community as scheduled tribe. An often used criterion is based on attributes such as:

- Geographical isolation - they live in cloistered, exclusive, remote and inhospitable areas such as hills and forests.
- Backwardness - their livelihood is based on primitive agriculture, a low-value closed economy with a low level of technology that leads to their poverty. They have low levels of literacy and health.
- Distinctive culture, language and religion - communities have developed their own distinctive culture, language and religion.
- Shyness of contact – they have a marginal degree of contact with other cultures and people.

Primitive Tribes

The Scheduled Tribe groups who were identified as more backward communities among the tribal population groups have been categorised as 'Primitive Tribal Groups' (PTGs) by the Government at the Centre in 1975. So far seventy-five tribal communities have been identified as 'primitive tribal groups' in different States of India. These hunting, food-gathering, and some agricultural communities, who have been identified as more backward communities among the tribal population groups need special programmes for their sustainable development. The primitive tribes are awakening and demanding their rights for special reservation quota for them.

Geographical Overview

There is a substantial list of Scheduled Tribes in India recognised as tribal under the Constitution of India. Tribal peoples constitute 8.2% of the nation's total population, over 84 million people according to the 2001 census. One concentration lives in a belt along the Himalayas stretching through Jammu and Kashmir, Himachal Pradesh, and Uttarakhand in the west, to Assam, Meghalaya, Tripura, Arunachal Pradesh, Mizoram, Manipur, and Nagaland in the northeast. In the northeastern states of Arunachal Pradesh, Meghalaya, Mizoram, and Nagaland, more than 90% of the population is tribal. However, in the remaining northeast states of Assam, Manipur, Sikkim, and Tripura, tribal peoples form between 20 and 30% of the population.

Another concentration lives in the hilly areas of central India (Chhattisgarh, Madhya Pradesh, Orissa and, to a lesser extent, Andhra Pradesh); in this belt, which is bounded by the Narmada River to the north and the Godavari River to the southeast, tribal peoples occupy the slopes of the region's mountains. Other tribals, including the Santals, live in Jharkhand and West Bengal. Central Indian states have the country's largest tribes, and, taken as a whole, roughly 75% of the total tribal population live there, although the tribal population there accounts for only around 10% of the region's total population.

There are smaller numbers of tribal people in Karnataka, Tamil Nadu, and Kerala in south India; in western India in Gujarat and Rajasthan, and in the union territories of Lakshadweep and the Andaman Islands and Nicobar Islands. About one percent of the populations of Kerala and Tamil Nadu are tribal, whereas about six percent in Andhra Pradesh and Karnataka are members of tribes.

THE PEOPLING OF INDIA

The concept of 'original inhabitant' is directly related to the initial peopling of India, which, due to the debate on topics such as the Indo-Aryan migration hypothesis, has been a contentious area of research and discourse. Some anthropologists hypothesize that the region was settled by multiple human migrations over tens of millennia, which makes it even harder to select certain groups as being truly aboriginal. One narrative, largely based on genetic research, describes Negritos, similar to the Andamanese adivasis of today, as the first humans to colonize India, likely 30-65 thousand years before present (kybp). 60% of all Indians share the mtDNA haplogroup M, which is universal among Andamanese islander adivasis and might be a genetic legacy of the postulated first Indians. Some anthropologists theorize that these settlers were displaced by invading Austro-Asiatic-speaking Australoid people (who largely shared skin pigmentation and physiognomy with the Negritos, but had straight rather than kinky hair), and adivasi tribes such as the Irulas trace their origins to that displacement. The Oraon adivasi tribe of eastern India and the Korku tribe of western India are considered to be examples of groups of Australoid origin.

Subsequent to the Australoids, some anthropologists and geneticists theorize that Caucasoids (including both Dravidians and Indo-Aryans) and Mongoloids (Sino-Tibetans) immigrated into India: the Dravidians possibly from Iran, the Indo-Aryans possibly from the Central Asian steppes and the Tibeto-Burmans possibly from the Himalayan and northeastern borders of the subcontinent. None of these hypotheses is free from debate and disagreement.

Ethnic origins and linguistic affiliations in India match only inexactly, however: while the Oraon adivasis are classified as an Australoid group, their language, called Kurukh, is Dravidian.

Khasis and Nicobarese are considered to be Mongoloid groups and the Munda and Santals are Australoid groups, but all four speak Austro-Asiatic languages. The Bhils and Gonds are frequently classified as Australoid groups, yet Bhil languages are Indo-European and the Gondi language is Dravidian. Also, in post-colonial India, tribal languages suffered huge setbacks with the formation of linguistic states after 1956 under the States Reorganisation Act. For example, under state-sponsored educational pressure, Irula children are being taught Tamil and a sense of shame has begun to be associated with speaking the Irula language among some children and educated adults. Similarly, the Santals are "gradually adopting languages of the areas inhabited, like Oriya in Orissa, Hindi in Bihar and Bengali in West Bengal."

DISRUPTIONS DURING MUGHAL AND COLONIAL PERIODS

Although considered uncivilized and primitive, adivasis were usually not held to be intrinsically impure by surrounding (usually, caucasoid - Dravidian or Aryan) caste Hindu populations, unlike Dalits, who were. Thus, the adivasi origins of Maharishi (Sanksrit: *Great Sage*) Valmiki, who composed the Ramayana Hindu religious epic, were acknowledged, as were the origins of adivasi tribes such as the Grasia and Bhilala, which descended from mixed Rajput and Bhil marriages. Unlike the subjugation of the dalits, the adivasis often enjoyed autonomy and, depending on region, evolved mixed hunter-gatherer and farming economies, controlling their lands as a joint patrimony of the tribe. In some areas, securing adivasi approval and support was considered crucial by local rulers, and larger adivasi groups were able to sustain their own kingdoms in central India. The Gond Rajas of Garha-Mandla and Chanda are examples of an adivasi aristocracy that ruled in this region, and were "not only the hereditary leaders of their Gond subjects, but also held sway over substantial communities of non-tribals who recognized them as their feudal lords."

This relative autonomy and collective ownership of adivasi land by adivasis was severely disrupted by the advent of the Mughals in the early 16th century. Similarly, the British beginning in the 18th century added to the consolidation of feudalism in India, first under the jagirdari system and then under the zamindari system. Beginning with the Permanent Settlement imposed by the British in Bengal and Bihar, which later became the template for a deepening of feudalism throughout India, the older social and economic system in the country began to alter radically. Land, both forest areas belonging to adivasis and settled farmland belonging to non-adivasi peasants, was rapidly made the legal property of British-designated zamindars (landlords), who in turn moved to extract the maximum economic benefit possible from their newfound property and subjects without regard to historical tenure or ownership. Adivasi lands sometimes experienced an influx of non-local settlers, often brought from far away (as in the case of Muslims and Sikhs brought to Kol territory) by the zamindars to better exploit local land, forest and labour. Deprived of the forests and resources they traditionally depended on and sometimes coerced to pay taxes, many adivasis were forced to borrow at usurious rates from moneylenders, often the zamindars themselves. When they were unable to pay, that forced them to become bonded labourers for the zamindars. Often, far from paying off the principal of their debt, they were unable even to offset the compounding interest, and this was made the justification for their children working for the zamindar after the death of the initial borrower. In the case of the Andamanese adivasis, long isolated from the outside world in autonomous societies, mere contact with outsiders was often sufficient to set off deadly epidemics in tribal populations, and it is alleged that some sections of the British government directly attempted to destroy some tribes.

Land dispossession and subjugation by British and zamindar interests resulted in a number of adivasi revolts in the late eighteenth and early nineteenth centuries, such as the Santal hul (or Santal revolt) of 1855-56. Although these were suppressed ruthlessly by the governing British authority (the East India Company prior to 1858, and the British government after 1858), partial restoration of privileges to adivasi elites (e.g. to *Mankis*, the leaders of Munda tribes) and some leniency in tax burdens resulted in relative calm, despite continuing and widespread dispossession, from the late nineteenth century onwards. The economic deprivation, in some cases, triggered internal adivasi migrations within India that would continue for another century, including as labour for the emerging tea plantations in Assam.

Tribal Classification Criteria and Demands

Population complexities, and the controversies surrounding ethnicity and language in India, sometimes make the official recognition of groups as adivasis (by way of inclusion in the Scheduled Tribes list) political and contentious. However, regardless of their language family affiliations, Australoid and Negrito groups that have survived as distinct forest, mountain or island dwelling tribes in India and are often classified as adivasi. The relatively autonomous Mongoloid tribal groups of Northeastern India (including Khasis, Apatani and Nagas), who are mostly Austro-Asiatic or Tibeto-Burman speakers, are also considered to be adivasis: this area comprises 7.5% of India's land area but 20% of its adivasi population. However, not all autonomous northeastern groups are considered adivasis; for instance, the Tibeto-Burman-speaking Meitei of Manipur were once tribal but, having been settled for many centuries, are caste Hindus.

It is also difficult, for a given social grouping, to definitively decide whether it is a 'caste' or a 'tribe'. A combination of internal social organization, relationship with other groups, self-classification and perception by other groups has to be taken into account to make a categorization, which is at best inexact and open to doubt. These categorizations have been diffused for thousands of years, and even ancient formulators of caste-discriminatory legal codes (which usually only applied to settled populations, and not adivasis) were unable to come up with clean distinctions.

Demands for Tribal Classification

An additional difficulty in deciding whether a group meets the criteria to be adivasi or not are the aspirational movements created by the federal and state benefits, including job and educational reservations, enjoyed by groups listed as scheduled tribes (STs). In Manipur, Meitei commentators have pointed to the lack of scheduled tribe status as a key economic disadvantage for Meiteis competing for jobs against groups that are classified as scheduled tribes. In Assam, Rajbongshi representatives have demanded scheduled tribe status as well. In Rajasthan, the Gujjar community has demanded ST status, even blockading the national capital of Delhi to press their demand. However Government of Rajasthan declined Gujjars demand by saying that they are treated as upper caste and they are by no mean a tribe. In several cases, these claims to tribalhood are disputed by tribes who are already listed in the schedule and fear economic losses if more powerful groups are recognized as scheduled tribes; for instance, the Rajbongshi demand faces resistance from the Bodo tribe, and the Meena tribe has vigorously opposed Gujjar aspirations to be recognized as a scheduled tribe.

Endogamy, Exogamy and Ethnogenesis

Part of the challenge is that the endogamous nature of tribes is also conformed to by the vast majority of Hindu castes. Indeed, many historians and anthropologists believe that caste endogamy reflects the once-tribal origins of the various groups who now constitute the settled Hindu castes. Another defining feature of caste Hindu society, which is often used to contrast them with Muslim and other social groupings, is lineage/clan (or *gotra*) and village exogamy. However, these in-marriage taboos are also held ubiquitously among tribal groups; and do not serve as reliable differentiating markers between caste and tribe. Again, this could be an ancient import from tribal society into settled Hindu castes. Interestingly, tribes such as the Muslim Gujjars of Kashmir and the Kalash of Pakistan observe these exogamous traditions in common with caste Hindus and non-Kashmiri adivasis, though their surrounding Muslim populations do not.

Some anthropologists, however, draw a distinction between tribes who have continued to be tribal and tribes that have been absorbed into caste society in terms of the breakdown of tribal (and therefore caste) boundaries, and the proliferation of new mixed caste groups. In other words, ethnogenesis (the construction of new ethnic identities) in tribes occurs through a fission process (where groups splinter-off as new tribes, which preserves endogamy), whereas with settled castes it usually occurs through intermixture (in violation of strict endogamy).

Other Criteria

Unlike castes, which form part of a complex and interrelated local economic exchange system, tribes tend to form self-sufficient economic units. For most tribal people, land-use rights traditionally derive simply from tribal membership. Tribal society tends to the egalitarian, with its leadership based on ties of kinship and personality rather than on hereditary status. Tribes typically consist of segmentary lineages whose extended families provide the basis for social organization and control.

Tribal religion recognizes no authority outside the tribe. Any of these criteria may not apply in specific instances. Language does not always give an accurate indicator of tribal or caste status. Especially in regions of mixed population, many tribal groups have lost their mother tongues and simply speak local or regional languages. In parts of Assam - an area historically divided between warring tribes and villages - increased contact among villagers began during the colonial period, and has accelerated since independence in 1947. A pidgin Assamese developed while educated tribal members learned Hindi and, in the late twentieth century, English.

Self-identification and group loyalty do not provide unfailing markers of tribal identity either. In the case of stratified tribes, the loyalties of clan, kin, and family may well predominate over those of tribe. In addition, tribes cannot always be viewed as people living apart; the degree of isolation of various tribes has varied tremendously. The Gonds, Santals, and Bhils traditionally have dominated the regions in which they have lived. Moreover, tribal society is not always more egalitarian than the rest of the rural populace; some of the larger tribes, such as the Gonds, are highly stratified.

The apparently wide fluctuation in estimates of South Asia's tribal population through the twentieth century gives a sense of how unclear the distinction between tribal and nontribal can be. India's 1931 census enumerated 22 million tribal people, in 1941 only 10 million were counted, but by 1961 some 30 million and in 1991 nearly 68 million tribal members were included. The differences among the figures reflect changing census criteria and the economic incentives individuals have to maintain or reject classification as a tribal member.

These gyrations of census data serve to underline the complex relationship between caste and tribe. Although, in theory, these terms represent different ways of life and ideal types, in reality they stand for a continuum of social groups. In areas of substantial contact between tribes and castes, social and cultural pressures have often tended to move tribes in the direction of becoming castes over a period of years. Tribal peoples with ambitions for social advancement in Indian society at large have tried to gain the classification of caste for their tribes. On occasion, an entire tribe or part of a tribe joined a Hindu sect and thus entered the caste system *en masse*. If a specific tribe engaged in practices that Hindus deemed polluting, the tribe's status when it was assimilated into the caste hierarchy would be affected.

Religion

The majority of Adivasi practice Hinduism and Christianity. During the last two decades Adivasi from Orissa, Madhya Pradesh, Jharkhand have converted to Protestant groups. Adivasi beliefs vary by tribe, and are usually different from the historical Vedic religion, with its monistic underpinnings, Indo-European deities (who are often cognates of ancient Iranian, Greek and Roman deities, e.g. Mitra/Mithra/Mithras), lack of idol worship and lack of a concept of reincarnation. The "centre of Rig Vedic religion was the *Yajna*, the sacrificial fire" and there was "no Atma, no Brahma, no Moksha, no idol worship in the Rig Veda." Two specific rituals held great importance and it is known that, "when the Indo-Aryans and the Persians formed a single people, they performed sacrifices (Vedic yajna: Avestan yasna), and that they already had a sacred drink (Vedic soma: Avestan haoma)."

Adivasi Roots of Modern Hinduism

Some historians and anthropologists assert that much of what constitutes popular Hinduism today is actually descended from an amalgamation of adivasi faiths, idol worship practices and deities, rather than the original Indo-Aryan faith. This also includes the sacred status of certain animals and plants, such as monkeys, cows, peacocks, cobras (nagas), elephants, peepul, tulsi (holy basil) and neem, which may once have held totemic importance for certain adivasi tribes.

Adivasi Saints

- Saint Buddhu Bhagat, led the Kol Insurrection (1831-1832) aimed against tax imposed on Mundas by Muslim rulers.
- Saint Dhira or Kannappa Nayanar, one of 63 Nayanar Shaivite saints, a hunter from whom Lord Shiva gladly

accepted food offerings. It is said that he poured water from his mouth on the Shivlingam and offered the Lord swine flesh.

- Saint Dhudhalinath, Koli, Gujarati, a 17th or 18th century devotee.
- Saint Ganga Narain, led the Bhumij Revolt (1832-1833) aimed against missionaries and British colonialists.
- Saint Girnari Velnathji, Koli, Gujarati of Junagadh, a 17th or 18th century devotee
- Saint Gurudev Kalicharan Brahma or Guru Brahma, a Bodo whose founded the Brahma Dharma aimed against missionaries and colonialists. The Brahma Dharma movement sought to unite peoples of all religions to worship God together and survives even today.
- Saint Jatra Oraon, Oraon, led the Tana Bhagat Movement (1914–1919) aimed against the missionaries and British colonialists
- Saint Sri Koya Bhagat, Koli, Gujarati, a 17th or 18th century devotee
- Saint Tantya Mama (Bhil), a Bhil after whom a movement is named after - the "Jananayak Tantya Bhil"
- Saint Tirumangai Alvar, Kallar, composed the six Vedangas in beautiful Tamil verse.

Sages

- Bhaktaraj Bhadurdas, Koli, Gujarati, a 17th or 18th century devotee
- Bhakta Shabari, a Bhil woman that offered Shri Rama and Shri Laxmana her half-eaten ber fruit, which they gratefully accepted when they were searching for Shri Sita Devi in the forest.
- Madan Bhagat, Koli, Gujarati, a 17th or 18th century devotee
- Sany Kanji Swami, Koli, Gujarati, a 17th or 18th century devotee
- Bhaktaraj Valram, Koli, Gujarati, a 17th or 18th century devotee.

Maharishis

- Maharshi Matanga, Matanga Bhil, Guru of Bhakta Shabari. In fact, Chandalas are often addressed as 'Matanga 'in passages like Varaha Purana 1.139.91
- Maharshi Valmiki, Kirata Bhil, composed the Ramayana. He is considered to be an avatar in the Balmiki community.

Avatars

- Birsa Bhagwan or Birsa Munda, considered an avatar of Khasra Kora. People approached him as Singbonga, the supreme spirit. He converted even Christians to his own sect. He was against conversions by missionaries. He wanted not only political, but religious freedom as well! He and his clan, the Mundas, were connected with Vaishnavite traditions as they were influenced by Sri Chaitanya. Birsa was very close to the Panre brothers Vaishnavites.
- Kirata - the form of Lord Shiva as a hunter. It is mentioned in the Mahabharata. The Karppillikkavu Sree Mahadeva Temple, Kerala adores Lord Shiva in this avatar and is known to be one of the oldest surviving temples in Bharat.
- Vettakkorumakan, the son of Lord Kirata.
- Kaladutaka or 'Vaikunthanatha', Kallar (robber), avatar of Lord Vishnu.

Other Tribals and Hinduism

Some Hindus believe that Indian tribals are close to the romantic ideal of the ancient silvan culture of the Vedic people. Madhav Sadashiv Golwalkar said: "The tribals "can be given yajnopavita (...) They should be given equal rights and footings in the matter of religious rights, in temple worship, in the study of Vedas, and in general, in all our social and religious affairs. This is the only right solution for all the problems of casteism found nowadays in our Hindu society." At the Lingaraja temple in Bhubaneswar (11th century), there are Brahmin and Badu (tribal) priests. The Badus have the most intimate contact with the deity of the temple, and only they can bathe and adorn it. The Bhil tribe is mentioned in the Mahabharata. The Bhil boy Eklavya's teacher was Drona, and he had the honour to be invited to Yudhisthira's Rajasuya Yajna at Indraprastha. Indian tribals were also part of royal armies in the Ramayana and in the Arthasastra. Bhakta Shabari was a Bhil woman that offered Shri Rama and Shri Laxmana 'ber' when they were searching for Shri Sita in the forest. Maharishi Matanga, a Bhil became a Brahmana.

Sarna

Some western authors and Indian sociologists refer to adivasi beliefs as animism and spirit worship, and hold them to be distinct from Hinduism, Christianity or Islam. In Jharkhand, Chattisgarh and Orissa states, their religion is sometimes called Sarna. The Jharkhand movement gave the Santals an opportunity to create a 'great tradition' of their own. As Orans reported, "The movement is spoken of in the following terms 'we should not leave our religion; we should continue to use rice-beer; we should have our worship at the sacred grove; also we should not stop eating beef. We will call our religion *Sarna Dhorom.*' *Sarna* is the Munda word for 'Sacred Grove' while *Dhorom* is the Oriya word meaning 'religion'.

Sarna involves belief in a great spirit called the *Sing Bonga*. Santhal belief holds the world to be inhabited by numerous spiritual beings of different kinds. Santhals consider themselves as living and doing everything in close association with these spirits. Rituals are performed under groves of Sal trees called *Jaher* (or *sacred grove*), where *Bonga* is believed to appear or express himself. Often, *Jaher* are found in the forests.

According to the mythology of the Santhal community, the genesis of the 'Sarna' religion occurred when the 'Santhal tribals had gone to the forest for hunting and they started the discussion about their 'Creator and Savior' while they were taking rest under a tree. They questioned themselves that who is their God? Whether the Sun, the Wind or the Cloud? Finally, they came to a conclusion that they would leave an arrow in the sky and wherever the arrow would target that will be the God's house. They left an arrow in the sky; it fell down under a Sal tree. Then, they started worshiping the Sal tree and named their religion as 'Sarna' because it is derived from a Sal tree. 4 Thus, Sarna religion came into existence. There are priests and an assistant priests called "Naikey" and "Kudam Naike" in every Santhal village.

Demands for a Separate Religion Code

Some adivasi organizations have demanded that a distinct religious code be listed for adivasis in the 2011. All India Adivasi Conference held on 01.01.2011 and 02.01.2011 at Burnpur, Asansol, West Bengal. 750 delegates were present from all part of india and casted their vote for Religion code as Sari Dhorom - 632, Sarna - 51, Kherwalism - 14 and others religion - 03 Census of India.

TRIBAL SYSTEM

Tribals are not part of the caste system, and usually constitute egalitarian societies. Christian tribals do not automatically lose their traditional tribal rules. When in 1891 a missionary asked 150 Munda Christians to "inter-dine" with people of different rank, only 20 Christians did so, and many converts lost their new faith. Father Haghenbeek concluded on this episode that these rules are not "pagan", but a sign of "national sentiment and pride", and wrote:

"On the contrary, while proclaiming the equality of all men before God, we now tell them: preserve your race pure, keep your customs, refrain from eating with Lohars (blacksmiths), Turis (bamboo workers) and other people of lower rank. To become good Christians, it (inter-dining) is not required." However, many scholars argue that the claim that tribals are an egalitarian society in contrast to a caste-based society is a part of a larger political agenda by some to maximize any differences from tribal and urban societies. According to scholar Koenraad Elst, caste practices and social taboos among Indian tribals date back to antiquity:

"The Munda tribals not only practise tribal endogamy and commensality, but also observe a jâti division within the tribe, buttressed by notions of social pollution, a mythological explanation and harsh punishments. A Munda Catholic theologian testifies: The tribals of Chhotanagpur are an endogamous tribe. They usually do not marry outside the tribal community, because to them the tribe is sacred. The way to salvation is the tribe. Among the Santals, it is tabooed to marry outside the tribe or inside ones clan, just as Hindus marry inside their caste and outside their gotra. More precisely: To protect their tribal solidarity, the Santals have very stringent marriage laws. A Santal cannot marry a non-Santal or a member of his own clan. The former is considered as a threat to the tribe's integrity, while the latter is considered incestuous. Among the Ho of Chhotanagpur, the trespasses which occasion the exclusion from the tribe without chance of appeal, are essentially those concerning endogamy and exogamy."

Inter-dining has also been prohibited by many Indian tribal peoples.

Education

Extending the system of primary education into tribal areas and reserving places for tribal children in middle and high schools and higher education institutions are central to government policy, but efforts to improve a tribe's educational status have had mixed results. Recruitment of qualified teachers and determination of the appropriate language of instruction also remain troublesome. Commission after commission on the "language question" has called for instruction, at least at the primary level, in the students' native tongue. In some regions, tribal children entering school must begin by learning the official regional language, often one completely unrelated to their tribal tongue.

Many tribal schools are plagued by high dropout rates. Children attend for the first three to four years of primary school and gain a smattering of knowledge, only to lapse into illiteracy later. Few who enter continue up to the tenth grade; of those who do, few manage to finish high school. Therefore, very few are eligible to attend institutions of higher education, where the high rate of attrition continues. Members of agrarian tribes like the Gonds often are reluctant to send their children to school, needing them, they say, to work in the fields. On the other hand, in those parts of the northeast where tribes have generally been spared the wholesale onslaught of outsiders, schooling has helped tribal people to secure political and economic benefits. The education system there has provided a corps of highly trained tribal members in the professions and high-ranking administrative posts. An academy for teaching and preserving Adivasi languages and culture was established in 1999 by the Bhasha Research and Publication Centre. The Adivasi Academy is located at Tejgadh in Gujarat.

Economy

Most tribes are concentrated in heavily forested areas that combine inaccessibility with limited political or economic significance. Historically, the economy of most tribes was subsistence agriculture or hunting and gathering. Tribal members traded with outsiders for the few necessities they lacked, such as salt and iron. A few local Hindu craftsmen might provide such items as cooking utensils.

In the early 20th century, however, large areas fell into the hands of non-tribals, on account of improved transportation and communications. Around 1900, many regions were opened by the government to settlement through a scheme by which inward migrants received ownership of land free in return for cultivating it. For tribal people, however, land was often viewed as a common resource, free to whoever needed it. By the time tribals accepted the necessity of obtaining formal land titles, they had lost the opportunity to lay claim to lands that might rightfully have been considered theirs. The colonial and post-independence regimes belatedly realized the necessity of protecting tribals from the predations of outsiders and prohibited the sale of tribal lands. Although an important loophole in the form of land leases was left open, tribes made some gains in the mid-twentieth century, and some land was returned to tribal peoples despite obstruction by local police and land officials.

In the 1970s, tribal peoples came again under intense land pressure, especially in central India. Migration into tribal lands increased dramatically, as tribal people lost title to their lands in many ways – lease, forfeiture from debts, or bribery of land registry officials. Other non-tribals simply squatted, or even lobbied governments to classify them as tribal to allow them to compete with the formerly established tribes. In any case, many tribal members became landless labourers in the 1960s and 1970s, and regions that a few years earlier had been the exclusive domain of tribes had an increasingly mixed population of tribals and non-tribals. Government efforts to evict nontribal members from illegal occupation have proceeded slowly; when evictions occur at all, those ejected are usually members of poor, lower castes.

Improved communications, roads with motorized traffic, and more frequent government intervention figured in the increased contact that tribal peoples had with outsiders. Commercial highways and cash crops frequently drew non-tribal people into remote areas. By the 1960s and 1970s, the resident nontribal shopkeeper was a permanent feature of many tribal villages. Since shopkeepers often sell goods on credit (demanding high interest), many tribal members have been drawn deeply into debt or mortgaged their land. Merchants also encourage tribals to grow cash crops (such as cotton or castor-oil plants), which increases tribal dependence on the market for basic necessities. Indebtedness is so extensive that although such transactions are illegal, traders sometimes 'sell' their debtors to other merchants, much like indentured peons.

The final blow for some tribes has come when nontribals, through political jockeying, have managed to gain legal tribal status, that is, to be listed as a Scheduled Tribe. Tribes in the Himalayan foothills have not been as hard-pressed by the intrusions of non-tribal. Historically, their political status was always distinct from the rest of India. Until the British colonial period, there was little effective control by any of the empires centred in peninsular India; the region was populated by autonomous feuding tribes. The British, in efforts to protect the sensitive northeast frontier, followed a policy dubbed the "Inner Line"; non tribal people were allowed into the areas only with special permission. Postindependence governments have continued the policy, protecting the Himalayan tribes as part of the strategy to secure the border with China.

Government policies on forest reserves have affected tribal peoples profoundly. Government efforts to reserve forests have precipitated armed (if futile) resistance on the part of the tribal peoples involved. Intensive exploitation of forests has often meant allowing outsiders to cut large areas of trees (while the original tribal inhabitants were restricted from cutting), and ultimately replacing mixed forests capable of sustaining tribal life with single-product plantations. Nontribals have frequently bribed local officials to secure effective use of reserved forest lands.

The northern tribes have thus been sheltered from the kind of exploitation that those elsewhere in South Asia have suffered. In Arunachal Pradesh (formerly part of the North-East Frontier Agency), for example, tribal members control commerce and most lower-level administrative posts. Government construction projects in the region have provided tribes with a significant source of cash. Some tribes have made rapid progress through the education system (the role of early missionaries was significant in this regard). Instruction was begun in Assamese but was eventually changed to Hindi; by the early 1980s, English was taught at most levels. Northeastern tribal people have thus enjoyed a certain measure of social mobility.

The continuing economic alienation and exploitation of many adivasis was highlighted as a "systematic failure" by the Indian Prime Minister Manmohan Singh in a 2009 conference of chief ministers of all 29 Indian states, where he also cited this as a major cause of the Naxalite unrest that has affected areas such as the Red Corridor.

PARTICIPATION IN INDIAN INDEPENDENCE MOVEMENT

There were tribal reform and rebellion movements during the period of the British Empire, some of which also participated in the Indian freedom struggle or attacked mission posts. There were several Adivasis in the Indian independence movement including Khajya Naik, Bhima Naik, Jantya Bhil and Rehma Vasave.

List of Rebellions against British Rule

During the period of British rule, India saw the rebellions of several backward-castes, mainly tribals that revolted against British rule. These were:.

1. Halba rebellion (1774–79)
2. Chamka rebellion (1776–1787)
3. Chuar rebellion in Bengal (1795–1800)
4. Bhopalpatnam Struggle (1795)
5. Khurda Rebellion in Orissa (1817)
6. Bhil rebellion (1822–1857)
7. Paralkot rebellion (1825)
8. Tarapur rebellion (1842–54)
9. Maria rebellion (1842–63)
10. First Freedom Struggle (1856–57)
11. Bhil rebellion, begun by Tantya Tope in Banswara (1858)
12. Koi revolt (1859)
13. Gond rebellion, begun by Ramji Gond in Adilabad (1860)
14. Muria rebellion (1876)
15. Rani rebellion (1878–82)
16. Bhumkal (1910)
17. The Kuki Uprising (1917–1919)in Manipur.

NOMAD

Nomadic people commonly known as itinerants in modern-day contexts, are communities of people who move from one place to another, rather than settling permanently in one location. There are an estimated 30-40 million nomads in the world. Many cultures have traditionally been nomadic, but traditional nomadic behavior is increasingly rare in industrialized countries.

Nomadic cultures are discussed in three categories according to economic specialization: hunter-gatherers, pastoral nomads, and "peripatetic nomads". Nomadic hunting and gathering, following seasonally available wild plants and game, is by far the oldest human subsistence method. Pastoralists raise herds, driving them or moving with them, in patterns that normally avoid depleting pastures beyond their ability to recover. Peripatetic nomads, who offer the skills of a craft or trade to those they travel among, are most common in industrialized nations.

Hunter-gatherers

Many groups of 'nomadic' hunter-gatherers (also known as foragers) moved from campsite to campsite, following game and wild fruits and vegetables. Known examples include:

- Some Adivasi tribal people of India
- Most Indigenous Australians prior to Western contact
- Various groups of Pygmies, such as the Mbuti of the Ituri Rain forest in the Democratic Republic of the Congo
- The Bushmen of Southern Africa
- Many Native Americans, such as the Nukak-Makú, Comanches and many other Plains Indians, the Yahi of California, indigenous inhabitants of Tierra del Fuego, or early people of Montana located at Barton Gulch.

Pastoralism

Pastoral nomads are nomads moving between pastures. Nomadic pastoralism is thought to have developed in three stages that accompanied population growth and an increase in the complexity of social organization. Karim Sadr has proposed the following stages:

- Pastoralism: This is a mixed economy with a symbiosis within the family.
- Agropastoralism: This is when symbiosis is between segments or clans within an ethnic group.
- True Nomadism: This is when symbiosis is at the regional level, generally between specialized nomadic and agricultural populations.

The pastoralists are sedentary to a certain area, as they move between the permanent spring, summer, autumn and winter (or dry and wet season) pastures for their livestock. The nomads moved depending on the availability of resources.

Origin

Nomadic pastoralism seems to have developed as a part of the secondary products revolution proposed by Andrew Sherratt, in which early pre-pottery Neolithic cultures that had used animals as live meat ("on the hoof") also began using animals for their secondary products, for example, milk and its associated dairy products, wool and other animal hair, hides and consequently leather, manure for fuel and fertilizer, and traction.

The first nomadic pastoral society developed in the period from 8500-6500 BC in the area of the southern Levant. There, during a period of increasing aridity, PPNB cultures in the Sinai were replaced by a nomadic, pastoral pottery-using culture, which seems to have been a cultural fusion between a newly arrived Mesolithic people from Egypt (the Harifian culture), adopting their nomadic hunting lifestyle to the raising of stock. This lifestyle quickly developed into what Jaris Yurins has called the circum-Arabian nomadic pastoral techno-complex and is possibly associated with the appearance of Semitic languages in the region of the Ancient Near East.

The rapid spread of such nomadic pastoralism was typical of such later developments as of the Yamnaya culture of the horse and cattle nomads of the Eurasian steppe, or of the Greko-Mongol spread of the later Middle Ages.

Increase in the Former Soviet Union

One of the results of the break-up of the Soviet Union and the subsequent political independence and economic collapse of its Central Asian republics is the resurgence of pastoral nomadism.

Taking the Kyrgyz people as a representative example nomadism was the center of their economy prior to Russian colonization at the turn of the C19/C20, when they were settled into agricultural villages. The population became increasingly urbanized after World War II, but some people continued to take their herds of horses and cows to the high pasture (*jailoo*) every summer, i.e. a pattern of transhumance.

Since the 1990s, as the cash economy shrunk, unemployed relatives were absorbed back on the family farm, and the importance of this form of nomadism has increased. The symbols of nomadism, specifically the crown of the grey felt tent known as the yurt, appears on the national flag, emphasizing the centrality of their nomadic history and past in the creation of the modern nation of Kyrgyzstan.

Sedentarization

By 1920, nomadic pastoral tribes represented over a quarter of Iran's population. Tribal pastures were nationalized during the 1960s. The National Commission of UNESCO registered the population of Iran at 21 million in 1963, of whom two million (9.5%) were nomads. Although the nomadic population of Iran has dramatically decreased in the 20th century, Iran still has one of the largest nomadic populations in the world, an estimated 1.5 million in a country of about 70 million. In Kazakhstan where the major agricultural activity was nomadic herding, forced collectivization under Joseph Stalin's rule met with massive resistance and major losses and confiscation of livestock. Livestock in Kazakhstan fell from 7 million cattle to 1.6 million and from 22 million sheep to 1.7 million. The resulting famine of 1931-1934 caused some 1.5 million deaths: this represents more than 40% of the total Kazakh population at that time.

In the 1950s as well as the 1960s, large numbers of Bedouin throughout the Middle East started to leave the traditional, nomadic life to settle in the cities of the Middle East, especially as home ranges have shrunk and population levels have grown. Government policies in Egypt and Israel, oil production in Libya and the Persian Gulf, as well as a desire for improved standards of living, effectively led most Bedouin to become settled citizens of various nations, rather than stateless nomadic herders. A century ago nomadic Bedouin still made up some 10% of the total Arab population. Today they account for some 1% of the total. At independence in 1960, Mauritania was essentially a nomadic society. The great Sahel droughts of the early 1970s caused massive problems in a country where 85% of its inhabitants were nomadic herders. Today only 15% remain nomads.

As many as 2 million nomadic Kuchis wandered over Afghanistan in the years before the Soviet invasion, and most experts agreed that by 2000 the number had fallen dramatically, perhaps by half. The severe drought had destroyed 80% of the livestock in some areas. Niger experienced a serious food crisis in 2005 following erratic rainfall and desert locust invasions.

Nomads such as the Tuareg and Fulani, who make up about 20% of Niger's 12.9 million population, had been so badly hit by the Niger food crisis that their already fragile way of life is at risk. Nomads in Mali were also affected.

SLUM

A slum, as defined by the United Nations agency UN-HABITAT, is a run-down area of a city characterized by substandard housing and squalor and lacking in tenure security. According to the United Nations, the percentage of urban dwellers living in slums decreased from 47 percent to 37 percent in the developing world between 1990 and 2005. However, due to rising population, and the rise especially in urban populations, the number of slum dwellers is rising. One billion people worldwide live in slums and the figure will likely grow to 2 billion by 2030. The term has traditionally referred to housing areas that were once relatively affluent but which deteriorated as the original dwellers moved on to newer and better parts of the city, but has come to include the vast informal settlements found in cities in the developing world.

Many shack dwellers vigorously oppose the description of their communities as 'slums' arguing that this results in them being pathologised and then, often, subject to threats of evictions. Many academics have vigorously criticized UN-Habitat and the World Bank arguing that their 'Cities Without Slums' Campaign has led directly to a massive increase in forced evictions. Although their characteristics vary between geographic regions, they are usually inhabited by the very poor or socially disadvantaged. Slum buildings vary from simple shacks to permanent and well-maintained structures. Most slums lack clean water, electricity, sanitation and other basic services.

Etymology

The origin the word slum is thought to come from the Irish phrase *'S lom é* (pron. s'lum ae) meaning "it is a bleak or destitute place." A 1812 English dictionary defined slum to mean "a room". By the 1920s became a common slang expression in England, meaning either various taverns and eating houses, "loose talk" or gypsy language, or a room with "low going-ons". In *Life in London* Pierce Egan used the word in the context of the "back slums" of Holy Lane or St Giles. A footnote defined slum to mean "low, unfrequent parts of the town". Charles Dickens used the word slum in a similar way in 1840, writing "I mean to take a great, London, back-slum kind walk tonight". Slum began to be used to describe bad housing soon after and was used as alternative expression for rookeries.

In 1850 Cardinal Wiseman described the area known as Devil's Acre in Westminster, London as follows: "Close under the Abbey of Westminster there lie concealed labyrinths of lanes and courts, and alleys and slums, nests of ignorance, vice, depravity, and crime, as well as of squalor, wretchedness, and disease; whose atmosphere is typhus, whose ventilation is cholera; in which swarms of huge and almost countless population, nominally at least, Catholic; haunts of filth, which no sewage committee can reach - dark corners, which no lighting board can brighten."

This passage was widely quoted in the national press, leading to the popularisation of the word *slum* to describe bad housing. Other terms that are often used interchangeably with "slum" include shanty town, favela, skid row, barrio, and ghetto although each of these may have a somewhat different meaning. Slums are distinguished from shanty towns and favelas in that the latter initially are low-class settlements, whereas slums are generally constructed early on as relatively affluent or possibly a prestigious communities. The term "shanty town" also suggests that the dwellings are improvised shacks, made from scrap materials, and usually without proper sanitation, electricity, or telephone services. Skid row refers to an urban area with a high homeless population and a term is most commonly used in the United States. Barrio may refer to an upper-class area in some Spanish-speaking countries and is used to describe only a low-class community in the United States. Ghetto refers to a neighbourhood based on shared ethnicity. By contrast, identification of an area as a slum is based solely on socio-economic criteria, not on racial, ethnic, or religious criteria.

Characteristics

The characteristics and politics associated with slums vary from place to place. Slums are usually characterized by urban decay, high rates of poverty, illiteracy, and unemployment. They are commonly seen as "breeding grounds" for social problems such as crime, drug addiction, alcoholism, high rates of mental illness, and suicide.

In many poor countries they exhibit high rates of disease due to unsanitary conditions, malnutrition, and lack of basic health care. However, some like Dharavi, Mumbai, are a hive of business activity such as leather work, cottage industries, etc. Rural depopulation with thousands arriving daily into the cities makes slum clearance an uphill struggle. In fact one could argue that the presence of slums reflects true democracy(free movements of people) as only a totalitarian state could 'eradicate' slums.

A UN Expert Group has created an operational definition of a slum as an area that combines to various extents the following characteristics: inadequate access to safe water; inadequate access to sanitation and other infrastructure; poor structural quality of housing; overcrowding; and insecure residential status. A more complete definition of these can be found in the 2003 UN report titled "Slums of the World: The face of urban poverty in the new millennium?". The report also lists various attributes and names that are given by individual countries which are somewhat different than these UN characteristics of a slum.

Low socioeconomic status of its residents is another common characteristic given for a slum. In many slums, especially in poor countries, many live in very narrow alleys that do not allow vehicles (like ambulances and fire trucks) to pass. The lack of services such as routine garbage collection allows rubbish to accumulate in huge quantities. The lack of infrastructure is caused by the informal nature of settlement and no planning for the poor by government officials. Additionally, informal settlements often face the brunt of natural and man-made disasters, such as landslides, as well as earthquakes and tropical storms. Fires are often a serious problem.

Many slum dwellers employ themselves in the informal economy. This can include street vending, drug dealing, domestic work, and prostitution. In some slums people even recycle trash of different kinds (from household garbage to electronics) for a living - selling either the odd usable goods or stripping broken goods for parts or raw materials.

Slums are often associated with Victorian Britain, particularly in industrial, northern English towns, lowland Scottish towns and Dublin City in Ireland. These were generally still inhabited until the 1940s, when the government started slum clearance and built new council houses. There are still many examples left of former slum housing in the UK, however they have generally been restored into more modern housing.

Growth and countermeasures

Recent years have seen a dramatic growth in the number of slums as urban populations have increased in the Third World. In April 2005, the director of UN-HABITAT stated that the global community was falling short of the Millennium Development Goals which targeted significant improvements for slum dwellers and an additional 50 million people have been added to the slums of the world in the past two years. According to a 2006 UN-HABITAT report, 327 million people live in slums in Commonwealth countries - almost one in six Commonwealth citizens. In a quarter of Commonwealth countries (11 African, 2 Asian and 1 Pacific), more than two out of three urban dwellers live in slums and many of these countries are urbanising rapidly. The number of people living in slums in India has more than doubled in the past two decades and now exceeds the entire population of Britain, the Indian Government has announced. The number of people living in slums is projected to rise to 93 million in 2011 or 7.75 percent of the total population almost double the population of Britain.

Many governments around the world have attempted to solve the problems of slums by clearing away old decrepit housing and replacing it with modern housing with much better sanitation. The displacement of slums is aided by the fact that many are squatter settlements whose property rights are not recognized by the state. This process is especially common in the Third World. Slum clearance often takes the form of eminent domain and urban renewal projects, and often the former residents are not welcome in the renewed housing. For example, in the Philippine slums of Smokey Mountain, located in Tondo, Manila, projects have been enforced by the Government and non-government organizations to allow urban resettlement sites for the slum dwellers. According to a UN-Habitat report, over 20 million people in the Philippines live in slums, and in the city of Manila alone, 50% of the over 11 million inhabitants live in slum areas. Moreover new projects are often on the semi-rural peripheries of cities far from opportunities for generating livelihoods as well as schools, clinics etc. At times this has resulted in large movements of inner city slum dwellers militantly opposing relocation to formal housing on the outskirts of cities.

In some countries, leaders have addressed this situation by rescuing rural property rights to support traditional sustainable agriculture, however this solution has met with open hostility from capitalists and corporations. It also tends to be relatively unpopular with the slum communities themselves, as it involves moving out of the city back into the countryside, a reverse of the rural-urban migration that originally brought many of them into the city.

Critics argue that slum clearances tend to ignore the social problems that cause slums and simply redistribute poverty to less valuable real estate. Where communities have been moved out of slum areas to newer housing, social cohesion may be lost. If the original community is moved back into newer housing after it has been built in the same location, residents of the new housing face the same problems of poverty and powerlessness. There is a growing movement to demand a global ban of 'slum clearance programmes' and other forms of mass evictions.

ORISSA TRIBAL COMMUNITY

Linguistically the tribes of India are broadly classified into four categories, namely:

(i) Indo-Aryan Speakers

(ii) Dravidian Speakers

(iii) Tibeto-Burmese speakers, and

(iv) Austric speakers.

There are four hundred tribal languages, which means that most of the tribes have their own languages. However, in a majority of cases, these languages are unwritten ones. In Orissa the speakers of the Tibeto-Burmese language family are absent, and therefore Orissan tribes belong to other three language families. The Indo-Aryan language family in Orissa, includes, Dhelki-Oriya, Matia, Halaba, Jharia, Saunti, Laria and Oriya (spoken by Bathudi and the acculturated sections of Bhuiyan, Juang, Kandha, Savara, Raj Gond etc.).

The Austric language family includes eighteen tribal languages namely, Birjia, Parenga, Kisan, Bhumij, Koda, Mahili Bhumij, Mirdha-Kharia, Ollar Gadaba, Juang, bondo, Didayee, Karmali, Kharia, Munda, Ho, Mundari and Savarna. And within the Dravidian language family there are nine languages in Orissa, namely: Pengo, Gondi, Kisan, Konda, Koya, Parji, Kui, Juvi and Kurukh or Oraon.

There was a general misconception that tribal communities did not possess languages but dialects. But with the extensive study of tribal languages Linguists have come to the conclusion that tribal, do possess languages. Tribal languages contain the same features which other languages possess, such as (i) duality of structure (phonemic and morphemic) (ii) productivity capability (creativity and novelty) (iii) arbitrariness (no correlation between linguistic morphs and their meanings) (iv) interchangeability (vocal and auditory functions are simultaneous) (v) specialization (codes and code-switching capability. (vi) displacement (abstractness of speech) (vii) prevarication (ability to misrepresent reality) and (viii) cultural transmission (learning and inculcation). Besides, tribal languages have all the four subsystems, such as (a) phonomorphemic (b) syntactic (c) semantic and (d) symbolic which other languages have.

The major difference between tribal and non-tribal languages is that the former are unwritten ones. Nd therefore have no literay traditions, but only oral traditions when one examines the entire range of folklore of a tribe, he finds that the oral tradition of that tribe is no less rich. Some of the major tribes have been trying to develop literary traditions of their own, for example, Santhals of Orissa have developed a script called Olchiki, for their language. Their cultural organization has been priting and publishing primary level text books, Santhals songs, myths,riddles, proverbs, anecdotes and dramas in this script. And in addition, the cultural organization has been printing newsletters and calendars of Santhal annual cycle festivals. The tribes of Orissa though belong to three linguistic divisions, yet they have lots of socio-cultural similarities amongthem. These communities signify homogeneity of their cultures and together they characterize the notion or concept of triblism.

Tribal societies share certain common characteristics and by these they are distinguished from complex or advance societies. in India tribal societies had apparently been outside the main historical current. Hence tribal societies manifested such cultural features which signified a simple socio – cultural parameter.

Habitat: A major portion of the tribal habitat is hilly forested. Tribal village are generally found in areas away from the alluvial plains close to rivers. Most villages are uniethnic in composition, and smaller in size. Village are often not planned at all.

Economy : Tribal economy is characterized as subsistence oriented. The subsistence economy is based mainly on collecting, hunting and fishing (e.g., the Birhor, Hill Kharia) or a combination of hunting ad collecting with shifting cultivation. Even the so-called plough-using agricultural tribes do often, whereever scope is available, supplement their economy with hunting and collecting. Subsistence economy is characterized by simple technology, simple division of labour, small scale units of production and no investment of capital. The social unit of production and no investment of capotal. The social unit of production, distribution and consumption is limited to the family and lineage. Subsistence economy is imposed cirecumstances which are beyond the Control of human beings, poverty of the physical environment, ignorance of efficient technique of exploiting natural resources and lack of capital for investment. It also implies existence of barter and lack of trade.

Considering the general features of their (i) eco-system (ii) traditional economy (iii) supernatural beliefs and practices, and (iv) recent "impacts of modernization" the tribes of Orissa can be classified into six types, such as (a) Hunting, collecting and gathering type (b) Cattle-herder type (c) Simple artisan type (d) Hill and shifiting cultivation type (e) Settled agriculture type and (f) Industrial urban worker type.

Each type has a distinct style of which could be best understood in the paradigm of nature, man and spirit complex that is, on the basis of relationship with nature, fellow men and the supernatural.

Tribes of the first type, namely, Kharia, Mankidia, Mankirdia and Birhor, live in the tiny temporary depend on forest resources for their livelihood by practicing hunting, gathering and collecting. They live in tiny temporary hunts made out of the materials found in the forest. Under constraints of their economic pursuit they live in isolated small bands or groups. With their primitive technology, limited skill and unflinching traditional and ritual practices. Their entire style of life revolves round forest. Their world view is fully in consonance with the forest resources is vary significant. Socio-politically they have remained inarticulate and therefore have remained in a relatively more primitive stage, and neglected too.

The Koya, which belongs to the Dravidian linguistic group, is the lone pastoral and cattle-breeder tribal community in Orissa. This tribe which inhabits the Malkangiri, district has been facing crisis for lack of pasture. Rehabilitation of Bangladesh refugees in the Koystraditional habitat has created certain socio-economic problems for the latter.

In Orissa, Mahali and Kol-Lohara practisc crafts, like basketry and black-smithy respectively. The Loharas with their traditional skill and primitive tools manufacture iron and wooden tools for other neighbouring tribes and thereby eke out their existence. Similarly the Mahalis earn their living by making baskets for other communities. Both the tribes are now confronted with the problem of scarcity of raw materials. And further they are not able to complete with others, especially in the tribal market where goods of others communities come for sale. Because of their primitive technology.

The tribes that practice hill and shifting cultivation are many. In northern Orissa, the juang and bhuiyan and in southern Orissa the kandha, saora, koya, parenga, Didayi, Dharua and Bondo practice shifting cultivation. They supplement their economy by food-gathering and hunting as production. In shifting cultivating the practitioners follow a pattern of cycle of activities which are as follows : (i) Selection of a patch cf hill slope or forest land and distribution or allotment of the same to intended practitioner, (ii) Worshipping of concerned deities and making of sacrificing (iii) Cutting of trees, bushes ferns etc. existing on the land before summer month (iv) piling up of logs, bushes and ferns on the land (v) Burning of the withered logs, ferns and shrubs etc..to ashes on a suitableday (vi) cleaning of the patch of land before the onset of monsoon and spreading of the ashes evenly on the land after a shower or two (vii) Hoeing and showing of seeds with regular commencement of monsoon rains (viii) Crude bunding and weeding activities follow after sprouting of seeds (ix) Watching and protecting the crops (x) Harvesting and collecting crops (xi) Threshing and storing and storing of crons, grains etc. and (xii) Merry –making in these operations all the member of the family are involved in some way or the other. Work is distributed among the family member according to the ability of individual Member.

However, the head of the family assumes all the responsibilities in the practice and operation of shifting cultivation. The adult males, between 18 and 50 years of age undertake the strenuous work of cutting free, ploughing and hoeing, and watching of the crops at night where as cutting the bushes and shrubs, cleaning of seeds for sowing and weeding are done by women. Shifting cultivation is not only an economic pursuit of some tribal communities, but it account for their total way of life, Their social structure, economy, political organization and religion are all accountable to the practice of shifting cultivation.

However, shifting cultivation has certain demerits. Whenever shifting cultivation is carried out on a steep slope it invariably invites the agents age is of erosion and degradation. By deforestation soil loses its water retention capacity. The subsoil gets washed away and the rocks and boulders are gradually exposed. Slowly and steadily the shifting cultivation process causes the streams down the hill to dry up. It also brings down heavy silts into the river basins, plains and valley. The extensive deforestation effects rainfall. It affects the life of animals and forest resources, and it also leads tonomadic habits among the practioners.

In the past, land in the tribal areas had not been surveyed and settled. Therefore, the tribals freely practiced shifting cultivation in their respective habitats assuming that land, forest, water and other natural resources belonged to them. There were two traditional systems of land tenure prevalent among the tribes of Orissa, Among the tribes of northern Orissa land the other resources were communally owned and thus the annual distribution of plots on the hill slopes for shifting cultivation was being done in a corporate manner. But among the tribes of southern Orissa all such lands and other natural resources were under the control of the village (tribal) head man, who on approach used to allot plots for use to individuals. And since the evolution of Indian Forest Policy in 1952 and completion of survey and settlement of land in tribal areas the traditional tribal land tenure system has dwindled. The tribals therefore, now have limited land forest resources for the practice of Shifting cultivation and for carrying on hunting, collecting and gathering activities. The pernicious, yet unavoidable, practice of shifting cultivation continues unchecked, and all attempts made to wean away the tribals from shifting cultivation have so far failed. The colonization scheme of the State Govt. has failed in Practice.

In certain hilly areas terraces are constructed along the slopes. It is believed to be a step towards settled agriculture. Terrace cultivation is practiced by the Saora, Kandha and Gadaba. The terraces are built on the slopes of hill with water streams. In terrace cultivation the available hill slopes are fully used, and the available water of hill streams are tapped for cultivation throughout the year as the water flows from one terrace to another in downward motion. The terrace walls are riveted and packed with stones and boulders, which cannot be washed out easily. In terraces paddy is mainly grown and the per acre yield is quite high. The quantity of terrace land under the possession of a family is not much.

Several Large tribes, such as, Santhal, Munda, Ho, Bhumij, Oraon, Gond, Kandha, Mirdha, Savera, etc, are settled agriculturists though they supplement their economy with hunting, gathering and collecting. Tribal agriculture in Orissa is characterized by unproductive and uneconomic holdings, land alienation indebtedness, lack if irrigation facilities in the undulating terrains, lack of easy soft credit facilities in the undulating terrains, lack of easy or soft credit facilities as well as use of traditional skill and primitive implements. In general, they raise only one crop during the monsoon, and therefore have to supplement their economy by other types of subsidiary economic activities.

Tribal communities practicising settled agriculture also suffer from further problems, viz., (1) want of record of right for land under occupation (2) land alientation (3) problems of indebtedness (4) lack of power for irrigation (5) absence of adequate roads and transport (6) seasonal migration to other places for wage earning and (7) lack of education and adequate scope for modernization.

Sizable agglomeration of tribal population of Orissa has moved to mining, industrial and urban areas for earning a secured living through wage- labour. During the past three decades the process of industrial urbanization in the tribal belt of Orissa has been accelerated through the operation of mines and establishment of industries. Mostly persons from advanced tribal communities, such as Santhal, Munda Ho, Oraon, Kisan, Gond etc. have taken to this economic pursuit in order to relieve pressure from their limited land and other resources.

In some instances industrialization and mining operations have led to uprooting of tribal villages, and the displaced became industrial nomads. They lost their traditional occupation, agricultural land, houses and other immovable assets. They became unemployed and faced unfair competition with others in the labour market. The aspiration gradually escalated, although they invariably failed to achieve what they aspired for. Thus the net result was frustration occasionally their disappointment has been reflected in unrest and agitation. They Jharkhand movement also capitalizes on these issues.

While it is neither possible nor desirable to halt the process of industrialization, the authorities must contemplate built – in safeguards for all those who are affected by it. In a discussion on tribal economy it is essential to dilate briefly on the concept of "Primitivism", Because tribal communities in general are branded as primitive. The concept of 'Primitive' has been subjected to increasing criticism by anthropologists. The term is considered as a cliché and a derogatory one it is contempyuous and obfuscating. The term represents an ortholinar view point and a less advanced technological stage. Tribal societies, labelled as primitive, are almost in a state of equilibrium. The change though is ubiquitous, its pace is slow in tribal societies, because of geo-historical reasons, Branding the tribal communities as 'primitive ' in an egregious error, because the more we understand the tribal communities, the better we understand the ourselves.

The term 'primitive' denotes a particular configuration of certain phenomena, that is (i) small scale homogeneous kin – based society. With simple division of labour (ii) social and political Organization go hand in hand (iii) relative isolation with a specific geographical location (iv) egalitarian society, lack of significant competition and the normative order rests on cooperation (v) techno-economic level is low with the lack of formal education and capitalistic orientation (vi) personality is endowed with an over powering sense of realism and pragmatism. (vii) religious beliefs and performances directly contribute to a strong sense of personal security, and (viii) monolingualism contributing to socio –cultural isolationism. Therefore, what one notices here is that the largest significant reference group is the 'tribe' or a segment of it, the sub-tribe' this is, a single, endogamous ethnic group occupying a more or less contiguous territory in some cases, e.g., Santhal, Munda and Ho describe themselves as 'Hor' meaning 'man,' which others are 'Diku' or 'aliens.' The tribes are segmented into exogamous (partilineal in Orissa) totemic (excepting the Saoras) clans. Frequently with territorial cohesion and strong corporate identity. Clans are segmented into lineages with known genealogical ties which function as effective corporate social units.

The overall kinship system of the tibes may be labelled as 'tempered classificatory.' In terminology the emphasis lies on the unolineal principle, generation and age, Descent and inheritance are patrilineal and authority is patripotestal among all tribal communities of Orissa, On the basis of kinship organization Orissan tribes can be divided into two categories. The kinship system of the tribes of the Dravidian language family is' bifurcate mergine' type' whereas the tribes of the other two language families is bifurcate collateral type.

As regards the acquisition of brides for marriage the most widely prevalent practice among the tribes of Orissa is through 'capture' although other practices such as, elopement, purchase service and negotiation are also there. With the passage of time negotiated type of marriage which is considered prestigious, is being preferred more and more. Payment of bride price is an inseparable part of tribal marriage, but has changed to the system of dowry among the educated sections. In the past tribal marriages used to be performed in the house of the groom, but In recent times well to do and educated tribal families have changed the marriage booth to the bride's parental home. After marriage the bride goes to the houses of her –in-laws. Therefore, family among all the tribal communities of Orissa is patrilocal. Among some of the Dravidian tribal communities of Orissa the custom of 'prescriptive' and 'preferential ' marriage are here, that is marriage with mother's brother's daughter or fathers's brother's daughter.

Excepting the Kandha this custom is in operation among other Dravidian tribes of Orissa. Among the tribes there is very little specialization of social roles. With the exception of role differentiation in terms of Kinship and sex and some specialization in crafts, the only other role specializations are headman, Priest, Shahman and the Haruspex.

There is very little rigid stratification in society. The tendency towards stratification is gaining momentum among several settled agricultural tribes under the impact of modernization. The tribes of Orissa are at different levels of socio-economic development.

The religion of the Orissa tribes is an admixture of animism,, animatism, nature worship, fetishism, shamanism, anthropomorphism and ancestor worship. Religious beliefs and practices aim at ensuring personal security and happiness as well as community well-being and group solidarity. Their religious performances include life-crises rites, cyclic community rites, ancestor and totemic rites and observance of taboos. Besides these, the tribals also resort to various types of occult practices. In order to tide over either a personal or a group crisis the tribals begin with occult practices, and if it dies not yield any result the next recourse is supplication of the supernatural force.

SANTHAL: LARGEST TRIBAL COMMUNITY IN INDIA

Largest tribal community in India, found mainly in the states of West Bengal, Bihar, Jharkhand and Orissa. Satars or Santhals are one of the most backward ethnic groups of the neighbouring country Nepal. They live in the districts of Jhapa, Morang and Sunsari. There is also a significant Santal minority in neighbouring Bangladesh. Santhals also call themselves Hor. They prefer to live in the peripheries of forests and rivers. They have their own unique religion and culture. They are animist. Hunting and fishing are their favourite occupations. Their ancestral deity is Thakurjiu and their paternal guardian deity is Maranburu. Bow and arrows are their traditional weapons. Their favourite meat is pork. Most Santals are engaged in farming and labour. They belong to the Austro-Asiatic group of human families. They have also been called as a subgroup speaking a language belonging to the Munda family (Dahal, BS2051/052). Their language is called Santhali. They have their own script, which was developed by Dr Raghunath Murmu in 1925. It is called Olchiki.

Racially the Santhals belong to the protoastraloid racial group, linguistically they belong to the Mundari group of Austro-

Asiatic linguistic family and economically they may be classified as plain agricultural type. The Santhals are very conscious about their identity and heritage. And this is the reason why they have, most probably consciously, built up a sense of solidarity amongst themselves. Their internal solidarity is often based on their principle of likeness, that is a shared cultural characteristic, which binds them together. The Santhals live in peace and harmony among themselves.

Population: The Jhapa district in Nepal has the highest population of Santhals and Morang district has slightly less. Their population, according to the census of 2001, is 42,689. The Southern part of the Bihar is called as 'Santhal Praganas' because of the density of the Santhal tribe in this area. They had multiplied from proto – Australoid origin. It is also believed that they had come from the Districts of 'Santha' and that is why they are called as 'Santan' or men of Santha state. The Munda-Santal of northeastern India and Nepal comprise of nine different, but very closely related people groups. They are distributed politically throughout the states of Bihar, West Bengal, and Orissa, India. Most of the tribes live in the hilly areas of the Chotanagpur Plateau, located in southern Bihar. Others prefer living in the plains. Beyond this region, they have spread widely throughout India as agricultural and industrial labourers.

The seven groups who occupy territory farther north include the Santhal (of India and Nepal), the Bhumij, the Koda, the Mahili, the Ho, and the Agariya. The two remaining groups, the Juango and the Gadaba, are located in the southern portion of India, nearer to the coast of the Bay of Bengal.

Language: The Santhali language is part of the Austro-Asiatic family, distantly related to Vietnamese and Khmer. The history of the Santals may be traced to Africa from where started the human migration. It was found that humans from Africa started to migrate towards the Eastern part of the world or Asia. The Santhali script, or Ol Chiki, is alphabetic, and does not share any of the syllabic properties of the other Indic scripts such as Devanagari. It uses 30 letters and five basic diacritics. It has 6 basic vowels and three additional vowels, generated using the Gahla Tudag.

Santhals did not have a written language until the twentieth century. Therefore the script is a recent development. A distinct script was required to accommodate the Santhali language, combining features of both the Indic and Roman scripts. The modern Ol Chiki script was devised by Pandit Raghunath Murmu in 1925. He wrote over 150 books covering a wide spectrum of subjects. Darege Dhan, Sidhu-Kanhu, Bidu Chandan and Kherwal Bir are among the most acclaimed of his works. Pandit Raghunath Murmu is popularly known as Guru Gomke among the Santhals, a title conferred on him by the Mayurbhanj Adibasi Mahasabh.

Judicial system: The Santhals traditionally had an organized judicial system for the management and solution of the various problems within the community. They make every effort to solve the social problems arising within their community by themselves. The head of the Santhal community is called Manjhi Hadam. He is the chief of the executive, judicial and all other functions within society. He is assisted by other office bearers like Paranik, Jagmanjhi, Jagparanik, Naike, Gudit, etc, who work in their respective fields to solve various kinds of problems. After the birth of a child, the Jagmanjhi and following the death of a person the Gudit and others are present. Manjhi Hadam undertakes the looking into judicial cases and the dispensing of justice and above him is Disham Manjhi, and above both is Diheri. The Diheri is the highest judicial office bearer of Santhals. The Santhals who generally like to live in concentrated settlements of their own near rivers and forests are divided into 12 thars or groups. As the groups are in accordance with professional specialization, this appears as a form of social system. The Murmu are the priests of Santhals and Murdi the businessmen, while Kisku are the rulers and Hemram judges. Similarly, the Tudu are musicians and Soren soldiers. The organizations of Santhals are village council (Manjhibaisi), Proganna Council (Pramatrabaisi) and the highest council (Labirbaisi).

3

Problems of the Tribal Communities

There are various problems, which are confronted to the tribal communities. These problems have been summarized as follows;

Problem Relating to Poverty and Backwardness

The poverty and indebtedness crisis comes to the forefront in tribal phenomena. It is though the tribal money lending system that the tribals are greatly exploited. The tribal economy is characterically subsistence type of economy and due to their type of economy and due to their somewhat traditional hedonistic type of worldview, they have meagre amount of saving. Naturally when they are in need of money, they are forces to depend on others particularly the non-tribal moneylenders. Under this system, a person who takes loan from moneylenders who are landowners is required to serve him like slaves according to the terms and condition of the debt.

Quite often, if he is unable to repay the loan, it descends to his son or even to his third generation. Considering the degree of exploitation and seriousness of the problem, the 'Fifth schedule' empowers the Governors to take special action. This system of forced bonded labours is in practice in many tribal settlements in the study area. It is a significant factor that the labour commission has taken steps to release the tribal children from the moneylenders or landowners in H.D.Kote taluk tribal settlements.

The lack of proper data in tribal indebtedness is a great hurdle. Although, some studies were made on tribal indebtedness long back about which some references are available in the reports of the commissioners for Scheduled Caste and Scheduled Tribes, Government of India, but no efforts have been made to get on up to date figures of tribal indebtedness at the micro-level or at the level of a particular ethnic group, so that immediate steps could be taken to remove the indebtedness.

In this study, it has been noted that the following factors are highly responsible for the tribal indebtedness:

- Merger income of the tribes.
- Ignorance of equitable price-system.
- Large-scale celebrations and festivals, especially on the occasions like birth, marriage, deaths etc.

Remedial Steps

The fifth schedule of the constitution empowers the Government of a state to regulate the carrying on the business as moneylenders by persons who lend money to members of scheduled tribes in scheduled areas. In pursuance of this provision various State Government of have promulgated and enacted various laws and acts. Planning commissions Reports of the study team in the Tribal Development Programmes have summed up the situation with clarity. It is of the view that the attack on tribal indebtedness should be two-prolonged if it is to be effective and enduring. On the one hand long-term credit should be provided to enable the tribes to free himself from the strong hold of the usurious moneylenders and on the other hand improving his economic condition should raise his repaying capacity.

Co-operative credit should forthcoming in an adequate measure and the procedure has to be simplified to attract the tribes to take advantage of the credit facilities by the society. But the crux of the problem still remaining i.e. needs political will, commitment with honesty and integrity on the part of those who are supposed to be the protectors of tribal interests. In the absence of these, the coming regulations, provisions and schemes shall continue to be treated are mere pieces of paper.

Land Alienation

Land is the main stay of the tribes and more than 80 percent of them arc dependent on agriculture and allied activities. Their economy is primarily agro-based. Land is the only tangible asset of a tribal family. Tribes have emotional attachment to land. However, with the opening up of the tribal areas, the tribal land is being alienated to the non-tribals. During 2000-2001, the cultivatable land was 71.04 percent in the study area. Remaining 28.46 percent of land has been alienated from non-tribais, followness and land has not been suitable for cultivation. Consequently a large number of tribal cultivators have been rendered landless labourers. The agricultural labourers were 30.49 percent in 1999-2000. Which is more than other occupationist. It shows the decrease in the number of cultivators (13.15 percent) and increase in the landless labourers is also an indication of the distributing trend of land alienation. The incidence of land alienation varies from region to region. Apart from the field survey (1999-2000), about 43.36 percent of the tribal households have been affected by the land alienation.

Ariofiler tendency fiignfrgfited by the survey was that in certain areas, although the tribes are the official owners of the land, the non-tribes have become its virtual owners. This problem is very acute in the Melukamanahalli and Moguvinhally tribal colonies of Gundlepet taluk. The study of land alienation among the tribes has not been studied in detail. A case study of land alienation in rural areas was conducted by tribal welfare organizations which brought to light the nature and agencies associated with land alienation. Regulations under which cases of alienation of last few years could be opened. Mere legislation is not enough, it is essential, firstly, to study the various patterns of land alienation covering the entire Scheduled Areas.

Remedial Steps

Taking into consideration of the three bases of land alienation of tribal people viz.,

(a) The lacunae in the laws,

(b) The ignorance of the tribal people, and

(c) The complicated legal procedures to be. Many state governments have been doing something to help the tribal. Before looking into various legislative steps taken to safeguard tribal interest in land, it will be in the fitness of things to study the crucial recommendations of Scheduled Areas and Scheduled Commissions, 1961, on the basis of which various states passed a number of legislations.

Some of the important legislation enumerated may be divided into two types; one is protective intended to prevent non-tribal acquiring tribal land and the other deals with question of land reforms. Both type of legislation has fallen short of the needs of the situation. The protective legislation could not be of much use as no sufficient arrangement for alternative credit was made. The land reform legislation could not help the tribes to a great extent because it was too intricated for him to fallow. But the most important factor in this state of affair is the lack of will and integrity on the part of administration to ameliorate the sufferings of the tribal masses. Hence the vested interests exploiting the tribes have been and still are in a position to carry in their nefarious and criminal activities some time with the help of indifference of officials and some time with the active connivance of officials at lower levels. Due to their growing contacts with radical political elements and sincere pro-peasantry cards of radical organizations, an explosive is fast growing up.

Shifting Cultivation

Under shifting cultivation a vast area of forestland is selected for shifting cultivation and the trees and plants of the forest are cut and burnt. Under this system a vast track of forest land is destroyed by cutting the forest, which is not only harmful for them but, it also creates ecological imbalances in the region. Therefore, the government has banned the practice of shifting cultivation, and hence, those tribes who have been practicing the shifting cultivation, are facing seasons problems.

Remedial Steps

The report of the Scheduled Area and Scheduled Tribes

Commission, 1961, has recommended some important suggestions for implementation. Some of the major suggestions are as follows:

1. The total replacement of this system, if it come at all, will be a long-term process. In the mean time there must be a proper course to regulate it, experiment with it, improve it and try other workable alternatives of shifting cultivation tied up with the tribal way of life and it is much more than a technical problem pertaining only to improve the techniques of forming and agriculture.
2. Shifting cultivation may be converted into terraced cultivation wherever the hill slopes are ideal and the soil is sufficiently deep. This holds out immerse possibilities of improvement, and in many places throughout the tribal areas it has been taken up with enthusiasm.
3. Establishment of agncultural/calonies may also be an effective solution to wean away the tribes from shifting cultivation to sedentary cultivation. Under this programme, tribal families may receive some cultivable wasteland, financial assistance for the construction of houses, reclamation of the land, bullocks, agricultural implements and high yielding verity seeds etc., Facilities for communications, drinking water, irrigation, medical aids, etc., were also proposed. However the following measures should be provided for sedentary agriculture and to improve the agriculture in tribal areas.
   - Setting up of a demonstration farms
   - Distribution of improved agricultural implements, manure, fertilizers and HYV seeds
   - Extending credit facilities.

Improved agricultural implements distributed to tribes have been such as would meet their approval.

Problem relating to Forests

The tribal people everywhere have lived in intimate relationship with forest and it has been linked with their very existence due to obvious factors. Forests have been sufficiently sustaining their inhabitants. Forests are their abode and source of livelihood. They get food, fruits, roots and honey from the forests. Thus the traditional tribal economy is mainly built around the forests. Also many flora and fauna have been the objects of worship for the tribes due to one reason or the other. And not less important is the fact that the tribal people achieved a harmony between their lives and nature through the forests.

But the forest policies are not encouraging the tribes in many aspects, like growing, collection of forest produces formation of settlement in dense forests, land reforms etc., Although the forest policies are not to disturb for tribal livelihood, it vary from region to region. The forest Act has enhanced harassment and exploitation of the tribal people. The forest offices have to work in an extremely different physical condition, therefore they are given legal protection of a far reaching character. Under this guard the poor tribes have certainly been placed at the mercy of the forest officials. The unscrupulous officials among them have been playing havoc with their lives and harass them at the slightest pretext.

Collection of minor forest products an is not at all likely to hinder the forest either in its growth or preservation. But at certain places the tribal inhabitants are not allowed to avail of this concession. Instead the forest officials get it collected and uses it for their benefits.

The large-scale deforestation leads to ecological imbalance, nonavailability of forest products and non-availability of raw material for forest based industries. It also influences the rainfall, atmospheric quality and causes floods, landslides, soil erosion and other natural disasters. The ultimate victims are the tribes.

Remedial Steps

There are several developmental policies launched by the government for the upliftment of tribes. But the basic defects of these policies are that they are fonnulated without taking into consideration of the ground realities existing in the different remote tribal pockets. A particular policy may be suitable in one area and may not be suitable to other areas, as there are differences in ecological situations. Therefore, the utmost care has to be taken while formulating to preserve the policies. The forest and creation of new forest areas to compensate the loss of green cover in the last few decades. Tribes all along used to get most of their necessities from the forests. They never know the technique and care of raising different plant species. They have been exploiting the forest resources since time immemorial. Therefore, necessary training should be important to them in this respect by forest extension workers at the village level. In tribal areas, the villages are usually very small and consists of only 10 to 15 houses. In such cases a group of villages should be checked together and the centrally located village should be considered as the key or model village. The village level workers both government and voluntary organisations can effectively make use of these model village for the implementation viable forest policies in the field of forest, healthcare, education etc., for the comprehensive development of the tribal areas.

Lack of Educational Facilities among the Tribes

In the past, education was one of the main considerations for hierarchical classification in the Hindu society. Lack of it is largely responsible for the exploitation and pitiable plight of the tribes. Education is the key catalyst for the development of human resources.

For the tribes, education is the pivot on which success depends. Education disseminates knowledge. Knowledge gives inner strength, which is very much essential for the tribes for attaining freedom from exploitation. Due to ignorance arising out of illiteracy, the tribes have not been able to take advantage of new economic opportunities. Opening of the tribal areas in the work of developmental process have brought in juxtaposition two distinct value systems one based on tradition and ignorance and the other on technologies and innovations. Harmonious syncronisation of the two systems is essential for the development of tribal society. In this process, education will play a key role. The most important aspect of education in the tribal areas is that of informing the community about the new innovations is science and technology as well as the development in economic and political fields. Thus education must be fruitful to the tribal people for the enhancement social and economic status.

Recognising the importance of education, the constitution has made specific provisions in Article 15(iv) and 46 for promoting education among the scheduled tribes. According to 1981 census the literacy among the scheduled tribes was 14.58 percent against the general literacy of 31.34 percent. A comparative position of literacy percentage among the general population and scheduled tribe population as per 1981 and 1991 census is given in table; Although, literacy among the tribes has increased considerable over a period of one decade it is still far below the general level. The position of female literacy is really a matter of concern. The rate of tribal literacy varies from region to region. There are some important causes for slow-progress in literacy among the tribes. Such causes are to be maintained specially in this study and they are follows.

Social Factors

More allocation of funds and opening of new schools are not far behind in providing education to the tribal people. A few obvious factors play the dominant role in this respect. Formal education is not very much necessary for the members of tribal societies to discharge their social obligations. Economic Factors

Some Economic factors, too, are responsible for the lack of interest shown by the tribal people in getting education. Since most of the tribal people are living in utter poverty under subsistence economy, it is not easy for most of them to send their children to school thus losing two healthy hands in their struggle for survival. Verrier Elwin (1963)' very appropriately sums up the situation in the following way: "For a tribal family, to send its grown up girls or boys to school, is essentially a matter of economics; and entails dislocation in the traditional pattern of division of labour many parents cannot just afford to send their children to school."

According to the present system of education any economic benefit that a tribal child can bring to his family will be only after 10 or 15 years of schooling. The parents have neither the patience nor the foresight to wait for such a long period. They can however, be convinced easily if the education for them can be made productive right from the very beginning.

Lack of Interest in Formal Education

Sharma (1976) has rightly pointed out that the "urban middle-class-orientated education system has got superimposed on the entire nation both in terms of its structure and content." In many states tribal children are taught the same books, which from the curriculum of non-tribal children of the urban and rural areas of the rest of the state. Obviously the content of such books rearly appeals the tribal children who come from different cultural backgrounds. Stories of scientific and technological progress, founders of modern India, history and geography of the country etc, of course, from necessary part of any curriculum but the situation demands that their education should start with teaching of demography, history and ecology of their own region. National consciousness should not be imposed from above or outside, but they should be made aware of it in a systematic manner.

Dedicated Teachers

Lack of dedicated teachers is one of the major reasons for the slow growth of education in tribal areas. Most of the teachers employed for imparting education to the tribal children show little appreciation of the tribal way of life and value system. They approach the tribal people with a sense of superiority and treat them as 'savage' and 'uncivilized' and hence fail to establish proper rapport with their students.

Lack of Facilities

Nature of habitat of tribes is also responsible for the slow growth of education. Most of the tribal villages are scattered. This entails long travels to attend schools. School builds in some cases, also plays an important role in the growth of education among the tribal folk. Due to mismanagement, buildings and some times financial constrains are seldom suitable to run an educational institution. Another factor related with the problem is the number of teachers. Most primary schools in tribal areas are "single-teacher managed whose presence in the school is more an exception than a duty." Over burdening may be one of the possible factors for this state of affairs.

Remedial Steps

Thus, it is evident that the tribes of India and Mysore district are in different stages of development and naturally the problems of education related to those living in different stages of development, will be different. Therefore in order to eradicate illiteracy among the tribes of India and more particularly in the study area an integrated approach at the micro level will highly useful.

Problem of Unemployment and Migration

The tribes have migrated to different Tea gardens in search of getting employment since many years. Tribal agriculture and allied activities are seasonal and it depended on rainfall. Jemikuruba and Soliga tribal communities in Gundlupet and Kollegal taluks were migrated to Kerala and nearly by regions. It supports the idea that in search of employment, the tribes have been migrating to far of places and whose descendants hardly return to their homeland.

The tribal labourers are hard working and they migrate with their family members. Except the kids, both husband and wife will be engaged as labourers.

But they are very much exploited by the contractors who pick them from their villages and take them with proper transportation arrangements to the work spot either at tea garden or at the factory site or at the road sites where constructions are going on. But the most unfortunate part of these migrants and the newly recruited tribal labourers is that they become unemployed as soon as the earthwork is over or the construction is completed..

In this way, the tribes of Chamarajanagar district, particularly the members of the minor tribes like the Jenukuruba, Kadukuruba etc., who are illiterate and innocent exploited more by the contractors. This is not, however, true with the members of other minor tribes because, they live in the inaccessible jungle areas and they depend totally on the forest. They are therefore, untapped by the labour contractors.

Remedial Measures

Planning to solve unemployment should be formulated tat micro or local level with due weightage for specific problems of a particular place because of variation from one tribal area to other. Priority should be given to local tribes while appointing forest workers, watcher, guards etc., by the concerned authority. But unfortunately this is not being done due to administrative bottle-necks.

Housing Problem

The problem of housing for tribal people has to be viewed in the following aspects;

- Shelter
- Sanitation
- Aesthetic tastes, and
- Comparative costs.

Environment occupies an important place in the above-mentioned aspects of housing scheme of tribes. Variations in climate coupled with differences in economic condition of tribes and structure posses a number of problems. All the tribal communities are fortunate enough that they have been endowed with natural bounty. They are living in eco-friendly surroundings. Melukamanahalli, Kaniyanapura, Baragi, punajnur, Budipadaga etc., are the eco-friendly regions, which are situated at Bandipur National Park in Gundlepet taluk and Biligirirangaswamy temple wild life sanctuary in yalandur taluk. Many of the tribal families have developed a real pride in having good houses. On the other hand many of tribal families completely lack in house sense.

Government has built and granted the houses for many needy tribes. But these houses are unimaginative and misfit for the life style of tribes this is happening because some one will prepare model of the tribal house who generally never exposed to the tribal surrounding and ascertain the facts that what type of houses are convenient to the tribes.

Hence. Any scheme of housing without considering tribal consciousness is bound to meet the disapproval of the perspective in habitants of the houses.

Moreover the forest department is also coming in the way of solving tribal housing problem. The unimaginative and reckless bureaucracy has posed many restrictions on use of forest for house construction by the tribes. The tribes can collect the house construction materials from the forest by obtaining permit. But it is very difficult for a tribal to obtain permit from forest officials for obvious reason, which are known to all. Hence the entire forest policy has become counter productive as for as the tribal welfare schemes is concern.

Remedial Steps

Housing schemes for many impoverished tribal groups like soiigas, Junukurubas, Kadukuruba, Hakkipikki, Meda etc, in the study area are to be implemented on top priority. In this direction many of the housing schemes like Ashraya schemes, Ambedkar vasathi scheme etc launched by the state government are to be effectively speeded up for the benefit of tribes. But it should be kept in mind that even an explosive house is useless for tribal people if they feel uncomfortable in unfamiliar house surroundings.

HYGIENE AND HEALTH PROBLEM

The tribes are suffering from many chronic diseases and the most prevalent which take heavy tolls of them are water-borne. This is mainly because of poor drinking water supply. Even though plenty of water is available in and around the tribal settlements, generally it is dirty and contaminated. Diarrhea, dysentery, cholera, etc, are often the results of this situation.

Apart from this deficiency of certain minerals and other elements are also in the water the causes for such diseases. In B,R Hills tribal region, sickle cell Anemia and Tuberculosis are common among many tribes. Added to this maternity problem is very serious in tribal colonies. Even today maternity work is done by the tribal women. One tribal woman known as Jallesiddamma (staying in Yarakanagadde podu) doing wonderful service in this field and she has been awarded by the government for her health service. Her service is incorporated with all the tribal settlement in B.R.Hills. Hence she has been recognised as "Soliga Thayandira Herige Doctor" (Doctor of maternity) by the tribes and local people.

Remedial Steps

There has been considerable expansion of medical and public health facilities for tribes during the last two Five Year Plans. Health centers are being opened with qualified doctors and with good medical facilities inspite of this it is very difficult to trace the improvement in their health condition.

Due to the lack of transportation and communication in tribal areas, they feel reluctant to go to the hospitals that are located far away from the tribal settlements. Hence primary health center should be established in the remote tribal areas with expert doctors. Moreover, mobile medical service has to be introduced for serving the tribal community. This will play a long inning in solving the health problems of tribes.

Apart from this non governmental organisations should be effectively involved in solving health problems of the tribes in this regard, Jayavijayam tribal hospital located in B.R. Hills in association with VGKK, a non-governmental organization, It serves the tribes with modern medical aids at free of cost. It also bridges the tribes with communicate the modern medical field.

Problem of Communication

Tribes are living in isolation for centuries. The main reason for this isolation is lack of communication. The problem of communication in tribal area may be examined from two angels: (1) needs of the tribes and (2) developments of the tribal areas as a whole. It has been ascertained that the communication facilities may not always prove to be a blessing to the tribal society. It also facilitates the entry of perspective exploiters and other anti-social elements from non-tribal areas, who takes the advantage of innocence of the tribes and exploit them in a variety of ways. But at the same time the march of events cannot be halted and the needs of defence, industrialisation, mining and development can also not be ignored.

Many tribes are good cultivators of some growing variety of crops. With a good network of roads and communication, their production will be able to reach far off markets and they can fetch handsome returns. In the absence of adequate means of communications and transportation. They have to sell their produce at comparatively low prices and are easily brow beaten by the local non-tribal traders to sell their produce at throwaway prices. Mukti colony is far away from the marketing place (24 Kins) in Gundlepet taluk without proper transportation and communication. Hence, they are forced to sell their agricultural produce at low prices after harvesting and it is inhavitable for them due to lack of storage facilities.

Post and Telegraph services are slowly percolating into the remotest tribal areas, but unfortunately the mail carriers and staff are not regular employees of the post and telegraph department. Beduguli is one of the best examples for this inadequate service.

Remedial Steps

Development of communication no doubt will provide good opportunities for the tribal folk to develop national consciousness and a healthier intellectual horizon. Also the importance of communication in the realm of tribal economy hardly needs an emphasis but what has to be guarded against the danger of greedy and cunning, elements from the plains invading tribal areas to exploit the poor tribes. The best solution in such a situation seems to be taking all sorts of precautions for safeguarding the tribal interest before throwing any of their areas open.

Rehabilitation Problem

As an example of general failure in tackling the problem of rehabilitation of displaced tribals more than 2000 tribal families in Karemala, Melukamanahalli, Moguvinahalli, Mukti colony, Maddur colony and Mukalli colony in Gundlupet taluk, Muneswara colony and Srinivasapura colony in Chamarajanagar taluk, Anehola, Kavalichalla dam in Kollegal Taluks are distributed. These are all rehabilitated tribal colonies. Government has taken care to fulfill their basic needs, but, it is far away from expectation and situation is not happier for the reason mentioned below. Very few of them have taken advantage of agricultural facilities offered in their habilitation camps. The attraction of easy money and industrial employment are too strong, especially for young tribes.

The alternative land offered by the authorities for cultivation is not irrigable and cannot offer adequate return to maintain the families on it. The cash compensation given to tribes seldom-utilised far productive purposes. It is almost invariably used for daily living expenses until alternative employment is found.

Remedial Steps

In the sense of rehabilitation Government should provide only fertile land for cultivation in and around accessible regions. If once the tribes are rehabilitated, the government should provide them clean drinking water, electricity, communication and as much as possible the irrigation facilities for agriculture under the Ganga Kalyana Scheme, Nooru Bavi (Hundred Well) Scheme etc.

PROBLEMS OF INDIAN RURAL LIFE

India is a vast country spreading over an area of 33.67 million square kilometer, having 7.78 thousand kilometer of coastline. The large variation in climatic condition soil types, water bodies, vegetation types encountered in the countries endows with an endless variety of life between the snow-bound mountains of great Himalayas and the dark tropical forests. To the outsider, baffled by the heterogeneity of its races and their languages, beliefs and traditions, this country means little more than a geographical unit. To its people it is a vast complex world whose organic unity is taken for granted. But, whether one tries to describe India in terms of its geography and natural resources, or explains it historically, the picture remains incomplete, and only a comprehensive view of the wide canvas of Indian life can lead to proper understanding of the country and its people.

The cultural unity of the Indian people springs largely from the agricultural character of the country. Even today, when industrialization is progressing and large scale migration taking place from rural areas to cities and towns, majority of the Indian people lives in villages and is dependent on land. Since time immemorial, agriculture has been a kind of religion in the country. The gods that are honoured belong to the soil and are more or less the same all over the country. To understand India, one must, therefore, study its village life.

INDIAN VILLAGE LIFE

Rural people are often stereotyped and simple, but they usually know much more about their environment than many well-trained outsiders be they government officials or academic researchers. Farmers know the soils, the plants, the pests, the seasons, and the problems and risks, which they face. Farmers on their fields experience the sequence and conditions of their cultivation as a whole and have or good insight of the problems. Their adaptations are often skilful, sensitive, subtle and sophisticated. Of late, they are also-getting exposed to newer technologies that are relevant to rural setting.

SCIENCE AND TECHNOLOGY FOR RURAL DEVELOPMENT

The principle that "simple is sophisticated" can apply in this scenario to choices made in research and development. Research and development decisions frequently lead to innovations, which are large-scale, costly, difficult to maintain and dependent on greater inputs, which have to come from outside the rural environment. The innovations may be profitable; but they tend to benefit those rural people, who are already better off, rather than the poorer marginal farmers and landless labourers.

In contrast, innovations which are small-scale, cheap, easy to maintain and use locally available and renewable materials and inputs, are more likely to benefit the poor. At times, the formal research and development can miss opportunities or point them in the wrong directions. For example, for a rice breeding concentrated heavily on responses to chemical nitrogen, which is often cornered by the larger farmers, to the neglect of improving nitrogen-fixation in the root zone of the rice plant, a biological technology which may be scale-neutral, cheap, renewable, and more readily available to many more of the smaller farmers. In this scenario, research and development need be directed towards those simple outcomes to which the poorer rural users will have better relative access.

The Indian subcontinent is one of the most fascinating ecological and geographical regions in the world. It lies at the confluence of the African, European and Southeast Asian biological systems. The variety of ecological systems sustain a huge amount of diverse forms. Among such ecological systems are the villages of rural India which support diverse forms of life with their vast natural resources. About 76% of India's population lives in about 5,76,000 villages. In the past, the villages were self sufficient. However, industrial transformation and population growth in the post-independence period accompanied by rising living expectations have resulted in tremendous pressure on the natural resources of the villages. The important life support systems such as cropland, wetland, woodland, grassland and rangeland/wasteland have been misused, overused and degraded. The system is no longer able to function properly.

Conservation and management of bioproductive systems and recycling of resources involve human labour as an important energy input. Sometimes a change in the physical environment disturbs the balance between men and natural resources of a village ecosystem leading to several changes in the socioeconomic and cultural life of the people. The aspect of culture that changes most radically is that linked to the environment. Several different methods have been employed to compute the human and animal energy used in work. The total food energy intake of a full-time farm worker (working 40 hours per week) can be used as a measure of the energy utilized in farm labour.

RURAL DEVELOPMENT

Out of the total population, 52.5% live below the poverty line and a majority of them live in Indian villages. Because of the unsatisfactory living condition of rural mass, one of the most formidable and fundamental aspects of India's effort towards development is rural development. Rural development is a dynamic process to improve the socioeconomic life of the rural poor. It involves extending the benefits of development to the poorest among those who seek livelihood in the rural areas. In the other words, it implies economic and social uplift of the under -developed and poor people in the rural areas who have been languishing below the poverty line and are unable to meet their basic minimum requirements.

It is imperative that each development program should be viable economically, and should pave the way for activities. The monetary value of natural resources used by rural communities for subsistence is important when addressing issues affecting the livelihoods of impoverished rural households. There is therefore the need to attribute monetary values to non-marketed products from smallholder production systems in order to reliably account for resource availability and usage.

MAJOR ENVIRONMENTAL PROBLEMS IN INDIAN VILLAGES

The following are among the major environmental problems, which seriously affect the Indian villages, and erode the socio-economic and health conditions of the rural poor.

Indoor Air Pollution

Indoor air pollution caused by burning traditional fuels such as dung, wood and crop residues adversely affects to the health of the villagers, particularly the women and children. There is evidence associating the use of biomass fuel with acute respiratory tract infections chronic obstructive lung diseases in children. Lung cancer has been found to be associated with the use of coal, however, there is no evidence associating it with the use of biomass fuels. Cataract and adverse pregnancy outcome are the other conditions shown to be associated with the use of biomass fuels. Finally, there is enough evidence to accept that indoor air pollution in India is responsible for a high degree of morbidity and mortality in the rural areas.

Loss Of Biodiversity

Biological diversity in general and agricultural diversity in particular is being depleted at an unprecedented rate in the past few decades. Much of the agricultural biodiversity that remains on farms today can be found on the semi-subsistence farms of developing countries like India. Even though a variety of plants and animals homestead gardens comprise a variety of plants and vegetables, although the species richness of these gardens has been considerably reduce. Nevertheless, it is heartening to note that, some awareness has now been generated to conserve biodiversity.

Change In Land-Use Pattern

Land-use change has important implications for sustainable livelihood of local communities where traditional crop livestock mixed farming is sustained with local inputs. Knowledge of recent changes in land use, driving forces and implications of changes within the context of sustainable development is limited. A study analyzed the changes in spatial patterns of agricultural land use, crop diversity, manure input, yield, soil loss and run-off from cropland, and dependence of agro-ecosystems on forests, during the 1963-1993 period in a small watershed in central Himalaya, India. Data obtained from existing maps, interpretation of satellite imagery, GIS-based land-use change analysis, participatory survey and field measurements were integrated to quantify changes at the landscape/watershed scale. During the 1963-1993 period the same group found that, agricultural land use increased by 30% at the cost of loss of 5% of forestland. About 60% of agricultural expansion occurred in community forests compared to 35% in protected forests and 5% in reserve forests. Agricultural expansion was most conspicuous at higher elevations (2600m) and on medium slopes (10 -30°).

Waste Management in Rural Indian Villages

A micro-level study was carried out in a typical south Indian village to assess the quantity and type of wastes generated and its present mode of management. This information was used to identify the appropriate technologies, which could enhance the value of the waste produced, and at the same time, improve the economic conditions of rural people. The study indicated that nearly 2364 tons of rural wastes in the form of crop residues, animal manure and human excreta are produced annually in the village with a population of 510. About 77% of the waste generated in the village was used as domestic fuel, animal fodder and organic fertilizer for crop production. The rest (23%) was left out in open fields for natural decomposition. The energy balance sheet of the village indicated that the present consumption of biomass resources was 50% less than that actually required for various domestic and agricultural applications. Anaerobic digestion of animal manure and human excreta produced in the village could yield 82% of the domestic energy required besides enriching the waste by 3-4 times as compared to conventional storage on the ground. If the traditional mud *chulha* (stove) were replaced by an improved *chulha*, each family unit could reduce its annual consumption of fuel wood.

The use of non-renewable energy in Indian villages is very low. In the agriculture it is minimal, as it is mostly based on human labour and animal power rather than oil and electricity. Cultivation in large areas is done by hoe and animal draught. The use of tractor for tilling the land is also common in some areas. Ground water is lifted variously by human power and by animal power. The tube well and water pumps are also becoming popular in many areas. Cooking and lighting use local energy sources such as biogas, solar energy, firewood, and dung. Part of the village's income comes from communal energy farming with *Eucalyptus* and different species of *Euphorbia* (a succulent) and other energy crops, which enable the village to be, by a small margin, a net exporter of energy. Even the tools and utensils used in the village are produced nearby in small regional centers using small quantities of non-renewable energy.

Means of transport, used in the villages utilize animal power as well as petrol or diesel. The villages produce little surplus for export to the rest of the economy and import little from several essential items nearby from the town. Most of the villagers do not often travel long distances, (except on the inter-village exchange program) partly because they are notable to afford to travel much.

Mahatma Gandhi, the Father of the Nation, said that "India is in villages". "If villages perish, India perishes". Therefore, village ecosystems need a closer study emphasising on the interactions between societal needs and life support systems. A village, being a typical unit of rural India, can be considered as an ecosystem taking into account its distinctive structure and function.

The term village ecosystem reflects the totality of settlement and its activities as a dynamic and organic whole. The function of a village ecosystem mainly depends on the major bio-productive systems such as agricultural lands, grasslands, forest and wetland, which together form important physical resource base. In developing countries like India, the rural sector with high population density and high level of poverty poses a serious threat to the environment. Impact of human activities on the resource base of an ecosystem sometimes leads to critical situations. Degradation of the environment is closely related to the pattern of resource use which is influenced by population level, migration pattern, market access and land use practices. Indeed, it is a bitter truth that despite having all the wealth, science and technology in our hands, our society can never escape its dependence, direct or indirect, on the earth's natural resources, and it is particularly true for Indian villages.

STANDARD OF LIVING IN INDIA

Standard of living in India is low but improving. The single most common indicator used to quantify standard of living is the per capita purchasing power parity (PPP) adjusted gross domestic product (GDP). In 2009, the per capita PPP-adjusted GDP for India was US$3,015. With one of the fastest growing economies in the world, clocked at an average growth rate of 8% between 2004–2005, India is fast on its way to becoming a large and globally important consumer economy. The Indian middle class, estimated to be 300 million people by Indian standard (but much lower by European or North American standard), is fast becoming used to Western culture. If current trends continue, Indian per capita purchasing power parity will significantly increase from 4.7 to 6.1 percent of the world share by 2015.. In 2006, 22 percent of Indians lived under the poverty line. India aims to eradicate poverty by 2020. The standard of living in India shows large disparity. For example, rural areas of India exist with very basic (or even non-existent) medical facilities, while cities boast of world class medical establishments. Similarly, the very latest machinery may be used in some construction projects, but many construction workers work without mechanisation in most projects.

Poverty

A 24.3% of the population earned less than $1 (PPP, around $0.25 in nominal terms) a day in 2005, down from 42.1% in 1981. 41.6% of its population is living below the new international poverty line of $1.25 (PPP) per day, down from 59.8% in 1981. The World Bank further estimates that a third of the global poor now reside in India.

On the other hand, the Planning Commission of India uses its own criteria and has estimated that 27.5% of the population was living below the poverty line in 2004–2005, down from 51.3% in 1977–1978, and 36% in 1993-1994. The source for this was the 61st round of the National Sample Survey (NSS) and the criterion used was monthly per capita consumption expenditure below Rs. 356.35 for rural areas and Rs. 538.60 for urban areas. 75% of the poor are in rural areas, most of them are daily wagers, self-employed householders and landless labourers.

Although Indian economy has grown steadily over the last two decades, its growth has been uneven when comparing different social groups, economic groups, geographic regions, and rural and urban areas. Between 1999 and 2008, the annualized growth rates for Gujarat (8.8%), Haryana (8.7%), or Delhi (7.4%) were much higher than for Bihar (5.1%), Uttar Pradesh (4.4%), or Madhya Pradesh (3.5%). Poverty rates in rural Orissa (43%) and rural Bihar (41%) are higher than in the world's poorest countries such as Malawi.

India has a higher rate of malnutrition among children under the age of three (46% in year 2007) than any other country in the world.

Despite significant economic progress, 1/4 of the nation's population earns less than the government-specified poverty threshold of $0.40/day. Official figures estimate that 27.5% of Indians lived below the national poverty line in 2004-2005. A 2007 report by the state-run National Commission for Enterprises in the Unorganised Sector (NCEUS) found that 25% of Indians, or 236 million people, lived on less than 20 rupees per day with most working in "informal labour sector with no job or social security, living in abject poverty."

Since the early 1950s, successive governments have implemented various schemes, under planning, to alleviate poverty, that have met with partial success. Programmes like *Food for work* and *National Rural Employment Programme* have attempted to use the unemployed to generate productive assets and build rural infrastructure.

In August 2005, the Indian parliament passed the *Rural Employment Guarantee Bill*, the largest programme of this type, in terms of cost and coverage, which promises 100 days of minimum wage employment to every rural household in 200 of India's 600 districts.

The question of whether economic reforms have reduced poverty or not has fuelled debates without generating any clear cut answers and has also put political pressure on further economic reforms, especially those involving downsizing of labour and cutting down agricultural subsidiary

Life expectancy in India by States

State	*Total*	*Male*	*Female*
Andhra Pradesh	63.1	61.6	64.1
Assam	57.2	57.1	57.6
Bihar	60.2	60.7	58.9
Gujarat	62.8	61.9	63.7
Haryana	64.5	64.1	65.0
Himachal Pradesh	65.6	65.1	65.8
Karnataka	64.0	62.4	65.5
Kerala	73.5	70.6	76.1
Madhya Pradesh	56.4	56.5	56.2
Maharashtra	65.8	64.5	67.0
Orissa	57.7	57.6	57.8
Punjab	68.1	66.9	69.1
Rajasthan	60.5	59.8	60.9
Tamil Nadu	64.6	63.7	65.7
Uttar Pradesh	58.4	58.9	57.7
West Bengal	63.4	62.8	64.3
India	61.7	60.8	62.5

Physical Infrastructure

Since independence, India has allocated nearly half of the total outlay of the five-year plans for infrastructural development. Much of the total outlay was spent on large projects in the area of irrigation, energy, transport, communications and social overheads.

Development of infrastructure was completely in the hands of the public sector and was plagued by corruption, bureaucratic inefficiencies, urban-bias and an inability to scale investment. Calcutta city was the first city in India to boast of a metro-system. Today the Calcutta metro is considered among the world's best in terms of service and infrastructure. India's low spending on power, construction, transportation, telecommunications and real estate, at $31 billion or 6% of GDP in 2002 has prevented India from sustaining a growth rate of around 8%. This has prompted the government to partially open up infrastructure to the private sector allowing foreign investment. India holds second position in the world in roadways' construction. As of 31 December 2005, there were an estimated 835,000 broadband lines in India. Low tele-density is the major hurdle for slow pickup in broadband services. Over 76% of the broadband lines were via DSL and the rest via cable modems.

A 2007 study by the Asian Development Bank showed that in 20 cities the average duration of water supply was only 4.3 hours per day. No city had a continuous water supply. The longest duration of supply was 12 hours per day in Chandigarh, and the lowest was 0.3 hours per day in Rajkot. Some 400 million Indians do not have access to a proper toilet.

Regional Imbalance

One of the critical problems facing India's economy is the sharp and growing regional variations among India's different states and territories in terms of per capita income, poverty, availability of infrastructure and socio-economic development. For instance, the difference in growth rate between the forward and backward states was 0.3% (5.2% & 4.9%) during 1980–81 to 1990–91, but had grown to 3.3% (6.3% & 3.0%) during 1990–91 to 1997–98. The five-year plans have attempted to reduce regional disparities by encouraging industrial development in the interior regions, but industries still tend to concentrate around urban areas and port cities.

Even the industrial townships in the interiors, Bhilai for instance, resulted in very little development in the surrounding areas. After liberalisation, the disparities have grown despite the efforts of the union government in reducing them. Part of the reason being that manufacturing and services and not agriculture are the engines of growth. The more advanced states are better placed to benefit from them, with infrastructure like well developed ports, urbanisation and an educated and skilled workforce which attract manufacturing and service sectors. The union and state governments of backward regions are trying to reduce the disparities by offering tax holidays, cheap land, etc., and focusing more on sectors like tourism, which although being geographically and historically determined, can become a source of growth and is faster to develop than other sectors.

ILLITERACY PROBLEMS IN RURAL INDIAN AREAS

Illiteracy Problems in Rural Indian Areas "We are bumbling along with this outmodeled system of elementary education, which is a real shame." (Tefft, 12) These are the words of Krishna Kumar, director of the Central Institute of Education in New Delhi, India. Unfortunately Kumars's views are shared with other educators concerning the state of India's deteriorating education system. Illiteracy rates in many third world countries are alarmingly high; nestled in the heart of Asia, India's education program is falling behind other nations. (UNESCO, 2) It is a country where the population will reach one billion people by the next century, while only one-third of them will be able to read. Due to various social and economic problems India's education program continues to be undercut. Of the biggest victims of the educational system are those living in rural areas. The attitudes of the children and teachers also affect the quality of the schools. Allocation of government funds and the conditions of the destitute rural schools contribute to the low quality of education by rural children. While there are many rural area school systems which are operating in poor conditions there is one in particular whose schools outperform most other rural schools and also those located in wealthy areas of India. Consequently, Kerala, a rural state of India remains a puzzle to many educators. Its illiteracy rate does not follow the trend of most rural schools.

Many children living in rural areas receive a level of education which is very poor. Overall enrollment in primary and middle schools are very low. Fifty percent of children living in these areas leave school before the fifth grade (Tefft, 12) These children leave school for variety of reasons: some leave because of lack of interest; most leave so that they can work in the fields, where the hours are long and the pay is low. A large percent of the dropouts are females. Forced by their parents, most girls perform chores and tend the family at home. These are some of the reasons why sixty percent of all females in India are illiterate, a figure much higher than those of males. (UNESCO, 25) As these children grow into adults, many are still illiterate by the age of forty. These uneducated adults are also reluctant to send their own children to school because of their failure in the education system. This in turn creates a problem for the next generation.

While the children living in rural areas continue to be deprived of a quality education, part of the reason why is due to their teachers. A large number of teachers refuse to teach in rural areas and those that do are usually underqualified. In recent years the number of qualified teachers has increased because of increased efforts by the government and private groups to improve the general education and professional training of teachers. (UNESCO, 19).

There is more of an emphasis on the training of rural teachers, whose educational backgrounds are generally not as sound as their urban counterparts. Those that refuse to teach in rural areas cite distance and lack of interest by students as problems. Many of the teachers also lack the enthusiasm to teach because of their meager salary - less than one hundred dollars per month. (Tefft, 12) Another obstacle faced by the schools is that obtaining more teachers for rural schools is difficult because of state guidelines that approve of high student-to-teacher ratios. As the lack of teachers creates many obstacles for children in rural schools, another setback is the lack of resources which becomes detrimental to the learning process. Lack of books and other reading materials seem to be a widespread problem. The use of high-tech devices such as computers is very rare. Another condition of the schools are the inadequate facilities the classes are actually taught in. Some schools are located in warehouses while others in small houses. Many of the rural schools operate without electricity.

While many rural schools search for the proper resources, the distribution of government funds is major hindrance to the educational system. According to a recent study done by the World Bank, thirty percent of the total educational funding goes toward higher educational institutions (Tefft, 12) This is an important issue because the number of students enrolled in these types of institutions represent such a small percent of India's students. Other examples of the government's plans to undermine rural education can be found in the Constitution of India. In the Constitution it stated that the primary education of rural area children was a low priority in budget outlays.

Though rural children continue to be deprived of a formal education, the education system of Kerala, India is an exception. Located in the southern peninsula of the country, Kerala's illiteracy rates are lower than most other rural areas in India. Because of its immense population of twenty nine million and high unemployment rate, a large number of its inhabitants are forced to work outside of Kerala. Many of the people of Kerala who work in a different country send lots of donations back to Kerala. These people believe that it is responsibility of them to donate back to their hometown.

It is these donations which have funded many of the programs that make Kerala stand out from other rural states. Coupled with the government and private donations the education system has been able to benefit. More schools are being built and more teachers are willing to work there. The unusually low illiteracy rate is attributed to the planned education programs. Although its economy is only growing slowly and unemployment rate is high, its illiteracy rates, mortality rates and life expectancy are comparable to richer regions of the country. Other rural areas can learn from Kerala so that its success can be duplicated. Receiving more private donations and government support is essential for those rural areas needing to improve the general lifestyle of its people.

High illiteracy rates in rural parts of India is an area of the Indian education system that cannot be overlooked. Hampered by the government and by other factors the quality of education in rural districts has been quite poor. High dropout rates and low enrollment by the children have contributed to the large illiteracy rate. Kerala, a rural state of India boasts many areas of progress and serves as a model for other rural areas and many of the wealthier parts of India. Without drastic changes by the government and by its citizens, India is well on its way to becoming the world's most illiterate nation.

RURAL TRANSPORT IN INDIA

The importance of rural transport to economic and social development is obvious. Three fourths of India's population of 960 million, i.e. 720 million, live in six lakh villages, which vary in population between 800 and 5000. Though migration to towns is reducing the percentage of rural population, in absolute numbers the rural population is increasing.

For instance, during the decade 1981–91, rural population has increased by 100 million. Bulk of the 300 million people below the poverty line and the 30 million handicapped are in rural areas. 50% of the rural population are illiterate. At least 50% does not have access to clean drinking water, schools and primary health care facilities. Adequate rural road transport will improve these conditions.

Such a dismal state of affairs continues even after massive governmental investment for rural development, poverty alleviation and employment generation. Only 15% of Rs 20,000 crores of annual subsidies and grants, under various schemes, has reached the beneficiaries. Increasing allocation for rural development in successive Five Year Plans has not improved the situation. Only an efficient Rural Transport (RT) system can allow people to take advantage of massive investment envisaged for rural development.

Lack of Infrastructure

It is well known that development is dependent on appropriate and adequate infrastructure, such as power, transport, communication, water and irrigation. Also, essential services, such as educational institutions, health care facilities, rural banks and co-operatives, markets, development boards, etc. are essential for balanced development. Rural development did not make much progress due to lack of such inputs.

Rural Transport and Low Priority

If a proper RT system had been provided, it would have functioned as a catalyst, facilitator and efficient instrument for accelerating rural development and bringing about social equity. But RT is now far behind requirements, and therefore, is unable to play this vital role. According to the National Transport Policy Committee (NTPC), Fair Weather Roads (FWR) connected only 55% of villages. In order to cover all the villages by All Weather Roads (AWR), investment required may be of the order of Rs 30,000 crores, which is beyond the scope of the existing priorities of the government for investment. Transport itself has been given very low priority by the government; and RT still less. AWRs will bring in connectivity and mobility. India's large area size and population, the scattered nature and small size of village settlements, poverty and illiteracy of rural people and low level of commercial activity do not provide sufficient incentive and economic justification for large investments in RT.

The deplorable condition of all categories of India's roads is well known too. Experts have estimated that the country loses thousands of crores by way of wastage of petroleum, damage to vehicles, accidents, delays, etc. Road accidents are more in India than in USA, though the latter has 100 times the number of vehicles. Solution lies in privatization of RT system and road laying and maintenance.

Kerala's Example

Passenger road transport was nationalized long ago in the name of socialism. State Road Transport Undertakings (STUs) have been unable to meet rural requirements, particularly of

RT. Most STUs are operated inefficiently, and also incur huge losses. In Kerala, private buses are operating very efficiently, connecting every village. Kerala has 34,000 buses, of which only 2000 are of the STU, which shows the importance given by government to private road transport. Kerala has shown how rural people can enjoy most of the facilities and amenities which the small towns possess. Kerala's villages have 10 to 15 taxis and an equal number of three wheelers, since rural roads are fit for motorized transport. Kerala's high standard of living is partly due to better roads and connectivity.

Kerala has demonstrated the concept of having excellent road transport and communication systems. All villages are connected by AWR or FWR. With such a high degree of connectivity, people live in their village homes and commute to nearby towns for work. They even travel, by buses/trains, for two hours either way, as they have the advantage of a congenial village life, without the ill effects of living in urban areas, which is costly and undesirable from many points of view. Migration to towns is avoided. Villages retain their elite. Elsewhere, villages are denuded of enterprise. Kerala has few urban slums. The whole state is a vast network of villages and small towns.

Underdeveloped Villages

Rural people migrate to urban areas for job opportunities. Government's efforts to induce doctors, teachers, administrators and other professionals to work in rural areas have failed. This is obviously because villages do not have basic facilities and amenities, such as markets, hospitals, schools and colleges, entertainment, clubs, workshops, places of worship, trained personnel, intellectual climate, etc. Companies do not wish to establish factories in rural areas, as they are unable to attract professionals and technicians to work there. All these handicaps and deficiencies can be remedied if an adequate and efficient RT system is operated.

RURAL TRANSPORT SYSTEM AND PLANNING

RT is concerned with transporting goods and people within the village, between villages and urban areas, linking village roads with district roads, state highways and national highways. Rural Transport System (RTS) consists of roads and vehicles of various types and capacities, ownership and investment patterns, maintenance of roads and vehicles, taxation and government regulations, etc. The efficiency of RTS will depend upon the perspectives and priorities given by the government. RTS has to be integrated into regional planning and state plans. Policies regarding state vs. private in laying roads and operation of vehicles have to be changed in order to make progress.

The government has slowly, but very reluctantly, opened up road building for private participation, based on the concept of build, operate and transfer. But the progress is very slow. If the responsibility of laying the national and state highways as well as their maintenance is given to the private sector, government can divert available funds for district and village roads, in which the private sector may not be interested, as it would not be profitable for them. Also, it is not easy for the private sector to earn revenue through tolls in such roads. Incidentally, all buses in the village and district roads in Kerala are operated by small private operators, thus showing that RTS is profitable under conditions created in Kerala. Equitable employment and operational efficiency become possible, since small operators work diligently, avoiding overheads.

While formulating the plan for 1981–2001, the NTPC noted that funds allocated and utilized were far below minimum requirements. The Committee also stressed that road transport is a basic and vital infrastructure, which is a prerequisite, though not a guarantee, for economic growth.

NTPC also laid down that all villages, with population above 500, should be connected by AWRs by the turn of the century. They also pointed out that road construction programme will be a major sector for employment generation. In 1981, total road length was 1.5 million km, out of which 46% were surfaced roads. For the same period, road density in kilometres per 100 sq. km stood at 0.46, as against three for Japan. NTPC estimated that road length required by India by the turn of the century should be 2.6 million kilometres for an area of 3.28 million sq. km.

Studies by IIM and NCAER

The Indian Institute of Management at Bangalore and the National Council for Applied Economic Research at New Delhi conducted a survey of RT in 1978–79, with a major focus on bullock cart transport. IIM, Bangalore, followed it up with another study in 1989, and highlighted salient changes during the decade.

They have estimated significant trends, comparing conditions in 1979 and 1989. Studies on freight movements conducted in 1989 showed that carts play a predominant role for movement within the village, while trucks and tractors dominate outflow.

There is substantial increase in outflows, as rural produce is being taken to more distant locations than in previous years. Large settlements have less number of carts, and more motorized vehicles. Trucks need AWR, while carts and tractors can use FWR. Per capita passenger trips increase with settlement size; so also bicycles. When more number of villages are connected by AWR, truck traffic increases rapidly.

Passenger transport is mainly by bicycles and motorized vans in FWRs, and buses of various sizes and capacities in AWRs. Three wheelers, scooters and motor cycles handle a small part. In states like Bihar, UP and MP, locally made improvized vehicles are operating, which are known by various names, e.g. jugis.

Bullock carts are not used exclusively for passenger transport. Vans and trucks of various sizes and capacity are making rapid inroads, particularly in areas where there are FWRs. Where there are no motorable roads, carts still play an important role in freight movement.

Studies conducted by IIM, Bangalore show that percentage of passenger traffic in different modes – walk, cycle, bus and others – in respect of settlements with less than 500 and over 5000 population is 63.5 and 25.8%, 18.1 and 20.9%, 17.7 and 52.2% and 0.7 and 1.1% respectively. Studies also show that more than 60% of passenger trips – by walk, bicycle or bus – are for agricultural operations, education and business, irrespective of the size of the settlement.

Animal-drawn Carts

Though it would be desirable to connect all villages by AWRs, yet, under the present conditions, where 50% of villages are not connected by motorable roads, use of bullock carts is inevitable for many years. Out of 15 million carts, 12 million are estimated to be in rural areas, which may be transporting about six billion tonne km of freight per year. Camel carts operate in Rajasthan and Gujarat in both urban and rural sectors. In Haryana, Punjab and Western UP, buffaloes also are used for carting. Bullocks are becoming costly. A pair costs as much as Rs 10,000 to 15,000 in parts of Karnataka. Therefore, use of buffaloes and donkeys should be encouraged. Donkeys work as pack animals in Gujarat, Rajasthan and parts of Tamil Nadu. There is good scope for increasing the population of donkeys through a massive breeding programme and introducing donkey carts. At present, there is no organized effort for breeding work animals.

The number of carts have remained almost the same during the last two decades, estimated to be about 15 million in the whole country. In the early forties, a British engineer estimated that road damage then due to the iron rim fitted to wooden wheels was as much as Rs 50 crores per year. In current terms, the damage may be 300 to 500 crores of rupees per year. But even such heavy social cost has not prompted the government to popularize improved designs of carts with pneumatic tyred wheels, which do not damage roads.

Improved Carts

The Dunlop company was the pioneer (1950) in introducing pneumatic tyred carts, fitted with smooth bearings, steel wheels and axles. These simple improvements increased the capacity from one to three tonnes, with less draught effort required from the animals. CARTMAN has been popularizing improved carts (ICs) for the last 20 years. ICs eliminate damage to roads, move faster and bring in increased income from higher carrying capacity. Further, animals need to exert less; and therefore can pull normal loads without goading and beatings, i.e. less suffering. Further, productive life of the animals increases. During the last three decades, ICs have become popular in semi-urban areas and for sugarcane transport. It has been estimated that one million ICs are in operation now, plying mostly in Haryana and Punjab, Western UP, parts of Tamil Nadu, Pondicherry and most sugarcane-growing areas. Cost of an IC (Rs 10,000 to 15,000) would be about 50% more than a traditional wooden wheel cart. But an IC could carry three times more load.

Significant potential gain through improved RT and development can easily justify the funds required for popularizing improved carts. At present, most of the 12 million rural-based carts are used for transporting only personal goods to markets and to bring inputs for agriculture. In small villages, carts are used only for 50 days a year, while in large villages, with a population of two to three thousand, carts are used for 100 days a year.

Over the years, carts are increasingly being used more intensely and for more number of days per year. But progress has been very slow, except in Haryana, Punjab and Western UP, where most carts are ICs. But, there is good scope for introducing ICs in rural areas where commercialization is at the required level. Solution lies in giving ICs to farmers under various government schemes, such as IRDP, poverty alleviation, employment guarantee, SC/ST welfare, etc.

Use of Motor Vehicles

In the case of registered motor vehicles, data is available. But for carts and bicycles, there is no published information. Also, no reliable information is available regarding vehicle penetration into rural areas. Studies revealed the following:

a) 50% of villages have a population less than 500.

b) 60% of villages did not have access to AWR.

c) Smaller the village, less the economic activity, and therefore, less the number of vehicles. Carts move only about 15% of the tonne km of goods while trucks carry much more, accounting for 83%.

RTS AND URBAN DEVELOPMENT

Planning and development of cities has not made any impact. Cities have been growing in a chaotic way since Independence.

Quality of life has deteriorated so much that some cities are no longer habitable. Pollution in Delhi and Bangalore is above the safety limits. Therefore, from the point of view of saving urban areas from further decay, migration to urban areas has to be slowed down, which means that quality of rural life has to be improved. One easy way to improve the quality of life in villages is to improve RTS, which will provide access to markets, facilitate social contacts, connect employment centres, etc.

Gandhiji had repeatedly pleaded for development of villages, which would concurrently reduce the current mad rush to cities. Experience all over the world ought to teach us about the ill effects of unplanned urbanization and denuding villages of wealth, job opportunities and facilities. Unfortunately, life in the villages has not improved much and hence migration to towns and cities continues. Job opportunities, markets, education and health facilities, cultural activities, social amenities, etc. are required for retaining rural talent and also for attracting professionals from cities to work in rural areas. In spite of a lot of rhetoric on rural development and massive investment of Rs 30,000 crores per year directly and indirectly during last 50 years, rural development has been slow. A conceptual understanding of the factors affecting city vs village will reveal the importance of RT.

In villages, space is plenty and cheap. Air and water are much cleaner. But many other essential requirements are non-existent or are of poor quality. Towns and cities have these facilities and amenities. If villagers get access to these, rural people will not migrate to urban areas. Also, professionals would start working in villages.

The average size of a village settlement is only 1,000. Obviously, it is not possible to provide these facilities and amenities in every village or even in a cluster of villages. But it is possible to connect a cluster of 50 to 100 villages with AWRs and to provide a good road transport system for goods and passengers. Thus, a network of villages, with a population of half to one lakh, can be provided with all the facilities a modern town now has. According to experts, provision of all the necessities for making life comfortable and attractive to professionals would cost only 10% of what they would cost in a modern city. Every facility and amenity that exists in a city can be accessed with a good road network and transport system. Doctors, engineers, teachers, administrators and others would then be willing to work in such conditions. Volume of transactions and levelof economic activities will be high enough for providing all these facilities and amenities on a self-sustaining basis, i.e. without subsidy. A critical size of population coverage will make a road transport system technically feasible, economically viable and ecologically desirable.

The only solution to remove poverty is to create employment, which can be increased through roads and road transport. Unfortunately, the government has not approached the problem from this point of view.

In the above concept, RTS should become an integral part of regional planning, which would connect towns, large villages with a population of 5,000 and all the surrounding villages with a population ranging from 500 to 5,000. RTS should be considered as the nerve system for such connectivity. Such regional planning ought to have been the main focus of development planning. But the government undertook this work with official machinery, which is bureaucratic and non-professional. Most districts get about Rs 60 crores per year for spending in 300 development schemes. But RTS has not been given priority under these schemes.

Infrastructure Development

After having neglected it since Independence, the government has at last woken up to the imperative need for improving infrastructure, such as power, transport, communication, etc. But there is no evidence of urgency in adopting liberal policies, which those would bring in the private sector to complement and supplement state effort. Discussions are centred around industry, ports, highways, etc. RT and rural infrastructure have not been given due importance. It may be recalled that the British put up 50,000 km of rail track, covering many towns, where there was no economic activity. The same concept should apply for RT. India should not wait for the demand to come first for justifying roads and road transport. It ought to be the other way round. Providing roads and road transport would spur economic activity. Roads and transport will then become economically viable for investment and operation. Thus RT is important from the overall development point of view. Such a macro vision has not been planned so far.

RURAL ELECTRIFICATION

Rural electrification is the process of bringing electrical power to rural and remote areas. Electricity is used not only for lighting and household purposes, but it also allows for mechanization of many farming operations, such as threshing, milking, and hoisting grain for storage; in areas facing labour shortages, this allows for greater productivity at reduced cost. One famous program was the New Deal's Rural Electrification Administration in the United States, which pioneered many of the themes still practiced in other countries. According to IEA (2009) worldwide 1.456 billion people do not have access to electricity, of which 83 % live in rural areas. In Sub Saharan Africa only 12 % of the rural population has access to electricity.

Benefits

In impoverished and undeveloped areas, small amounts of electricity can free large amounts of human time and labour. In the poorest areas, people carry water and fuel by hand, their food storage may be limited, and their activity is limited to daylight hours. Adding electric-powered wells for clean water can prevent many water-borne diseases, e.g. dysentery, by reducing or eliminating direct contact between people (hands) and the water supply. Refrigerators increase the time that food can be stored, potentially reducing hunger, while evening lighting can lengthen a community's daylight hours.

Drawbacks

Depending on the source, rural electrification (and electricity in general) can bring problems as well as solutions. New power plants may be built, or existing plant's generation capacity increased to meet the demands of the new rural electrical users. A government may be inclined to use the cheapest generation source, which may be highly pollutive, and locate the power plant next to vulnerable minorities or rural areas.

Technology

One of the least expensive, most reliable, and best proven mains electricity distribution systems for rural electrification is single wire earth return. This system is widely used in countries such as Australia with very low populations densities. Also, there are some geographical requirements necessary for its use. There are many instance where these two systems are used together in the same system to serve remote and less remote rural populations. Since modern power distribution networks can cheaply include optic fibres in the centre of one of the wires, telephone and internet service may become available with rural electrification.

Locally generated renewable energy is an efficient technology, particularly compared to electrification with diesel generators. Higher installations costs are coupled with significantly lower running costs. Hybrid systems (renewables combined with diesel generators) are a widely acknowledged technology for rural electrification in developing countries.

INTEGRATED RURAL DEVELOPMENT PROGRAMME

Rural development in general is used to denote the actions and initiatives taken to improve the standard of living in non-Urban neighbourhoods, countryside, and remote villages. These communities can be exemplified with a low ratio of inhabitants to open space. Agricultural activities may be prominent in this case whereas economic activities would relate to the primary sector, production of foodstuffs and raw materials.

Rural development actions mostly aim at the social and economic development of the areas. These programs are usually top-down from the local or regional authorities, regional development agencies, NGOs, national governments or international development organizations. But then, local populations can also bring about endogenous initiatives for development. The term is not limited to the issues for developing countries. In fact many of the developed countries have very active rural development programs. The main aim of the rural government policy is to develop the undeveloped villages.

The Integrated Rural Development Programme (IRDP) is a rural development program of the Government of India launched in Financial Year 1978 and extended throughout India by 1980. It is a self-employment program intended to raise the income-generation capacity of target groups among the poor. The aim is to raise recipients above the poverty line by providing substantial opportunities for self-employment. During the 7th five year plan, the total expenditure under the program was Rs 33.2 million, and Rs 53.7 million of term credit was mobilized. Some 13 million new families participated, bringing total coverage under the program to more than 18 million families. These development programs have played an important role in increased agricultural production by educating farmers and providing them with financial and other inputs to increase yields.

The objective of IRDP is to enable identified rural poor families to cross the poverty line by providing productive assets and inputs to the target groups. The assets which could be in primary, secondary or tertiary sector are provided through financial assistance in the form of subsidy by the government and term credit advanced by financial institutions. The program is implemented in all the blocks in the country as a centrally sponsored scheme funded on 50:50 basis by the Centre and State. The Scheme is merged with another Scheme named *swarnjayanti gram swarozgar yojana* (SGSY) since 01.04.1999.

RURAL DEVELOPMENT PROGRAMS

The panchayat raj is a South Asian political system mainly in India, Pakistan, and Nepal. "Panchayat" literally means assembly (*yat*) of five (*panch*) wise and respected elders chosen and accepted by the village community. Traditionally, these assemblies settled disputes between individuals and villages. Modern Indian government has decentralized several administrative functions to the village level, empowering elected gram panchayats. Gram panchayats are not to be confused with the unelected khap panchayats (or caste panchayats) found in some parts of India. Panchayati Or Panchaayati Raj is a system of governance in which gram panchayats are the basic units of administration. It has 3 levels: village, block and district.

The term 'panchayat raj' is relatively new, having originated during the British administration. 'Raj' literally means governance or government. Mahatma Gandhi advocated *Panchayati Raj*, a decentralized form of Government where each village is responsible for its own affairs, as the foundation of India's political system. His term for such a vision was "Gram Swaraj" (Village Self-governance). It was adopted by state governments during the 1950s and 60s as laws were passed to establish Panchayats in various states. It also found backing in the Indian Constitution, with the 73rd amendment in 1993 to accommodate the idea. The Amendment Act of 1993 contains provision for devolution of powers and responsibilities to the panchayats to both for preparation of plans for economic development and social justice and for implementation in relation to twenty-nine subjects listed in the eleventh schedule of the constitution.

The panchayats receive funds from three sources – (i) local body grants, as recommended by the Central Finance Commission, (ii) funds for implementation of centrally-sponsored schemes, and (iii) funds released by the state governments on the recommendations of the State Finance Commissions. In the history of Panchayati Raj in India, on 24 April 1993, the Constitutional (73rd Amendment) Act, 1992 came into force to provide constitutional status to the Panchayati Raj institutions. This Act was extended to Panchayats in the tribal areas of eight States, namely Andhra Pradesh, Bihar, Gujarat, Himachal Pradesh, Maharashtra, Madhya Pradesh, Orissa and Rajasthan from 24 December 1996. Now panchayati raj system exists in all the states except Nagaland, Meghalaya and Mizoram. Also all the UTs except Delhi.

The Act aims to provide 3-tier system of Panchayati Raj for all States having population of over 2 million, to hold Panchayat elections regularly every 5 years, to provide reservation of seats for Scheduled Castes, Scheduled Tribes and Women, to appoint State Finance Commission to make recommendations as regards the financial powers of the Panchayats and to constitute District Planning Committee to prepare draft development plan for the district.The 3-tier system of Panchayati Raj consists of a) village level panchayat b) block level panchayat c) district level panchayat. Powers and responsibilities are delegated to Panchayats at the appropriate level :-

- Preparation of plan for economic development and social justice.
- Implementation of schemes for economic development and social justice in relation to 29 subjects given in Eleventh Schedule of the Constitution.
- To levy, collect and appropriate taxes, duties, tolls and fees.

Village Level Panchayat

It is called a Panchayat at the village level. It is a local body working for the good of the village. The number of members usually ranges from 7 to 31; occasionally, groups are larger, but they never have fewer than 7 members. The block-level institution is called the Panchayat Samiti. The district-level institution is called the Zilla Parishad.

Intermediate Level Panchayat

Panchayat samiti is a local government body at the tehsil or Taluka level in India. It works for the villages of the Tehsil or Taluka that together are called a Development Block. The Panchayat Samiti is the link between the Gram Panchayat and the district administration. There are a number of variations of this institution in various states. It is known as Mandal Praja Parishad in Andhra Pradesh, Taluka panchayat in Gujarat, Mandal Panchayat in Karnataka, etc.In general it's a kind of Panchayati raj at higher level.

Constitution

It is composed of ex-officio members (all sarpanchas of the panchayat samiti area, the MPs and MLAs of the area and the SDO of the subdivision), coopted members (representatives of SC/ST and women), associate members (a farmer of the area, a representative of the cooperative societies and one of the marketing services) and some elected members.

The samiti is elected for 5 years and is headed by the chairman and the deputy chairman.

Departments

The common departments in the Samiti are as follows:

1. General administration
2. Finance
3. Public works
4. Agriculture
5. Health
6. Education
7. Social welfare
8. Information Technology and others.

There is an officer for every department. A government appointed block development officer is the executive officer to the samiti and the chief of its administration the dapartment of

Functions

1. Implement schemes for the development of agriculture.
2. Establishment of primary health centres and primary schools.
3. Supply of drinking water, drainage, construction/repair of roads.
4. Development of cottage and small-scale industries and opening of cooperative societies.
5. Establishment of youth organisations.

Sources of Income

The main source of income of the panchayat samiti are grants-in-aid and loans from the State Government.

District Level Panchayat

In the district level of the panchayati raj system you have the "zilla parishad". It looks after the administration of the rural area of the district and its office is located at the district headquarters. The Hindi word Parishad means Council and Zilla Parishad translates to District Council. It is headed by the "District Collector" or the "Distric Magistrate" or the "Deputy Comminissioner". it is the link between the state government and the panchayat samiti (local seld government at the block level)

Constitution

Members of the Zilla Parishad are elected from the district on the basis of adult franchise for a term of five years. Zilla Parishad has minimum of 50 and maximum of 75 members. There are seats reserved for Scheduled Castes, Scheduled Tribes, backward classes and women.

The Chairmen of all the Panchayat Samitis form the members of Zilla Parishad. The Parishad is headed by a President and a Vice-President.

Functions

1. Provide essential services and facilities to the rural population and the planning and execution of the development programmes for the district.
2. Supply improved seeds to farmers. Inform them of new techniques of training. Undertake construction of small-scale irrigation projects and percolation tanks. Maintain pastures and grazing lands.
3. Set up and run schools in villages. Execute programmes for adult literacy. Run libraries.
4. Start Primary Health Centers and hospitals in villages. Start mobile hospitals for hamlets, vaccination drives against epidemics and family welfare campaigns.
5. Construct bridges and roads.
6. Execute plans for the development of the scheduled castes and tribes. Run ashramshalas for adivasi children. Set up free hostels for scheduled caste students.
7. Encourage entrepreneurs to start small-scale industries like cottage industries, handicraft, agriculture produce processing mills, dairy farms, etc. implement rural employment schemes.
8. They construct roads, schools,& public properties.And they take care of the public properties.
9. They even supply work for the poor people.(tribes, scheduled caste, lower caste)

Sources of Income

1. Taxes on water, pilgrimage, markets, etc.
2. Fixed grant from the State Government in proportion with the land revenue and money for works and schemes assigned to the Parishad.

SWARNJAYANTHI GRAM SWAROZGAR YOJANA

The objective of Swarnjayanti Gram Swarozgar Yojana (SGSY) is to bring the assisted poor families (Swarozgaris) above the poverty line by organising them into Self Help Groups (SHGS) through the process of social mobilisation, their training and capacity building and provision of income generating assets through a mix of Bank credit and Government subsidy. The programme aims at establishing a large number of micro-enterprises in the rural areas, building upon the potential of the rural poor. Emphasis under the programme is on group approach and developing activity clusters. However, individuals are also eligible for assistance to acquire assets for income generation.

Scope

Launched on 1st April, 1999, the programme replaces the erstwhile self-employment and allied programmes - IRDP, TRYSEM, DWCRA, SITRA, GKY and MWS, which are no longer in operation. The programme covers families below the poverty line in rural areas of the country. Within the target groups special safeguards have been provided forthe benefit of the vulnerable groups i.e. SCs/STs, women and physically handicapped persons. Accordingly, SCs/STs should account for 50 per cent of the Swarozgaris, women for 40 per cent and the disabled persons for 3 per cent.

Funding

SGSY is a Centrally sponsored scheme and funding is shared by the Central and State Governments in the ratio of 75:25.

Strategy

SGSY is a credit-cum-subsidy programme, wherein credit is the key component. It covers all aspects of self-employment, such as organization of the poor into self-Help Groups (SHGs), training, credit, technology, infrastructure and marketing. One of the key areas of the SGSY therefore, is social mobilization of the poor through the SHGS.

The social mobilization process helps the poor to be self-reliant and realize their own strength and advantage of group behaviour. Fifty per cent of the groups formed in each block should be exclusively for women.

In other SHG's also efforts would be made to involve women members in each Self- Help Groups. SGSY lays emphasis on activity clusters. About I 0 activities will be identified for each block with the approval of Panchayat Samitis, however emphasis will be on 4-5 activities for cluster development. The Gram Sabha will authenticate the list of families below the poverty line identified in BPL census. Identification of individual families suitable for each key activity will be made through a participatory process involving Gram Panchayat, Block functionaries (i.e. BDO or his representatives) and the banker.

How to Seek Assistance

For assistance under the programme, District Rural Development Agencies and Block Development Officers may be contacted.

SAMPOORNA GRAMEEN ROZGAR YOJANA

Pursuant to the announcement made by the Hon'ble Prime Minister in his Independence Day speech, a new Centrally Sponsored Scheme, namely, Sampoorna Grameen Rozgar Yojana (SGRY) was launched on 251h September, 2001 by merging the on-going schemes of EAS and the JGSY.

Objectives

The objectives of the programme is to provide additional wage employment in the rural areas as also food security alongside the creation of durable community, social and economic infrastructure in the rural areas. The programme is self-targeting in nature with special emphasis to provide wage employment to women, scheduled castes, scheduled tribes and parents of children withdrawn from hazardous occupations.

Strategy

The Programme is being implemented in two streams :

1. The First Stream of the Programme will be implemented at the District and Intermediate level. Panchayats. Fifty per cent of the funds available under the SGRY are earmarked for First Stream, these are distributed between the Zilla Parisad and the Intermediate Panchayats in the ratio of 40:60.
2. The Second Stream of the Progarmme will be implemented at the Village Panchayat level. Fifty per cent of the SGRY funds are earmarked for this Stream. The entire funds are released to the Village Panchayats through the DRDAs/Zilia Parishads.

Salient features of SGRY

The salient features of the proposed Scheme are as under:-

- The Sampoorna Grameen Rozgar Yojana (SGRY) is a Centrally Sponsored Scheme (CSS) being implemented with a total outlay of Rs.10,000 crores.
- Under the Scheme, 50 lakh tonnes of food grains amounting to Rs.5,000 crores (at economic cost) will be provided every year, free of cost to the State Governments and Union Territory Administrations.
- The remaining funds (Rs.5,000 crores) will be utilized, to meet the cost component of wages and material cost.
- The cost of the cash component of the Programme will be shared by the Centre and States in the ratio of 75:25.
- The payment for food grains will be made by the Ministry of Rural Development to the Food Corporation of India (FCI) directly.
- About 100 crore mandals of employment are envisaged to be generated every year in the rural areas through the SGRY.
- Fifty per cent of the total available funds under the SGRY will be provided to each stream.
- Every worker seeking employment under the SGRY will be provided 5 kg. of food grains (in kind) per mandal as part of wages.

- The balance of wages will be paid in cash so that they are assured of the notified minimum wages.
- The State Governments and UT Administrations will be free to calculate the cost of food grains (paid as part of wages) at either BPL rates or APL rates or anywhere between these two rates.
- The SGRY has been in operation from the financial year 2002-2003. Since the Scheme was launched in the middle of 2001-02, the ongoing schemes of the EAS and the JGSY were merged with the new Scheme.

The Programme permits works which lead to the creation of additional wage employment, durable assets and infrastructure, particularly those which assist in drought proofing such as soil and moisture conservation works, watershed development, promotion of traditional water resources, afforestation and construction of rural infrastructure and link roads, primary school buildings, dispensaries, veterinary hospitals, marketing infrastructure and Panchayat Ghars in rural areas.

Monitoring and Evaluation

The overall supervision of the programme rests with the Zilia Parisad.

The programme will be regularly monitored by the Department of Rural Development in accordance with the in-built monitoring mechanisms, including periodical reports and returns, Vigilance and Monitoring Committees, visits by officers of the Central and State Governments and by the Area officers of the Ministry of Rural Development.

The programme would also be evaluated through the studies conducted by reputed institutions, organizations and sponsored by the Central/State Governments.

How to Seek Assistance

Village Pradhan/Panchayat Members, Block Development Officers, Chief Executive Officer or Zilia Parishad, District Collector of District Rural Development Agency may be contacted.

PRADHAN MANTRI GRAM SADAK YOJANA

There is a yawning gap between 'Urban India' and 'Rural Bharat'. Villages have not been able to keep pace on the path of progress. A critical link on this path is a national network of All-weather roads in the Rural Areas. There is a close link between Rural Connectivity and Growth, be it in the area of Trade, Employment, Education or Healthcare. States with poor connectivity are also States that reflect poor socio-economic indices. Acritical link for progress is, therefore, a nationwide network of All-weather roads in our rural areas. While over the last five decades, the length of Rural Roads has been increasing, there are still more than 40% of India's villages, numbering over 2.5 lakh, which remain unconnected.

For the first time, a Programme is being launched, that is dedicated solely to the construction of Rural Roads- the Pradhan Mantri Gram sadak Yojana(PMGSY). The Programme envisages connecting every Habitation with a population of over 1,000 persons through Good, all-weather roads, by the year 2003; and those with a population of more than 500 persons, by the year 2007.

Besides providing connectivity to about 1,00,000 habitations, the Programme also aims to upgrade, to specifications, about 5 lakh kilometres of existing Rural Roads. In order that a Programme of this nature and magnitude is effective, PMGSY incorporates the following key elements:

- Preparation of Master Plans- District Rural Roads Plans to be generated based on Block-level Plans.
- Project Implementation Units to be formed to ensure professional and timely completion.
- Execution on a Project Mode.
- Ensuring Standard Specifications, including adequate cross-drainage works.
- Time-bound Execution- completion in 9-12 months; Penalty clauses for time overruns; No Escalation permitted.
- Strict Quality Control - independent Monitors to inspect works.

- Innovative Financing - for assured funding.
- Extensive Use of Information Technology- for on-line monitoring etc.
- Audit - Internal and External.

The Programme further envisages

- Ready availability of Land for the Roads;
- Maintenance of the Roads by Panchayati Raj Institutions;
- Encouraging Use of locally available materials for construction of roads;
- Planting of trees on either side of roads.

Pradhan Mantri Gram Sadak Yojana

A Programme with vision, clarity of purpose, professionalism, transparency and accountability. A Programme to transform the lives of 30 crores people through Roads that would bring Change, Employment and Growth. A Programme that would enable 10 crores rural poor to cross the Poverty line.

RURAL HOUSING

INDIRA AWAAS YOJANA (IAY)

The objective of Indira Awaas Yojana (IAY) is primarily to help construction of new dwelling units as well as conversion of unserviceable Kutcha houses into Pucca/semi Pucca by members of Scheduled Castes/Scheduled Tribes, freed bonded labourers and also non-SC/ST rural poor below the poverty line by extending them grant-in-aid.

Scope

IAY is a beneficiary-oriented programme aimed at providing houses for SC/ST households who are victims of atrocities, households headed by widows/unmarried women and SC/ST households who are below the poverty line. Its scope has been expanded to conversion of unserviceable Kutcha houses into Pucca/semi Pucca houses with effect from 1st April, 1999.

Funding

Indira Awaas Yojana is a Centrally Sponsored Scheme

funded on cost-sharing basis between the Government of India and the States in the ratio of 75: 25. In case of Union Territories, the entire resources under this scheme are provided by the Government of India.

Strategy

Grant of Rs. 20,000/- per unit is provided in the plain areas and Rs.22,0001- in hilly/difficult areas for construction of house. For conversion of a Kutcha house into Pucca/semi Pucca, Rs. I 0,0001- is provided.

Sanitary latrine and smokeless chullha are an integral part of the house. In construction/upgradation of the house, cost effective and environment friendly technologies, materials, designs are encouraged. The house should be allotted in the name of the female member of beneficiary households, alternatively it can be allotted in joint names of both husband and wife.

How To Seek Assistance

The eligible person who desires to seek assistance under the Scheme should contact the Village Panchayat or Village Level Worker on the Block Development Officer or District Rural Development Agency.

INNOVATIVE STREAM FOR RURAL HOUSING AND HABITAT DEVELOPMENT

The objective of the Innovative Stream for Rural Housing and Habitat Development is to promote/propagate innovative and proven housing technologies, designs and material in the rural areas.

Scope

With a view to encouraging the use of cost effective, environment-friendly, scientifically tested and proven indigenous and modern designs, technologies and materials, a scheme called Innovative Stream for Rural Housing and Habitat Development has been launched. The Innovative Stream for Rural Housing and Habitat Development has been conceived to be implemented on project basis.

Funding

Funds under the scheme are provided on project basis. The total grant for implementing a project by an NGO/Autonomous Society should, in normal circumstances, not exceed Rs.20.00 lakh and for eminent educational technical/research institutions and Government agencies it should not exceed Rs.50.00 lakh.

Strategy

The project should contain innovative elements, especially in regard to convergence of shelter and habitat development and inter-departmental and inter-disciplinary implementation at the ground level. The project should also possess potential and replicability after the pilot stage is over. The project relating to areas which are remote, inaccessible, disaster affected and extremely backward in social and economic infrastructure, shall be preferred.

How to seek assistance

All recognized Government and Non-Governmental agencies with experience in technology promotion and propagation of cost effective and environment-friendly rural housing technologies/designs and material may apply for funding to the Ministry of Rural Development.

SAMAGRA AWAAS YOJANA

The basic objective of the Samagra Awaas Yojana (SAY) is to improve the quality of life of the people and overall habitat in the rural areas.

Scope

The Scheme in due course is proposed to be implemented all over the country. However, in the first phase, the scheme is proposed to be implemented in one block each of 25 districts in 24 States and one Union Territory.

Various components of this Scheme will be implemented by different line departments, namely, the DRDA, Housing, Public Health, Agriculture, Forest, etc. In view of this, it would be necessary that the scheme is supervised, coordinated and monitored by the District Collector.

Funding

The existing schemes of housing, drinking water, sanitation etc. follow the normal funding pattern. However, under the SAY, special assistance of Rs.25 lakh (Rs.5 lakh for IEC and Rs.20 lakh for Habitat Development) is additionally provided by the Central Government.

Contribution received in cash and kind from the people to the extent of 10 percent is of critical importance for ensuring long term sustainability and public involvement.

Strategy

The underlying philosophy of Samagra Awaas Yojana is to provide convergence to the existing rural housing, sanitation and water supply schemes with special assistance on technology transfer, human resource development and habitat improvement with people's participation.

How to seek assistance

Since this is an area development and awareness generation scheme, the concerned DRDA is to seek assistance from Ministry of Rural Development by giving details of activities by which these objective shall be fulfilled.

RURAL BUILDING CENTRE

The objective behind the setting up of Rural Building Centres is transfer of technology and dissemination of information on cost effective and environmental friendly technologies, materials, methods, etc. and skill up- gradation through training and production of cost effective building components.

These Rural Building Centres will be involved in transfer of technology from lab to land.

Scope

The scope includes Government institutions, NGOS, private entrepreneurs, autonomous institutions, etc. with an outreach in the rural areas desirous of engaging in the task of transfer of technologies, materials, methods, designs from lab to land for promotion of cost effective rural housing.

Funding

The one time grant of Rs. 15 lakh is released through HUDCO by the Ministry of Rural Development.

Strategy

The eligible organization shall set up these centres to provide training to professionals, skilled, workmen,etc. on cost effective, environmental friendly technologies, materials and methods and shall produce cost effective building components.

How to Seek Assistance

The State Government, District Rural Development Agencies/Zilla Parishads, credible NGOS, private entrepreneurs, professional association, autonomous institutions and corporate bodies including public sector agencies can set up and operate the rural building centre.

NATIONAL MISSION FOR RURAL HOUSING

National Mission for Rural Housing has been set by the Ministry of Rural Development to enable the induction of science and technology inputs on a continuous basis, in the sector. It also seeks to provide convergence of technology, habitat and energy-related issues in order to provide affordable shelter for all in rural areas, within a specified time frame, and through community participation.

Scope

The Mission has to provide guidance and lay down policies for achievement of set objectives throughout the country.

Funding

A National Mission for Rural Housing and Habitat Development is not a scheme, but an organization laying down policies and procedures for achieving the broad objectives of providing and improving rural habitat. The funding shall continue to be done under different schemes.

Strategy

The National Mission shall integrate efforts under all schemes to improve rural habitat by providing guidance and laying down policies through people's participation.

CREDIT-CUM-SUBSIDY SCHEME FOR RURAL HOUSING

The objective of the Credit-cum-Subsidy Scheme for Rural Housing is to facilitate construction of houses for rural families who have some repayment capacity. The scheme aims at eradicating shelterlessness from the rural areas of the country.

Scope

The scheme provides shelter to rural families who have not been covered under Indira Awaas Yojana and who are desirous of possessing a house. All rural households having an annual income up to Rs.32,000/- are covered under the Scheme.

Funding

The funds shared by the Centre and the State is in the ratio of 75 : 25.

Strategy

The rural poor just above the poverty line are also entitled to get the benefits of the scheme. A maximum subsidy of Rs. I 0,000/- per unit is provided for construction of a house. Sanitary latrine and smokeless chullah are an integral part of the house. Cost effective and environment friendly technologies, materials, designs, etc. are encouraged. Sixty per cent of the houses are allocated to SC/ST rural poor.

How to Seek Assistance

State Governments decide the implementation agency, which may be the State Housing Board, State Housing Corporation, specified Scheduled Commercial Bank, Housing Finance Institution or the DRDA/ZP. The person desirous of getting benefit of the Scheme may approach the implementing agency.

ACCELERATED RURAL WATER SUPPLY PROGRAMME (ARWSP)

Rural water supply being a State subject, States take up projects and schemes from their own resources. However, Government of India has been supplementing State efforts in providing safe drinking water in rural areas. The National

Agenda for Governance of the Government envisages provision for safe drinking water to all rural habitations in the country by 2004.

To accelerate the coverage of uncovered and partially covered rural habitations with safe drinking water, the Central Government has launched the Accelerated Rural Water Supply Programme (ARWSP), with the following priorities:

- Coverage of no safe source habitations
- Coverage of quality affected habitations with acute toxicity
- Upgradation of source level of safe source habitations, which get less than 40 liters per capita per day (Ipcd)
- Coverage of schools and Angwadis.

Norms

To take up projects/schemes under ARWSP, following norms are to be followed:

- 40 lpcd of drinking water for human beings;
- 30 lpcd of additional water for cattle in areas under the Desert Development Programme;
- One hand-pump or stand post for every 250 persons; and,
- Availability of water source in the habitation or within 1.6 km in the plains and I 00 m elevation in hilly area.

Funding

Funds are provided to States for making provision of safe drinking water in rural habitations. The State Governments are to provide matching funds from their own resources. To tackle water quality problems and to ensure source sustainability, up to 20 per cent of the fund can be utilized.

Projects/schemes on sustainability of sources can also be taken up under this programme for rainwater harvesting, artificial recharge, revival of traditional systems like Kundis, Johads, dugwells, etc. Further, 15 per cent of the funds released can be spent on operation and maintenance (O&M) of the existing systems/sources of rural water supply.

Sector Reform: Community Participation

A certain proportion of the ARWSP funds are set aside for implementation of Sector Reforms projects for institutionalizing community participation in the Rural Water Supply Programme. This programme has been introduced in 67 pilot districts across the country, under which, the community is equipped to plan, sanction, implement, manage, operate and maintain rural water supply schemes of their own choice so as to ensure their sustainability. Under these projects, people's contribution amounting to at least 1 0 per cent of the capital cost and I 00 per cent of the O&M cost are also envisaged. The contribution towards capital cost can be ion the form of cash, kind or labour.

Role of Panchayats

After the 73ra Amendment to the Constitution of India, the subject of rural water supply was placed under the Panchayati Raj Institutions, arid the Panchayats/local community have the power to implement schemes, particularly in selecting the location of hand pumps, standposts and spot sources; in management of sources and schemes.

SWAJALDHARA

A new initiative " SwajalDhara "was launched on 25th December, 2002, to open up the reform initiatives in the rural drinking water supply sector throughout the country.

The strategic elements of the Scheme are: (i) demand driven and community participation approach; (ii) panchayats/ communities to plan, implement, operate, maintain and manage all drinking water schemes; (iii) partial capital cost sharing by the communities upfront in cash; (iv) full ownership of drinking water assets with Gram Panchayats; and (v) full operation and maintenance by the users/Panchayats. The unique feature of the scheme is that the rural people should feel as the owners of the Scheme.

Scope

Beneficiary Groups, Gram Panchayats and Blocks adopting the reforms principles will be eligible for Swajaldhara Projects. The Swajaldhara Scheme is meant for taking up only simple and basically community oriented schemes. This scheme can be implemented by the States/U.Ts in Gram Panchayats/Blocks/ Beneficiary Groups. The entire district can be taken up in phases. Providing water supply facilities in schools and uncovered, partially covered and water scarcity habitations and revival of traditional water sources to ensure drinking water sustainability can also be implemented under Swajaldhara.

Funding

The Swajaldhara proposals will be approved and sanctioned only, if the proposals are found to have the commitment of the concerned District Implementing Agency and the State Government for compliance of reform principles and IO per cent of the estimated capital cost of the schemes (5 per cent in case of predominantly SC/ST habitations) is paid by the community, in cash upfront, as their contribution. The cost of the project excluding community contribution will be fully met by the Government of India. The Gram Panchayat must also be willing to take up the Operation & Maintenance (O&M) responsibility after the Scheme is completed and taken over by Gram Panchayat.

CENTRAL RURAL SANITATION PROGRAMME

The Centrally sponsored Rural Sanitation Programme (CRSP) strives to provide sanitation facilities to the rural populations, generate awareness about use of toilets and safe sanitation by providing individual household latrine, women complex, school sanitation and garbage disposal system. Significant activities under this scheme include construction of individual sanitary latrines with 80 per cent subsidy to the poor below the poverty line, stress on school sanitation, encourage other households to have facilities on their own, launch intensive awareness campaigns, establish sanitary complexes exclusively for women and promote total sanitation of villages. Implementation is done through the State Government Department, namely Public Health Engineering Department/Panchayati Raj Department and Rural Development Department with the active involvement of NGOs through campaign approach.

Strategy

The programme will be implemented as community-led and people-centred. A demand driven approach will be adopted with increased stress on awareness building and meeting the demand with alternate delivery mechanism (rural sanitary marts/production centres). School sanitation is included as a major component.

INTEGRATED WASTELANDS DEVELOPMENT PROGARMME (IWDP)

The Integrated Wastelands Development Programme (IWDP) strives to develop nonforest wasteland on village/micro watershed basis and helps in generating employment in rural areas, besides, enhancing people's participation in wasteland development leading to equitable sharing of benefits and sustainable development.

Scope

Watershed development approach has been adopted for all area development progammes including IWDP. Under this programme, village/micro-watershed plans are taken up after taking into consideration the local capabilities, site condition and local needs of the people living in and around the project area.

Strategy

Major activities taken up under this programme are soil and moisture conservation, afforestation and pasture development, promotion of horticulture/agro-forestry, encouraging natural regeneration, wood substitution and fuel wood conservation measures, and dissemination of technology, as decided by the user groups living in or around the project.

Funding

The Government of India provides I 00 per cent grant for implementation of the Programme. Each year, the project proposals are prioritized in consultation with the State Governments. Prioritized projects are sanctioned during the year keeping in view the funds available for the Programme after meeting the liability for the ongoing projects, progress made in ongoing projects, spread of treatable wastelands in the States, implementation capacity, etc. subject to conformity with the Guidelines for Watershed Development. The projects are sanctioned at a rate of Rs.4,000/- per hectare for treatment of wastelands over a period of five years.

It is a demand-driven programme. Prioritized projects are prepared by the ZPs/DRDAs and submitted to this Department through the State Governments every year and sanctioned in favour of DRDA/ZPs by Department of Land Reforms (DoLR).

DROUGHT PRONE AREAS PROGRAMME

The Drought Prone Areas Programme (DPAP) aims at mitigating the adverse effects of drought on the production of crops and livestock and productivity of land, water and human resources. It strives to encourage restoration of ecological balance and seeks to improve the economic and social conditions of the poor and the disadvantaged sections of the rural community.

Scope

DPAP is a people's programme with Government assistance. There is a special arrangement for maintenance of assets and social audit by Panchayati Raj institutions. Development of all categories of land belonging to Gram Panchayats, government and individuals fall within the limits of the selected watershed for development.

Funding

Allocation is to be shared by the Centre and State Governments on 75: 25 basis. The watershed community is to also contribute for maintenance of the assets. Funds are directly released to Zilla Parisads (ZPs), District Rural Development Agencies (DRDAS) to sanction projects and release funds to Watershed Committees and Project Implementation Agencies.

Strategy

Village community, including self-help/user groups, undertake area development by planning and implementation of projects on watershed basis through Watershed Association and Watershed Committees constituted from among themselves.

Asset less poor in the watershed area would be organized with self- help groups and provided with financial assistance to start a suitable income generating activity. The Government supplements their work by creating social awareness, imparting training and providing support through project implementation agencies.

DESERT DEVELOPMENT PROGRAMME

The Desert Development Progaramme (DDP) aims at combating drought and desertification, mitigating the adverse effects on crop production, livestock and people; encouraging restoration of ecological balance by harnessing, conserving and developing natural resources i.e. land, water vegetative cover and raising land productivity. The programme also strives to improve the economic conditions of the resource poor and disadvantaged sections of the society through creation, widening and equitable distribution of resources and increased employment opportunities. It is envisaged as an essentially land based activity for combating desertification.

Scope

It is a people's programme with Government assistance and special arrangement for maintenance of assets. Social audit is done by Panchayati Raj institutions. All categories of land belonging to Gram Panchayats, Government and individual failing within the limits of the project area can be developed.

Strategy

Area development is on watershed basis. A watershed project of about 500 hectares is the unit for implementation. There is direct participation of local people in planning, development and maintenance.

Funding

It is a Centrally sponsored programme with the share of the Centre and State in the ratio of 75: 25. Funds are released directly to Zilia Parishads (ZPs)/District Rural Development Agencies (DRDAs). ZPs/DRDAS are empowered to sanction projects and release funds to Watershed Committee and Project Implementation Agencies.

HARIYALI

In order to enhance the participation of the Panchayati Raj Institutions (PRIs) in the development process, a new initiative 'Hariyali' was launched on 27th January, 2003. The aim is to strengthen and involve PRis in the implementation of Watershed Development Programmes.

Under this initiative, Gram Sabha will replace the Watershed Association and the Gram Panchayat would execute the watershed project with technical support from the Block Panchayat/Zilla Panchayat who would act as the Project Implementing Agency for all watershed projects in a particular block. In case the Block/Zilla Panchayat has no technical support to support the Gram Panchayats, a suitable Government Line Department/Autonomous Agency will be identified for the purpose. Failing all these options, a reputed voluntary Organization of good operational/financial standing in the district with adequate technical expertise and experience will be identified to act as the Programme Implementing Agency.

LAND REFORMS

The Land Reforms Programme strives to fulfill all the principles of the national land reforms policy which consist of abolition of intermediary tenures tenancy reforms, ceiling on agricultural holdings and distribution of surplus land, consolidation of agricultural holdings, computerization of land records and strengthening of revenue administration and updating of land records.

Computerization of land records facilitates easy maintenance and updating of the changes which occur in the land data base and provides for comprehensive scrutiny to make the land records tamper-proof. Its objectives include providing the required support for implementation of development programmes for which data about distribution of land holding is vital. It also includes preparation of annual set of records thereby producing documents for recording details. Land holders can get updated copy of Record of Right (ROR) quickly and at cheaper rates.

For taking up re-survey and settlement operations, adoption of new technology in the field of survey, settlement, updation/

reproduction of cadastral maps and updation of revenue records is emphasized.

Scope

Initiatives undertaken focus on elimination of exploitation in land relations, realizing the goal of land to the tiller, enlarging the land base of rural poor, increasing agricultural productivity and production of infusing equality in local institutions. The Centrally sponsored scheme for computerization of land records presently being implemented in all the districts of the country except those where land records are not maintained. Similarly, 33 Pilot Projects on Digitization of Cadastral Surveys Maps in 22 States in the country are going on.

Funding

Specific schemes like computerization of land records and strengthening of revenue administration and updating of land records are funded by the Central Government. The funding pattern is I 00 per cent for the Scheme of Computerization of Land Records and 50:50 basis between the States and the Centre under the scheme of Strengthening of Revenue Administration and Updating of Land Records but the Union Territories are provided I 00 per cent Central assistance.

COUNCIL FOR ADVANCEMENT OF PEOPLES ACTION AND RURAL TECHNOLOGY

The Council for Advancement of People's Action and Rural Technology (CAPART), a registered society under aegis of the Department of Rural Development, strives to encourage, promote and assist voluntary action in implementation of projects for the enhancement of rural prosperity. It strengthens and promotes voluntary efforts in rural development with the focus on injecting new technological inputs. It also acts as a catalyst for development of technology appropriate for rural areas. It strives to promote, plan, undertake, develop, maintain and support projects/schemes aimed at all-round development, creation of employment opportunities, promotion of self-reliance, generation of awareness, organization and improvement in the quality of life of the people in rural areas through voluntary action.

Scope

While CAPART seeks to associate the voluntary sector in several schemes that are part of the planned development and are being implemented on national basis, it also supports several innovative projects keeping the needs of specific areas in view.

Strategy

With a view to bringing CAPART nearer to the people and to ensure closer interaction between CAPART and voluntary agencies at the grassroots level, the functioning of CAPART has been decentralized by the setting up of nine Regional Commiftees/Regional Centres at Jaipur, Lucknow, Ahmedabad, Bhubneswar, Patna, Chandigarh, Hyderabad, Guwahati and Dharwad. The Regional Committees are empowered to sanction projects to voluntary agencies up to an outlay of Rs,20.00 lakh in their respective regions.

Funding

The quantum of assistance is normally decided on the nature of the project and capability of the organization to take up the project and handle the funds requested. On acceptance of the terms and conditions, CAPART releases sanctioned funds in suitable instalments depending upon the nature of the project, quantum of assistance involved and the proportion of assistance to be mobilized from other sources including contribution by beneficiaries.

DRDA ADMINISTRATION

Training is one of the tested tools for performance improvement as well as upgradation of knowledge and skills of the personnel engaged in rural development activities and poverty alleviation progarmmes. As training, research and development are inextricably linked, continuing education of both policy makers and progarmme implementers is imperative. Towards facilitating this, the National Institute of Rural Development (NIRD) was set up in 1965 to impart training to the rural development functionaries as well as Panchayati Raj Institutions through classroom interaction and field work. The Institute is I 00 per cent funded by the Ministry of Rural

Development, Government of India. The Institute strives to facilitate the rural development efforts by improving the knowledge, skills and attitudes of rural development officials and non-officials through organizing training courses, workshops and seminars.

The Institute also undertakes research, action research and provides consultancy in the field of rural development. It advises and assists the State Institutes of Rural Development (SIRDS) and other organizations in training and research.

The training efforts of the Institute aim at creating knowledge base, development of appropriate skills and bringing about of requisite attitudinal changes in rural development officials and non-officials. Various empirical studies are undertaken to understand and analyze rural development issues to facilitate identification of new areas for policy intervention, assess training needs and evaluate the impact of rural development programme. Action research is undertaken to learn through action process and field intervention methodologies and to determine their implications for the policies and procedures of implementation of rural development programmes. The Institute provides consultancy services which are made available to national and international organizations.

In order to cater to the distinctive physical and socioeconomic features of the North-Eastern region, a NIRD North Eastern Regional Centre was established in 1983.

For intensifying training related activities throughout the country, schemes on strengthening/establishment of State Institutes of Rural Development (SIRDs), strengthening/establishment of Extension Training Centres (ETCS) and Organization of training courses, seminars/workshops (OTCs) are also being implemented by the Ministry of Rural Development.

MIGRATION IN RURAL INDIA

25% of the country's poor live in urban areas.

31% of the urban population is poor.

Traditional rural-urban migration exists in India as villagers seek to improve opportunities and lifestyles. In 1991, 39 million people migrated in rural-urban patterns of which 54% were female. Caste and tribe systems complicate these population movements.

Seasonal urban migration is also evident throughout India in cities like Surant where many migrants move into the city during periods of hardship and return to their native villages for events such as the harvest.

Fifty-six Biharis were murdered in Assam in November 2003, over a week of sustained ethnic violence. In the face of intense competition for the semi-skilled D category of jobs (requiring a minimum of eighth standard education) in the Indian Railways (the single largest employer in the world), targeted bloodshed was the answer. A mere 2,750 vacancies in Assam had attracted 20,000 prospective applicants from Bihar. This prompted the local ULFA (United Liberation Front of Assam) to call for protection of employment opportunities for the sons-of-the-soil, a long-standing ideology of Bal Thackeray's Shiv Sena in Maharashtra. In the days of violence, 11 wage labourers were also brutally murdered because they hailed from Bihar. But what is the root of a force so vicious and desperate that it instigates mass murder on ethnic lines?

Jobless Growth: Trends in India

This incident can be interpreted as a symptom of a larger malaise. The root of the problem is 'jobless growth' in the Indian economy, that is, despite an acceleration in the growth rate in India; the pace of creation of work opportunities has not kept pace with the growing requirement. In the post-liberalisation period, unemployment on a Current Daily Status basis rose from 6.0 percent in 1993-94 to 7.3 percent in 1999-2000 resulting in an additional 27 million job seekers. The most disturbing fact is that of these, 74 percent are in the rural areas and 60 percent among them are educated.

There is substantial decline in employment elasticity (e.g. increase in employment for every unit rise in GDP) in almost all the major productive sectors, except for transport and finance. In agriculture, the employment elasticity has dropped to near zero. The reason for the phenomenon of jobless growth could be that growth in India has essentially been capital intensive.

Further, the public sector is in the process of shedding excess labour in the name of downsizing for meeting the efficiency challenges of market competition.

Regional Imbalances

This trend of rising unemployment is compounded by the existence of regional imbalances in development within the country, which have collectively accelerated the phenomenon of migration. All theories of migration concede that migration occurs when the region of origin lacks the opportunities which the destination promises. It is inherently a combination of pull and push factors. Variation in economic development across regions is a primary motive for migration to greener pastures. The rural poor are concentrated in eastern India, and in the rainfall-dependant parts of central and western India, which continue to have low agricultural productivity, while the bulk of the jobs are being created in western and southern India.

Inter-state labour migration is an important feature of the Indian economy. Most of this movement has been from the most populous and poorest states with net in-migration being higher for the more developed states. Gujarat and Bihar provide an interesting contrast in terms of migration. The population entering Bihar was 364,337 and that exiting the state was more than three times higher at 1,226,839. (Census 1991) In contrast, the in-coming population for Gujarat was double that of Bihar at 716,190 and the out-going population 305,738, a quarter of the population leaving Bihar. Further, there exist intra-district movements. In Surat, labourers from the eastern talukas move to the irrigated western talukas like Ucchal and Nirzar, which are irrigated by the Ukai project. Census 2001 migration tables have not yet been released.)

This increase in migration is essentially due to regional differences in the population pressure on land, inequality of infrastructure, industrial development, and modernization of agriculture. In particular, the developed areas have increased demand for labour during specific seasonal activities, especially sowing and harvesting in the case of agricultural activities. As this demand often supersedes the availability of local labour, these developed regions offer a higher wage rate and/or greater number of days of employment. The agriculturally developed regions are invariably areas which have extensive canal irrigation and HYV (high yielding variety) technology. The demand for labour also exists in seasonally based agro-industries e.g. rice mills, sugar factories, canal construction, road construction, etc.

Implications of Migration

However, in the Indian context in recent decades, certain new migratory trends can be discerned, which indicate that its effects may be unfavourable both at the macro and micro level. There is evidence from different secondary studies in Gujarat to identify these new trends.

One is excessive migration. In Gujarat, rural-rural migration, especially from the drought-prone to the agro-climatically better-endowed districts, seems to have created overcrowding in the districts of destination.

This is reflected in the fact that some of the most drought prone districts such as Amreli, Kachchh, Surendranagar and Rajkot, have relatively higher labour productivity vis-à-vis the agriculturally prosperous districts like Junagadh, Kheda and Mehsana. Invariably, migrant labour is paid at lower wages compared to local labour, and the implementation of the Interstate Migrant Workman (Regulation of Employment and Conditions of Service) Act of 1979 is largely on paper. Migrants from backward regions are willing to accept any distress wages that are offered as long as they have access to employment. In the bargain they undercut the employment prospects of local labour. Their excess supply also contributes to reducing the wage rate.

The phenomenon of overcrowding appears to be both a cause and a symptom of the exploitative labour process of distress migration. The growing phenomenon of rural-rural migration also has important implications for future generations who would also suffer from the same debilitating lack of opportunities and low productivity. For example, whole families of tribals from the Dang district of South Gujarat migrate for six to eight months to work in the sugar factories in the plains, resulting in their children being unable to enrol in schools.

Secondly, Jan Breman draws attention to a new phenomenon of circulatory migration in South Gujarat. Employers prefer to hire migrant labour, as they are considered to be cheaper and more docile than local labour. Consequently, labourers need to migrate in search of jobs, which they are denied in their native region. This perpetuates a vicious cycle of migration. Also, there often seems to be an inherent specialisation among labourers according to their place of origin, resulting in region and task specific movements. For example, road workers originate from the Panchmahals, quarry workers from Bharauch, cane cutters into South Gujarat from Maharashtra, and rice mill workers from the Jalan district of Rajasthan. These location-specific 'skills' however often are inconsequential for unskilled jobs with high content of physical labour. They are nevertheless perpetuated as a justification among employers to hire outstation labour.

These processes of seasonal migration have even developed into semi-formalised systems with the active participation of contractors or mukadams as middlemen who gather migrant labourers for prospective employers. The seasonal movements are often debt induced as the mukadam often provides a wage advance to the migrants. According to the NCRL (National Commission of Rural Labour), there were approximately 10 million seasonal/circular migrants in the rural areas alone in 1999-2000. This includes an estimated 4.5 million inter-state migrants. There were large numbers of migrants in agriculture and plantations, brick kilns, quarries, construction sites and fish processing.

Theory and Impact of Migration

While migration enables workers from underdeveloped regions to find employment, its impacts have been evaluated variably by academics. Todaro's neo-classical model regards migration as a product of rational economic decision-making. The migrant makes a rational free choice to improve his economic condition by seeking more favourable employment conditions, even if the decision is being taken under distress. The policy recommendations of this theory are therefore in favour of migration and suggest reducing the cost of migration, i.e. improve the bargaining power of migrants, improve information and conditions of work, etc.

In contrast, the structuralist theories view the personal choice to migrate not at a product of individual freedom but rather as structured by the larger mechanisms of capitalistic production. In case of the poor, their choice to migrate is often the only option that they possess for survival, and their decision is a reflection of lack of choice rather than freedom of opportunity. Breman views the creation of migrant 'wage hunters' as representative symptoms of the larger processes of global capitalistic development resulting in a race to the bottom. Given that capitalistic production is motivated by profit as the only determining factor, it would invariably lead to regional imbalances and employers would hire labour at the lowest available cost.

Also, the reality of migrants at a micro-level ensures that their constant motion and inherent insecurity of employment reduces their ability and inclination to unionise or enhance their bargaining positions for fear of instant dismissal. The policy recommendations of this group of academics would therefore be in favour of strict implementation of programs to reduce regional development imbalances, minimum wage regulation and right to work, for example, employment assurance schemes like the Maharashtra Employment Guarantee Scheme (EGS).

4

Government Policy and Programme for Rural Tribal Development

CHHATTISGARH TRIBAL DEVELOPMENT PROGRAMME

India is a vast and diverse country, which is also a home for over one-fourth of world's absolute poor. IFAD, therefore, focuses on using its limited resources to develop innovative approaches that have a catalytic effect in leveraging additional resources for assisting the most vulnerable groups.

The proposed programme has defined its target group and geographical area on this basis and has built on the experiences of the programmes, which are nationally funded as well as assisted by International donors, particularly in the area of rain fed farming and watershed management, and has combined these approaches with IFAD's own experience in India with participatory development process through the development of community based institutions. This is the first project in India to adopt watershed management as an intervention methodology. Among the social groups in India, scheduled tribes (STs) have the highest proportion of the poor. While they account for only 8% of the total population, they comprise 40% of the displaced population. Literacy rate among STs is only is less than half of the general population, and that of rural tribal women about one-fourth. The Government of India has allocated significant amount of resources for tribal development, but the impact has been rather limited. The approach adopted has been more welfare-oriented, and there has been less emphasis on the issue of empowerment. This programme proposes to use the opportunity created by the recent constitutional amendment concerning the extension of the Panchayats Act to Scheduled Areas and would assist the state governments in putting into practice the principles established by this act in empowering the local communities and in establishing collaborative relationships with communities for designing resource management strategies which meet their perceptions and aspirations.

The programme covers two tribal populated states of India viz. Chhattisgarh and Jharkhand. The target groups comprises all households in the selected villages, i.e. villages with tribal, Primitive Tribal Groups (PTGs) and scheduled caste population of not less than 50% of the total population where the majority of the households live below the poverty line. The objective of the Programme is to develop and implement a replicable model that ensures household food security and improves livelihood opportunities and overall quality of life of the tribal population based on the sustainable and equitable use of natural resources. To achieve this, the Programme :- i) empowers tribal grassroots associations and users' groups, including women and other marginal groups; ii) promotes activities which generate sustainable increases in production and productivity of land and water resources; and iii) generates sources of income outside of agriculture, particularly for the landless.

The basic approach is to promote processes of awareness generation, legal literacy, social analysis and mobilisation for self-selecting group formation among disadvantaged women and marginalised groups. The programme supports initiatives identified, planned and implemented by beneficiaries and provides the required resources and support. The resources are managed directly by the beneficiaries after appropriate training and capacity building. These are supplied through NGOs with a proven experience in applying such approaches. The proposed programme has three main components. Under the beneficiary empowerment and capacity building component, the programme finances broad based awareness raising of tribal rights and of gender and equity issues, legal and managerial strengthening, and technical training. Similarly, under livelihood systems enhancement, the programme finances all production-related activities as well as enabling measures, namely land and water management/watershed development, including community-based small infrastructures; production systems improvement; rural micro-finance; and health and nutrition. Under the programme management and implementation component, the programme finances salary and allowances for Programme Implementation Unit (PIU) staff at District level, the relevant running costs for the Tribal Development Society and a skeleton Programme Management Unit (PMU), a legal defence fund, specialised and baseline studies, training for the staff and the development of training material, exposure visits, study tours, and technical assistance, and the costs of capacity building of facilitating NGOs and their contractual support services.

A gradual and phased approach is adopted to allow for the satisfactory empowerment of Gram Sabhas and for building up grassroots institutions. Therefore the programme has been carried out in two phases - a pilot phase and a scaling up phase- with a reassessment and evaluation at the end of the pilot phase and three years after commencement of the scaling up phase. It is envisaged that the programme would be completed over a eight year period. The total programme cost over nine years, inclusive of contingencies, duties and taxes, is estimated at INR 2 276 million (USD 41.7 million). The programme funds, forming part of IFAD's assistance, having passed through the Government of India is received by each Tribal Development Society, Chhattisgarh (TDS, who then releases the funds to the districts programme implementation units (DPIUs). The DPIU releases the funds related to the NGO capacity building and overhead costs directly to the NGOs. The funds planned for the activities to be undertaken by the communities is passed on either to special purpose committees established under the programme, or to the Gram Sabha.

TRIBAL DEVELOPMENT SOCIETY

The programme manageses by involving Community-based Organisations, Tribal Development Society, Programme Management Unit, District Programme Implementation Units,

Non-Governmental Organisations, and relevant line agencies belonging to the government of both States. At the village level, the Gram Sabha (GS) is the basic unit for planning, co-ordinating and monitoring programme activities. The programme finances the establishment of a comprehensive M&E framework comprising a computerised programme management system (CPMS) and a MIS, a participatory process monitoring system based on annual beneficiary workshops, periodic planning and budgetary process, a mid-term review and impact assessments systems. Participatory M&E mechanisms is designed to enable the communities to monitor and evaluate their own performance, identify constraints and take corrective measures, when needed. Since the programme's activities is demand driven, an environmental screening system (ESS) is set up a screening procedure of all requests for financing emanating from Gram Sabhas/users' groups.

The programme would benefit an estimated 74 000 households located in 1 080 natural villages: over 51 000 households would be located in Chhattisgarh, the remainder in Jharkhand. Almost 6 000 families form the primitive tribal groups (PTGs) are expected to benefit from programme interventions. With an estimated average household size of 5, there would be almost 370,000 beneficiaries. Over a 20 year period, the economic rate of return is estimated to be 14.2% for the programme aggregated over both states. While this ERR is not high, it represents reasonably good returns for a situation where grassroots institution development and capacity building is a primary focus.

The programme has a number of risks. Failure to promote community participation through creation of local leadership would cause the programme to degenerating into a conventional tribal development programme and this is the principal risk to the Programme. Secondly, the NGOs in the region, especially those in Madhya Pradesh/Chhattisgarh, are relatively inexperienced. Risks are also associated with provision of services required under the programme like Farmers Field School. Lastly, the program involves changing relationships within the development process and overcoming dependency attitudes of communities. As mentioned, most tribals have become overly dependent on Government subsidies while the proposed program expects beneficiaries' contributions in practically all the activities envisaged. This could be a risk for the program. The programs will be implemented in two phases-

- The first phase is called the pilot phase of approximately three years, during which the program activities has been undertaken 114 natural villages.
- The second phase will be a scaling up phase of about five years, which will complete the Program outreach in 750 natural villages of the Program Area with about fifty one thousand beneficiaries.

GRASS-ROOT EMPOWERMENT AND TECHNICAL CAPACITY BUILDING COMPONENT

Notification and Empowerment of the GS, Tribal population, especially women and other marginal groups, through awareness raising on Tribals and women's rights, and specifically as under:

Explaining project concept to villagers: Broad based awareness-creation on tribal rights, as espoused by the Panchayati Raj Legislation and on Gender & Equity issues. Legal and managerial strengthening training shall be conducted in all villages, through orientation training in legal literacy, program planning, implementation and management. A legal defense fund shall be set up to assist the tribal population in defending its rights.

WADI DEVELOPMENT

BAIF Development Research Foundation is an Agency working to create opportunities of gainful self employment for the rural families' especially disadvantaged sections, ensuring sustainable livelihood, enriched environment, improved quality of life and good human values. Its Operational area is spread over 12000 villages in Maharashtra, Karnataka, Gujarat, Rajashthan, Uttar Pradesh, Uttaranchal, Andra Pradesh and Madhya Pradesh.

The unique programme of developing orchards, popularly known as 'Wadi', on wastelands owned by the poor tribal families was launched by BAIF. This programme ensures the active involvement of the entire family, particularly the women. 'Wadi' ensures complete authority of women over the income generated from vegetable cultivation in their backyards. Many other income generation activities have now been introduced as 'Wadi' to broad base the programme. This programme has checked seasonal migration and ensured women's empowerment, food security, improved quality of life and a clean environment.

The experts has supported project team for the implementation of integrated livelihood programme in selected villages. In 2006-07 year total 552 beneficiaries have been selected in 48 villages in all the three districts of programme area. District wise details of beneficiaries mentioned in the table where with the expertise of BAIF personnel Wadi Vikas model is being implemented.

Study and Action Research

Following Research Studies have been initiated in the Programme Area. One Research Study is conducted to study different factors responsible for the diminishing population of the hill Korwa(Pahari Korwa) in Jashpur & Surguja districts focusing on the nutritional, health, sociological & anthropological aspects. This is conducted by the Post Graduate Department of Sociology, Gramya Bharti Vidhyapeeth, Hardi Bazar, Korba. From these districts 03 Blocks-namely Bagicha, Kusmi & Lundra (where maximum concentration of Hill Korwa lies) has been selected purposely. On the basis of the same criterion 14 villages were selected. It has started in the month of June and Total time for the study is 6 Months.

The second study is conducted jointly by IFAD and WFP. In the context of its new Initiative to Mainstream Innovations (IMI). Main purpose of the study is to document innovative approaches and best practices to poverty targeting in projects that use demand-driven approaches to determine allocation of project resources. Goal of the study is to illustrate how poverty targeting can be achieved under demand-driven approaches and how these approaches can be replicated and upscale. Objectives were:

- To document processes and mechanisms through which the CTDP has ensured access to project benefits and services by the poorest communities and sections of the population (and in particular women and Schedules tribes) while using demand-driven approaches to determine resource allocation;

- To illustrate to what extent and in what way these approaches have been innovative for the context in which they have been applied;
- To draw lessons from this experience in terms of institutionalization and replication of these approaches.
- The Study Team comprised of Ms. Annina Lubock-Technical Advisor, Gender and Household Food Security, Ms. Daniela- Associate Professional officer and Ms. Nisha Shrivastava- Research Coordinator. Data collection was done with the help of Samarthan, a NGO in Chhattisgarh.

Another monographic study conducted on Birhore Primitive Tribal Group by Budhadev Jankalyan Samiti specially focuses the anthropological, social, cultural and economic status in or programme area. The report also provides different social, agricultural, educational and social problems among these groups and their fruitful remedial measures.

TRIBAL POPULATION OF MADHYA PRADESH

Madhya Pradesh has the largest Tribal population of all the states. The rich diversity in the tribal communities, spread over in various parts of the state, is clearly seen not only in matters of lifestyle and cultural traditions, but also in social and economic structure, religious beliefs, language and speech, customs *et cetera*. Due to the varied socio-cultural and geographical environment and its parameters, the diverse tribal world of Madhya Pradesh not only has been largely cut-off from the mainstream of development but has, on this account, also been a cause of concern and special effort for the Central and State Governments since Independence.

After Independence, special arrangements were made for the upliftment of the Scheduled Tribes. The foundation of The Tribal Research and Welfare Institute at Chhindwara, M.P. on 20th April 1954, under the Department of Tribal Welfare in

Madhya Pradesh, was part of the Impetus in this direction. Subsequently the Institute was shifted to Bhopal, the capital of the state of M.P.

Activities

The Institute has carried out extensive ethnographic studies on the tribes of Madhya Pradesh and maintains a rich database in its documentation centre. Evaluation and impact assessment studies of schemes of the government related to development and empowerment of the scheduled tribes, are undertaken. The Institute apprises the government of its findings on the above and related issues with suggestions for appropriate policy or implementation change

The Institutes undertakes anthropological reference studies. It also furnishes its considered opinion to the government in cases where communities claim to belong to the scheduled tribes. Training is imparted to field level government functionaries to orient and sensitize them regarding the way of life of tribal communities. Seminars and workshops are held to discuss issues relating to the tribes.

Dictionaries are under preparation, of Gondi, Korku and Bhili tribal dialects. Fairs and festivals are held from time to time to create awareness of the richness of tribal culture. The Institute maintains a comprehensive library of books, documents, photographs and films relating to the tribes.

Encouragement and facilitation of academic research on tribal issues, partly through implementation of the scheme of Fellowships awarded by the Government of India for doctoral and post doctoral research, is part of the Institute's programmes. The Tribal Museums at Bhopal and at Chhindwara showcase a fascinating collection of artifacts. A new museum building is under construction at Bhopal. The Institute has been declared a Nodal TRI to co-ordinate with the TRIs of Himachal Pradesh, Uttar Pradesh, Rajasthan and Chhattisgarh states.

OVERVIEW OF SOCIO-ECONOMIC SITUATION OF THE TRIBAL COMMUNITIES

This study was carried out by the FAO Investment Centre on the socio-economic situation of tribal communities and livelihoods in selected areas in Madhya Pradesh and Bihar. Some of the key livelihood issues looked at were: below subsistence production; declining availability and control over common property and forest resources; deficit-induced indebtedness leading to loss of control over private resources; insecure or lack of land tenure among some of the poorest groups, and dependence on low return seasonal labour migration. It also considered specific development concerns of tribal women.

The information presented is based on the data collected in 1997 by formulation missions to Madhya Pradesh and Bihar and other studies undertaken for the present reformulation mission, including Participatory Rural Appraisal (PRAs) studies done in both states. This has been complemented by additional information gathered by this reformulation mission from village women and men, different Government offices and non-governmental organizations (NGOs).

RURAL POVERTY AND THE STATUS OF WOMEN AT NATIONAL LEVEL

The household consumer expenditure (HCE) survey conducted during 1993/94 showed that India had slightly less than 40% of the population, or over 325 million people, under the officially defined poverty line. Of these, over 280 million lived in rural areas. In other words, 35% of the households and about 40% of the population in rural areas live below the poverty line.

In the first two and a half decades after independence, the incidence of poverty fluctuated but showed no sustained decline. Since 1977/78, however, the proportion of poor has been declining. Available statistics show that this trend became particularly visible during 1983-1993/94, when the proportion of the poor as measured by headcount ratio (HCR) decreased by 16%, the depth of poverty as measured by the poverty gap index (PGI) by 30%, and the severity of poverty as measured by the relative squared poverty gap by 45%.

The rate of decrease in the proportion of the poor, however, is slow, at about 2% per annum in the 1980s, and poverty remains widespread. In absolute terms, the number of poor in

India increased from about 164 million in 1951 to over 325 million in 1993. Of the estimated 1.3 billion poor in the world, about 27% are in India. Given that India's share of world population is only about 15%, it has a disproportionately higher share of the world's poor.

The key features of the rural poverty in India are as follows:

- Among rural households, landless agricultural labourers have the highest incidence of poverty (51%), followed by non-agricultural rural labour (35%). Of the total rural poor, almost 42% are agricultural labourers and about 33% self-employed households in agriculture. Overall, 42% of rural poor households are landless and over 80% of them cultivate less than 1 ha of land.
- Among the social groups, scheduled tribes (STs) have the highest proportion of the poor (54%), followed by scheduled castes (SCs, 50%). Of the total rural poor population, scheduled castes account for 27% and scheduled tribes about 15%, although their share in the entire population is only 18 % and 11%, respectively. In essence, caste and, to some extent, ethnicity continue to determine the ownership of land and thus poverty.
- Scheduled tribe populations in India suffer from other forms of human deprivation than the lack of material well being. While the tribal population accounts for only about 8% of the total population, it constitutes 40% of the displaced population. The literacy rate among STs is only 24%, compared to 52% in the general population in 1991. Among the rural women of the tribal population, the literacy rate is only 13%. Similarly, while gross primary-school enrolment among STs has increased over time, and the gap with the rest of the population may disappear very soon, the dropout rate remains high.
- There is a significant inter- and intra-state variation in the incidence of rural poverty in India. Among the states having the highest proportion of the poor in 1993/94, Bihar ranks first (66%), followed by Assam (57%), Orissa (57%), West Bengal (52%), Maharashtra (51%) and Arunanchal Pradesh (48%). The three eastern states of

West Bengal, Bihar and Orissa account for over 42% of the rural poor.

- Disaggregated data at sub-state level show highly uneven change in the headcount ratios within the state and a very high incidence of poverty in certain regions. Overall, there is an almost contiguous region encompassing four regions of eastern Maharashtra, two southern regions of Madhya Pradesh, all of Uttar Pradesh except the western region, all of Bihar and West Bengal, and five regions of the northeastern states.

In the last quarter of a century, Indian women have significantly improved their overall well being. Yet women in India remain one of the most disadvantaged groups in society. The sex ratio has been in more or less constant decline since 1901 (when it was 944) and has dropped to 927. Only 39% of women are literate (against 64% for men) and only 34% of births are attended by trained health personnel. The maternal mortality rate is high, and India accounts for about one fourth of total maternity-related deaths in the world. The death rate for female children under five is 29 per thousand, against 25 among male children of the same age group. Of the 324 million illiterates enumerated in the 1991 census, 61% were women and girls. Some 39% of the girls drop out before completing primary education and 57% before completing upper primary. The average age at marriage has increased but is still low at 19.5 years, and some 30% of the girls are married between 15 and 19.

Over 90% of rural women workers are unskilled and about 90% of women are engaged in the informal/unorganized sector. Wage rates in agriculture are on average 30-50% less than for men. Women shoulder the entire burden of household activities and child-care responsibilities and 58% of women's work time is spent in such activities. Female casual labourers in rural India show the highest incidence of poverty of any occupational category, male or female. A disproportionate burden of poverty is suffered by female-headed households. At the same time, the delivery structures of credit, technical advice, etc., do not reach them, because institutions are slow to recognize women as heads of households.

National Tribal Policy

India has about 532 scheduled tribes (STs) speaking over 100 different languages, with each tribe having its own ethnic and cultural identity. According to the 1991 census, the population of STs in the country was 67.8 million constituting around 8% of the total population. Over half the tribal population is concentrated in five states - Madhya Pradesh (15.4 million), Bihar (6.6 million), Orissa (7.0 million), Andhra Pradesh (4.2 million) and West Bengal (3.8 million). Madhya Pradesh accounts for 23% and Bihar 9.7% of the total tribal population in the country.

Historically, tribal communities were characterized by a lifestyle distinct from agrarian communities. They subsisted on different combinations of shifting cultivation, hunting and gathering of forest products: all activities closely linked with forests. Their cultures celebrated and fostered this close bond with nature while also emphasizing communal ownership and consumption, closely-knit kinship structures, and minimal hierarchies.

The British colonial rule either appropriated their forests or drastically curtailed their access to them while suppressing shifting cultivation. It also imposed a system of revenue collection, which, while re-constructing natural communities into administrative 'revenue villages', also opened the doors for exploitative non-tribal moneylenders and traders to start settling in tribal areas. Tribal rebellions, both against State interventions curtailing their access to local natural resources and exploitation by outsiders, resulted in special laws being framed for many tribal areas in recognition of the unique self-regulatory cultural traits of tribal communities.

The Scheduled District Act promulgated in 1874 delineated tribal areas as 'scheduled areas'. The Government of India Act of 1935 further classified these areas into two categories, i.e. the northeastern tribal region and other backward tribal regions. The former was totally excluded from the ambit of major Indian laws, whereas the latter were partially excluded.

After Independence, the tribals were accorded special rights and protection under Article 342 of the Constitution with the

Government of India's tribal development policy aiming to bring them the benefits of economic development without eroding their traditional culture and identity. Independent India has continued with the 'scheduling' of tribal areas and tribes introduced by the British.

Tribal areas outside the northeastern region, including the study area, come under the Fifth Schedule of the Constitution. The State Governor, or a Tribal Advisory Council Chair, can make special provisions for the administration of Schedule Five areas besides waiving or amending any existing law considered detrimental to tribal interests or in conflict with their traditional values and culture. The Fifth Schedule also makes the states responsible for promoting the educational and economic interests of the tribals and to protect them from social injustice and exploitation. The Central Government provides special financial assistance to the states under Article 275 for implementing schemes for the development of scheduled tribes. Tribal development policy under the Eighth Plan (1992-97) and the approach paper for the Ninth Five Year Plan stress people's initiative and participation as key elements in the development process and in protecting the interests of the tribals. High priority has been accorded to elimination of their exploitation and removal of all forms of oppression.

Today, the tribal majority areas, which overlap with the country's major forest areas, are also areas with the highest concentrations of poverty.

Demographic Trends

Madhya Pradesh. MP has the largest tribal population in the country with the STs comprising 23.27% of the state's population in 1991. The percentage of both the scheduled tribe and scheduled caste population in MP has increased during the last two decades (from 20.1% in 1971 to 23.3 in 1991 for the ST population, and 13.1% to 14.5% for the SC population) due to their relatively higher fertility rates. In 1991, the fertility rate of the state's SC population was 4.71, of the ST population 4.05 and that of the remaining population 3.76.

No separate data is available on key demographic parameters for the tribal population. Average life expectancy in Surguja district is 51.9 years. The crude birth rate ranges from 32 to 36 per thousand females in the two districts.

Bihar. According to the 1991 census, the total tribal population in Bihar was 6,616,914 (7.7% of the state population). 91% of the state's tribal population is concentrated in the 18 districts of south Bihar out of which the tribals constitute the majority only in 3 districts - Gumla, Lohardaga and West Singhbhum. The tribals are predominantly rural (93%) in spite of the fact that the level of urbanization in the region is 20.3% compared to 13% for the state as a whole. The density of population of the state as a whole is 497 whereas the density of population of the ST areas is 273.

In contrast to Madhya Pradesh, the fertility rate of the tribal population in Bihar at 3.42 is the lowest in the state compared to that of 3.95 among the SCs and 4.06 among the general population. The proportion of the ST population declined by over one full percentage point in 20 years.

SCHEDULED TRIBES IN THE STUDY AREA

The area studied in both the states has a combination of a variety of tribes and occupational artisan castes which have lived in a symbiotic relationship for a few hundred years. The tribes in the area belong to two linguistic groups. One group speaks the Austro-Asiatic or Mundari group of languages and includes the Santhal, Ho and Munda. The other group of tribes speaks a language of the Dravidian group - this includes the Oraon, Chero and Gond. The tribes themselves range from surviving remnants of almost pure hunter-gatherers among the 'Primitive Tribal Groups' (PTGs) to the settled agriculturist tribes like the Santhal, Ho, Munda, Oraon and Gond. However, until today, even the agricultural tribes do a considerable amount of gathering and all tribes share a historically strong collectivism in economic activities.

Madhya Pradesh. No recent data are available on the population by tribe for the programme blocks in MP. However, according to the 1961 census data, three main tribes, namely Gond, Oraon and Kanwar predominate in the three districts, accounting for more than 80% of their total tribal population. The main tribal groups in the three districts are:

- Raigarh/Jashpur: Oraon, Kanwar, Gond, Nagwanshi, Sawara, Kharia, Korwa, Baiga and Birhor
- Surguja: Gond, Oraon, Kanwar, Nagesia, Korwa, Baiga, Binjhwar Bihar. 30 tribes have been notified as scheduled tribes in Bihar. The most numerous STs are the Santhal, Oraon, Munda, Ho, Kharwar, Kharia and Bhumij which constitute about 86% of the total tribal population of the state. The major STs in the Bihar programme districts are:
- Ranchi: Oraon, Munda, Bhumij, Bedia (in Angara Block only), Mahali, Lohra and Kharia;
- East and West Singhbum: Santhal, Ho, Bhumij, Bathudi, Munda and Oraon.

Primitive Tribal Groups

Madhya Pradesh. 7 Scheduled Tribes have been recognized as 'Primitive Tribal Groups' in MP These are : Pahari Korwa, Baiga, Avujhmariya, Bhariya, Kamar, Sahariya and Birhor. The MP government has set up separate development agencies, registered as autonomous societies, for each of the PTGs excepting the Birhors. The PTG development agencies devote funds, in addition to those available for STs in general, exclusively for the PTGs. Their basic strategy for promoting more focused development of the PTGs is to form clusters of 4 to 5 PTG villages and make teams of officials from the revenue, rural development, education and the tribal welfare departments responsible for each cluster.

Bihar. Nine scheduled tribes have been classified as PTGs in Bihar: Asur, Birhor, Birjia, Korwa, Parhaiya, Savar, Hill Kharia, Mal Paharia and Sauria Paharia. Their total population is estimated at about 190,000 persons. The Birhor population in the study area is only 210 of which 190 live in only two villages in Angara block. There is no separate development agency for the PTGs in Bihar.

Migration

Madhya Pradesh. Information collected by this mission, as well as by the PRAs and Non-Timber Forest Products (NTFPs) marketing study, suggests very low rates of migration from some of the programme blocks in MP. According to the BDO of Dharamjaigarh block for example, barely 50 families from the entire block migrate seasonally due to the availability of different NTFPs from the forests most of the year. This was despite the fact that out of the 24,000 families below the poverty line in the 1996-97 survey, as many as 7000 (29%) were landless. In Odgi block, however, all the able-bodied persons in some villages migrate and return only just prior to the onset of the rains. The more general pattern in the block is that one or several members of half to one-third of the households in each village migrate for 3 to 4 months in the dry season.

Bihar. Although no precise information is available for the study area, the Chotanagpur Plateau is known to have high rates of migration, including to distant states such as Punjab and to Delhi. The PRAs done in Bihar came across seasonal migration particularly among the PTGs.

Sex Ratios

Madhya Pradesh. A striking demographic feature of the study area is the significantly higher female to male ratio compared to the all India ratio of 927 and the MP state ratio of 931 females per 1000 males. Sex ratios among the STs in the programme blocks in Surguja district range from 950 (Odgi) to 985-6 (Mainpat, Lundra and Udaipur). The relatively low sex ratio among the tribals in Odgi block is surprising due to the reportedly high levels of migration from the block. In Raigarh/Jaspur districts, all the programme blocks have over 1000 females per 1000 males ranging from 1003 (Bagicha) to 1028 (Manora). With almost no migration from Dharamjaigarh block, a female to male ratio of 1016 is again striking probably indicating the superior status of tribal women in the area.

Literacy

Madhya Pradesh. Literacy rates among the tribal population in the study area are very low, particularly among women. Overall, both ST male and female literacy rates in Raigarh/Jaspur districts are significantly higher than the literacy rates in Surguja district. ST male literacy in the programme blocks ranges from 17% (Odgi and Mainpat) to 39% (Manora). ST female literacy ranges from as low as 4.3% (Odgi) to 23% (Manora). Literacy rates among the PTGs are even lower - barely 5% among the Pahari Korwas and almost nil amongst the women. Although the government has built residential schools for them, Pahari Korwa children tend to leave them and run away.

Bihar. Literacy among the tribal population at 23.6% in 1991 continues to be less than half that of for the total population of the state (52.2%) although it has increased fourfold over the last four decades. While the state male literacy is 64.1%, the tribal male literacy is 32.5%. The tribal female literacy rate is particularly low at 14.5% compared to 29.3% for the total female population.

Both the male and female literacy rates in all the programme blocks are significantly lower than the literacy rates for the state as a whole. Male literacy in all but 2 of the programme blocks (Tonto 24.7%, Goelkera 29%) is higher than the state ST male literacy of 32.5%. Rajnagar block has the highest male literacy (44.2%). Female literacy, however, is lower than the state ST female literacy rate of 14.5% in *all* the programme blocks ranging from 5.9% (Tonto) to 13.9% (Rajnagar).

Literacy rates also vary among different tribes. In 1981, the Kharias had the highest literacy rate among the STs followed by the Oraons and the Mundas. These tribal groups have also adopted Christianity to a greater extent. Literacy among the PTGs was the lowest, ranging from 5.7% among the Birhors to 7.6% among the Mal Maharias. Literacy among the PTG female population in 1981 was about 2.5%.

Health Status

The most common diseases among tribal communities are parasitic infections, diarrhoea, dysentery, skin diseases, respiratory infections, whooping cough and measles. Serious diseases such as tuberculosis, leprosy and malaria are also common in the study areas. Health facilities do not reach them because the norms prescribed by the State Governments for establishing Primary Health Centres and Health Sub-Centres are inappropriate for a dispersed population in small settlements in inaccessible areas. When health facilities happen to be available, most tribal villagers can neither pay the doctor nor pay for the medicines.

Tribal women's health is at risk during their reproductive years. Around 68 % of pregnant and lactating women suffer from anemia. Around 72 % of all births are attended by untrained traditional birth attendants (*dais).* Of particular interest, the maternal mortality rate is reported to be around 2 per 1000 live births compared to the national average of 4.4 per 1000 live births.

In interior villages with good forest cover, the communities rely on their traditional herbal medicine practices. In mixed villages, adoption of allopathic treatment has become a major source of indebtedness. Women members of Self Help Groups reported that they borrow from their savings group for health care; others obtained loans from money lenders.

The prevalent nutritional disorders are anemia and avitaminosis with the associated common deficiency diseases of a) angular conjunctivitis and angular stomatitis and pellagra, all assumed to be caused by riboflavin deficiency; b) night blindness and skin dryness or roughness attributed to vitamin A deficiency; c) endemic goitre, the principal aetiological factor of which is iodine deficiency.

The children portray a classic picture of chronic malnutrition with lower size, weight and height, for their age. This is undoubtedly related to the poor nutritional status of women, with an inter-generation transmission of malnutrition resulting in the very high incidence of low birth weight in India. 60% of the pre-school children are underweight and 25% severely underweight. Pre-school children are the weakest section of the population. Mortality rates for ST children under five was 136 in Bihar and 167 in MP.

Settlement Patterns

Topography, socio-cultural characteristics, livelihood systems and to some extent, historical factors have shaped the settlement patterns in the study area. In terms of size and density, the settlements may be characterized as (i) small and scattered (only 10 to 15 houses), (ii) medium sized compact or dispersed (up to 100 houses in 1 to 3 or 4 hamlets) and (iii) larger usually more compact settlements. Revenue villages in Bihar tend to be smaller than those in MP: 67% of the villages in the former have less than 500 inhabitants, compared to 39% in MP, where 56% of the population lives in villages of 500 to 2 000 inhabitants. The more compact and larger settlements tend to be in the plains and are inhabited by the more agriculturally advanced tribes. A revenue village may have between 2 to 7-8 'natural' villages consisting of settlements at considerable distance from each other. Most revenue villages do not represent social units of organization nor do they function as collective units of decision-making.

PTG settlements are primarily found in remote, forested and hilly tracts with some villages having only 10 to 15 houses. The Birhors make their *tandas* in isolated patches with large gaps between two *tandas* to ensure that each community has adequate forest area for hunting and gathering. Pahari Korwa settlements often lack permanency as the entire settlement is abandoned if a number of deaths take place in the same neighbourhood. The settlements may be of a single ethnic group or of several STs and castes. Traditional PTG settlements were uni-ethnic but subsequent to their resettlement outside forest areas, they often comprise hamlets within larger, mixed villages.

Local Level Institutions

Traditional Institutions. The settled tribes in the study area have at least two levels of traditional leadership - within the village and for a cluster of villages of the clan for dealing with inter-village issues and disputes. Some of them also have a third and higher leadership level for addressing issues confronting the larger community. In almost all the settled tribes, the posts of the traditional leaders are hereditary often reserved for the male lineage of the 'original reclaimers' of the land. The traditional village assembly has virtually been an all-male institution with women provided access only under highly exceptional circumstances.

PTGs. By virtue of their dependence on foraging, and the nature of collectivism and cooperation it requires, the social institutions of PTGs are the least hierarchical to facilitate consensual decision-making. In the absence of any attachment to private property, gender relations have been particularly egalitarian among the PTGs. Birhor settlements have traditionally had a council of elders composed of all elders of the group, both male and female. Regular political participation by women in the village council has also been reported in the case of the Korwa, a tribe that has only recently come into settled agriculture.

An overview of the present status of traditional village institutions in the study area in both states indicates the following patterns:

- The tradition of taking collective decisions based on consensus among most communities is still strong, particularly in the more remote villages.
- While in some cases traditional/hereditary leaders are still respected, in others they are being replaced by a new generation of young and educated leaders who have gained the community's respect and trust.
- In more heterogeneous communities, where socio-economic stratification and differentiation within tribals has increased, the new leadership represents the economically better off sections interested in increasing their political power.
- Within this pattern, small numbers of educated tribal women leaders are also beginning to emerge, in part, due to the reservation of one third seats for women in PRIs. There is considerable openness to creating institutional space for women to start participating in community affairs.
- Traditional institutions continue to perform a number of regulatory functions within villages besides mobilizing the community for undertaking tasks of common interest when required. These have become weakest near the urban towns.

Modern Institutions. By far the single most pervasive modern village institution introduced in post independence India has been the *Gram Panchayat* as the lowest rung of local government. Intended to put into practice Mahatma Gandhi's vision of gram swaraj (village self rule) the *Gram Panchayat* effectively reconstructed the village for administrative convenience. Superimposition of statutory *Panchayats* in tribal areas has had many adverse impacts on their self governing traditional institutions. Concentration of power in the elected *Panchayat Pradhans*, combined with a lack of transparency and accountability in their functioning, slowly converted many panchayats into centres of corruption, political manipulation and factional rivalry.

During the last 10 to 15 years, with increasing recognition of the importance of people's participation for increasing the effectiveness of development interventions, an extensive array of 'people's' institutions have been created in the villages for the implementation of sectoral programmes. These include joint forest management (JFM) committees being set up by the Forest Department, education committees by the Education Department, watershed associations and committees by the DRDA, water and health committees by the Public Health Department, water users association by the Irrigation Department, and Mahila Mandals (women's associations) by the Women and Child Department. Under a number of special programmes such as the Bihar Education Programme, selected village women are trained as animators to organize women not only for accessing literacy but also for dealing with their other problems.

New Institutions Promoted by NGOs. Many NGOs have also been promoting a variety of new institutions within villages. Their nature and tenor varies with the ideology and perspective of the concerned NGO. Some NGO-promoted village institutions have traits similar to those promoted by government departments while others focus on leadership development and community mobilization. Some NGOs are also providing support to self-initiated forest protection associations of the villagers. Training and supporting cadres of village animators for organizing and mobilizing predominantly male youth groups is another NGO focus.

Among the more dynamic new institutions being promoted by NGOs, although on a limited scale and only by a few NGOs, are women's associations for advocacy and local action on issues affecting women's lives and self-help groups (SHGs) engaged in savings and credit and/or income generation activities.

LIVELIHOOD SYSTEMS IN THE STUDY AREA

Livelihood systems in the study area are primarily dependent on various combinations of agriculture, forests and labour. Livestock and fish rearing are closely integrated in the farming systems. There are also a number of artisanal castes and tribal groups who depend either on providing services to the community or on small-scale processing and marketing. The traditional livelihood system of the PTGs consisted of shifting cultivation, hunting and gathering forest foods and other produce. They are undergoing a painful process of enforced transition to settled cultivation outside the forests. Although many still depend to some extent on hunting and forest products, these are no longer their main source of livelihood. Instead they are grappling with survival on poor quality non-forest lands without agricultural implements. Women's work is regarded as crucial for the survival of tribal households in terms of provisioning for food, income earning, as well as management of resources.

Typology of Livelihood Systems

The tribal livelihood systems identified in the study area can be classified according to the degree of dependence on forest resources. Forest dependent upland systems, usually located in upper watersheds where most PTG Villages are also located, are estimated to represent about 20% of the study area. Communities in these watersheds live in small, scattered settlements located near or within reserve or protected forests. PTGs in such areas are under transition from pure forest dependence to a mixed forest/agriculture/wage labour system due to resettlement, and declining forest productivity. Characteristics include a continuing dependence, often unsustainable, on harvesting of firewood and some NTFPs such as roots/tubers, bamboo, tendu, sal leaves and fibre collected for consumption or sale. Limited permanent or shifting cultivation is practiced within a defined village forest territory, providing food security for 2 to 4 months. Small stock consists of poultry, pigs and goats which are sold when cash is needed. In Bihar, there is substantial reliance on seasonal migration for wage work outside the village (in brick kilns, mining or road construction) to supplement incomes. Headloading is often an important source of income, particularly for women: according to the PRA study in Bihar, 90% of the households in such villages were practicing headloading as a survival strategy, an activity primarily undertaken by women.

Mixed systems, located in middle watersheds, comprise about 65% of the study area. These are partially hilly areas with communities having lesser dependence on forest than the former and in place of this there is added reliance on agriculture. Farming is mainly single crop with some paddy and vegetable cultivation. Some farmers may own bullocks and use manure for maintaining soil fertility. Food security extends to 3 to 4 months. Access is interrupted at certain times of the year and so market orientation is somewhat limited with a greater focus on subsistence production. Migration can involve up to 50% of households in this system.

Lowland systems, located in lower watersheds and covering about 15% of the study area. These communities extend into the lower plains and may have relatively little forest access. They tend to be more multi-ethnic, have smaller but more intensively farmed landholdings and own more bullocks. Double cropping is more common and, where irrigation is available, even a third crop may be grown. There is a greater reliance on paddy, vegetable cultivation occurs year round and overall food security can extend to 5 to 7 months. A much greater market orientation is present due to year-round market access. Many fields may already be bunded as the terrain is generally flatter and there is better information about water management techniques. In general, farming has been carried out for a longer period and this is demonstrated in greater productivity per hectare. Distant migration may be less prevalent with greater availability of wage work locally.

Components of Livelihood Systems

Land Holding Patterns. In Bihar 56% of the farmers operate an average of 0.4 ha whilst 71% of the holdings are less then

2 ha; the average of holdings with less than 2 ha is 0.6 ha. In Madhya Pradesh about 51% of the cultivators are marginal farmers (average holding 0.4 ha), accounting for only 11% of the cultivated area. About 20% of the farmers are small farmers with an average size of 1.5 ha accounting for 16% of the cultivated area. The rest of the farmers (23%) cultivate 73% of the land. These figures, however, refer to all holdings in the study blocks, including those of non-tribals. Broadly speaking, holding patterns of tribals tend to be more egalitarian and holding sizes smaller. About 75% of the tribal households have firm title to their land. Land tenure issues mainly concern 'encroached' forest land. Information about the extent of landlessness is not readily available except for the PTGs in Surguja district.

PTGs. 55.3% of Pahari Korwas in the study blocks are landless. As the PTGs never had titles to the forests in which they traditionally subsisted, 'landlessness' among them is a product of delegitimization of their traditional livelihood system. Although the government is allotting them non-forest land, it is normally unproductive and many remain landless or lack proper land titles. Even if they have titles, the actual possession is often in the hands of other tribals or non-tribals with the land owners working as labourers on their own land. Many PTGs sell off the land allotted to them to people of other tribes at low rates and revert to their traditional life style of living in the forest.

Agricultural Production Patterns. Agriculture in the study area is predominantly rainfed and monocropped: only about 8% of the cultivated land in the Bihar study area and 4% in MP is under irrigation. Less than 25% of the gross-cropped area is double cropped. Paddy is the major crop accounting for about 60 to 70% of the cultivated land during the *kharif* season, with productivity ranging from 450 kg to 1100 kg/ha. The other crops are maize, a variety of millets sorghum, wheat, barley, pulses and oil seeds. Food grains occupy about 95% of the cropped area. Paddy, maize, millets, arhar, niger and groundnut are the important *kharif* crops while the main crops grown in the *rabi* season are wheat, oilseeds (rapeseed, mustard, linseed, groundnut, pigeon pea and niger), pulses (lentil and gram), and vegetables. Horticulture is little developed in the study area with the present area under fruits, vegetables, and spices accounting for only about 2.5% of the cultivated area. Vegetable cultivation is picking up very fast. These are preferably grown on *Bari* land (homestead). Women participate in all agricultural operations excepting ploughing and sowing of rice seed, contributing between 70 to 80% of the total labour.

Household Food Security. The extent to which the tribals are able to meet their food requirements from agriculture is determined by the type of land they own, the size of the holdings and the size of the household. The PRAs as well as the seasonality analysis done by the mission agronomists, indicate a declining role of agriculture in household food security which lasts for 2 to 6 months of the year for the majority of farming households. It is estimated that average households in upland systems are only able to meet 20 to 40% of their food requirements; those in the middle system 30 to 40% and those in lowland systems between 50 to 70% of their needs. Food insecurity peaks in the post-sowing monsoon period (August-September) and again around March when the *kharif* harvest has been exhausted. In the past, most tribals were able to cover most of the shortfall with foods gathered from the forests. Forest degradation and curtailed forest access has reduced the availability of natural foods on which they depended compelling the tribals, especially those in the upland and mixed systems, to depend more and more on purchased foods to meet their minimum survival needs. Impoverished villagers have to choose between migrating for wage work or resorting to unsustainable harvesting of firewood for survival income. Many tribals have become caught in a debt trap because of the precariousness of their food security situation.

Forests in the Livelihood System. In extent, forests cover approximately 28% of the geographical area of the program districts in Bihar and 46% in MP. Forests supply timber, fodder, fuelwood and a large number of Non-Timber Forest Products. Despite forest degradation, NTFPs contribute significantly to the economy of the study area. Almost all households living in the forest belt depend upon collection of NTFPs for consumption and sale. Mahua and tendu leaf are economically the two most important items, both primarily collected by women. According to the NTFP study done in MP for the reformulation mission, as many as 50 NTFPs are still gathered from the forests in the study area. Income per household (including an allowance for the value of non-marketed NTFPs) ranges from just over Rs.2000 to more than Rs.5000 and includes collection activities (e.g. edible plants, tendu leaf, seeds, etc.) and processing activities (e.g. basket-making, rope-making, de-seeding, etc.). This is in addition to the value of grazing, firewood and timber for house construction derived from the forests.

Gender Roles in Forest Use

Among the PTGs such as Birhor, Pahari Korwa and Savar, women play important roles in (a) food gathering from the forests; (b) rope-making from the bark of trees and sabai grass (Birhor); (c) honey collection; (d) herbal medicinal plant collection and processing, sale; (e) hunting and trapping; (f) basket-making; (g) shifting cultivation; (h) labour; and (i) fishing. Among the Birhors, sale or barter of rope in exchange for cash or grain is the exclusive work of women.

Food gathering is a vital economic activity even for women of the settled tribes. Various types of roots, stems, leaves, fruits, flowers and mushrooms are collected through the year. Roots and stems are the most important forest foods which constitute a major part of their diet. Leaves, vegetables and mushrooms are often consumed as complete meals.

The extent of women's income from NTFPs in the study area can be gauged from the fact that in Surguja district, Rs.14 crores are paid as wages for Tendu leaf collection annually, a product primarily gathered by women. In Surguja's east forest division in which 3 of the programme blocks (Kusmi, Lundra and Shankargarh) fall, Rs.4 crores are paid as wages for Tendu leaf collection and Rs.2 crores for Sal seed collection annually. Another Rs.2 to 3 crores are earned annually through the collection of other NTFPs in the unorganized sector.

Livestock

Livestock raising is an important component of the tribal culture and of the production systems and is fully integrated with crop production. Cattle and buffaloes provide draft power, manure, play an important role in threshing operations and livestock constitutes a cash reserve for times of distress. Traditionally, livestock is grazed on common and wasteland and also in the forest during the monsoon season. Once produce is harvested, the stubbles and volunteer grasses become the main grazing areas throughout the rest of the year. Overall 70-90% of households in the programme districts in MP own livestock excluding poultry (mainly cattle and pigs) and the proportion increases to over 90% if poultry is included. Livestock is mostly of local breed. Tribal communities generally do not milk the cattle and milk is not a traditional part of their diet.

Dependence on Labour

Most tribal households depend on wage labour to eke out a living. Dependence on wage labour is much higher in villages away from forests, (for over half the year) when food from their own lands is not available. Wage work is done both within the village and in neighbouring towns. Within the village, it is mostly agricultural work whereas outside, the villagers work in brick kilns and as unskilled construction labour.

Women's participation in wage work is equal to that of the men. However, agricultural wages paid to women are almost always lower than those paid to men. Landless SC women are often the poorest and most dependent on wages. In many tribal villages, agricultural wage-rates are fixed in *Gram Sabha* meetings based on the paying capacity of the landowners. The tradition of keeping women's wages lower than those of men, while sustaining the low return agricultural economy, also means that it relies heavily on poor women's cheap labour.

Indebtedness. According to the rural financial sector study conducted for this mission, 58% of the tribal households in Bihar and 47% in Madhya Pradesh were indebted: the estimated average debt per indebted household was INR 2917 in Bihar and INR 5918 in Madhya Pradesh. Degree of indebtedness was found highest amongst marginal farmers in Bihar (75% of the sample) and landless labourers in MP (52%). In MP, around 67% of borrowing was for productive purposes and 33% for consumption. Borrowing for repayment of old debt was also a major feature of borrowing for non-productive purposes. Of the total borrowings, about 67% in Bihar and 50% in MP was from informal sources.

Availing of loans. A major reason for women not being able to avail IRDP loans is their not having any land or property which can be used as collateral by the banks. Even the studies done on rural finance for the mission found that women had next to no access to the formal credit institutions. In the study area in Madhya Pradesh, only about 13% of the sample households and in Bihar, only 11% households had availed of loans from formal credit institutions in women's names.

SOCIAL AND ECONOMIC STATUS OF TRIBAL WOMEN

It is widely recognized that tribal women enjoy a better status within their own communities than women in mainstream Indian society. There are few restrictions on their mobility. Women have considerable freedom of choice in the selection of marriage partners and tribal cultures have liberal norms related to divorce and remarriage by women. Due to their important role in the agriculture-cum-forest based tribal economies, women have traditionally enjoyed respect as economically-valued members of their communities. This is reflected in the tradition of bride price instead of dowry among most tribal communities. A major indicator of tribal women's better status even in the study area is the highly favourable tribal female to male ratio in almost all the blocks compared to those of other communities.

Among the settled agricultural tribes, however, there have been two crucial areas of gender inequality by tradition - property rights and political participation. Among most agricultural tribes in the study area, property, particularly land, passes through the male lineage and under customary law, women do not have inheritance rights to land. Under Section 3 of the Indian Succession Act of 1925, the State Government of Bihar has exempted most STs in the state from the purview of normal succession laws. Matters of inheritance and rights to property among these tribes are governed by their customary laws.. The second important area of gender inequality among the settled tribes has been that of political participation with women being excluded from traditional community institutions The second important area of gender inequality among the settled tribes has been that of political participation with women being excluded from traditional community institutions.

Women of even settled tribes, however, have traditionally had control over their own income from wages or the sale or processing of NTFPs that they collect from common lands and forests. To some extent, this has countered the gender inequality in property rights by providing women a certain degree of economic independence and greater control over household food security. However, as discussed below, this position of tribal women is under threat of rapid erosion.

GENDER ROLES, KNOWLEDGE AND TABOOS IN AGRICULTURE

The majority of labour for agricultural production (between 70-80% by different estimates) in the study area is provided by women, yet government, and even most NGO interventions in the agricultural sector are generally blind to women's role in the farming system. Demonstrations and training in new technology, distribution of seeds and fertilizer as well as loans and subsidies are being targeted only at men. The same is the case with the schemes of the horticulture and animal husbandry departments with all fruit plants, ducks, goats and chicken being distributed primarily to men. Such an acute gender imbalance in access to new agricultural knowledge and resources created by such interventions is tending to undermine women's traditionally respected role in the production system. There is not a single woman agricultural extension worker in the programme districts in MP. A recent directive of the state government, however, has reserved one-third of future recruitment of agricultural extension workers for women.

Age-old taboos also forbid women to perform certain tasks. These include ploughing, sowing the seed of the main rice crop (although the backbreaking work of transplanting paddy is considered exclusively women's work) and tiling the roof of a house. The women are liable to social punishment if they violate any of the three taboos. In essence, these prevent women from gaining independent capability in agricultural production.

or in acquiring shelter. There were no such taboos for women of the foraging tribes. Seed broadcasting under shifting cultivation was done by women and women participated equally in house construction. Ploughing was absent in any case. With many of the PTGs shifting to settled agriculture, their women are rapidly internalizing the gender roles and practices of the settled tribes.

Changing Attitudes to Women's Political Participation

Considerable attitudinal changes towards women's traditional exclusion from political participation at both the community and higher levels are evident among the settled tribes. Three major processes have contributed to such change. Perhaps the most significant ones have been the political struggles of the tribals themselves. During the most dynamic phase of the Jharkhand Mukti Morcha's movement in the mid-1970s in the Chotanagpur plateau, women were encouraged to form women's associations in every village to fight against the 'internal' enemies of polygamy and rampant alcoholism among men to revitalize tribal society. Large numbers of women were active participants in this struggle.

Secondly, under the ambit of different government programmes, mahila mandals (women's associations) have been formed in many villages as forums for reaching development inputs to women. Women's associations were also formed during the total literacy campaign for increasing literacy among women. Under the Bihar Education Programme, which is now being extended to all districts of the state, trained women animators organize women's associations for literacy and dealing with their other problems. Under the Government of India's DWCRA (Development of Women and Children in Rural Areas) scheme, women's groups are being organized in many villages for income generation activities. The reservation of one third seats for women in PRIs has had a visible impact in MP. Due to no panchayat elections having been held in Bihar for 19 years, such impact is less evident in Bihar. Other government programmes, such as JFM and Watershed Development, under which new village institutions are being promoted, are also encouraging women's participation in community affairs.

Lastly, there have been many NGO initiatives to organize and mobilize women. These include women's savings and credit groups, and advocacy groups for women's rights and against domestic violence. Although uneven, the cumulative impact of all these interventions has increased acceptance of women's participation in government or NGO promoted groups and community institutions. The traditional male-only village assembly has either learnt to co-exist with such new institutions or has started to transform by accepting women in its ambit. Women still do not attend the traditional male gatherings unless specifically invited. When invited by the male leaders, they often turn up in large numbers. In the context of the continuing high levels of illiteracy among tribals, educated tribal women enjoy special respect in their communities and are gaining acceptance in leadership roles.

Trends of Change in Women's Rights

Despite women not having inheritance rights to land under customary law among most settled tribes, various social arrangements have existed to ensure adequate care of women in situations of widowhood, breakdown of marriage, single women and for families having only daughters.

Thus, widowed women acquired use rights to their husband's property for maintenance for life. On their death, the property passed into the hands of the husband's nearest male relatives. Both unmarried daughters and daughters who returned to their paternal homes due to breakdown of marriage, similarly acquired use rights in their paternal property for life maintenance. In the case of families having only daughters, sons-in-law could inherit their parental property if they agreed to settle in their wife's paternal village. Severe social sanctions for violation of these norms reduced the vulnerability of women in such situations. The weakening of traditional institutions has reduced such traditional social protection enjoyed by tribal women. The rising value and scarcity of land are leading to a breakdown in women's maintenance rights. Several incidents of women inheriting land being labelled witches and being hounded out (occasionally even killed) by male relatives to grab the land, have been reported from the Jharkhand area. The worst sufferers in this category are widowed women in the age group of 55 and above.

During the field visits, it was found that unmarried daughters of Ho families are now allocated only one acre of their paternal land for life maintenance, while the rest is divided equally among the brothers, irrespective of the total size. Given the taboos against women ploughing, sowing and building roofs, such women remain dependent on their male relatives both for cultivating the land and for shelter. With many such women continuing to live with one of the brothers after the parents' death, their status and condition within such households needs to be understood better. There were also indications that the number of daughters remaining unmarried may be increasing for a variety of reasons.

Women Supported Households

In most of the villages visited, an effort was made to identify the number of women headed and women supported households to understand their status and food security situation. In the limited time available it was difficult to communicate the concept of women *supported* households (with the man either away, sick or prone to excessive drinking), due to which the villagers only estimated the widows in their villages. Between 7 to 10% of the households appeared to be headed by widowed women. The percentage of women *supported* households must be considerably higher in villages with rampant alcoholism and male migration. While in the case of some widows, land ownership had been transferred to their names, in others it had been transferred to their sons. Among the Gond Manjhi tribe in Pathalgaon, the widows now receive only 50% of their husband's land, the other half going to the woman's younger brother-in-law. In a mixed Oraon-Dehadi Korwa village, the tradition had changed to no land being transferred to the widow's name with all of it being given to the sons. In most cases, daughters inherited land only when there were no sons.

Agricultural Produce

Traditionally, ownership and control over income earned through one's labour from non-private property strictly belonged to the person who expended the labour. Thus income from collection and processing/sale of NTFPs from forest lands belonged to the man, woman or child who had invested the labour in the activity.

In the case of produce or income from private land owned by the men, by and large the ownership rested with the land owner. This is most strictly observed among the Munda. Among the other tribes, although the ownership generally rests with the male 'head' of the household, its management and control were shared by husband and wife. Due to tribal women's major role in trade and marketing, and having primary responsibility for household provisioning, they have also been the effective 'managers' of household income and agricultural produce.

Women's Income and Status

Women in all the villages visited, categorically stated that they kept and controlled their own income (usually from wages, NTFPs and petty processing/trading). As far as the husband's income was concerned, while some said that even the husbands handed over their incomes to their wives for household maintenance, in other cases, it either depended on individual husbands or the men kept their income in their own hands.

Women's ability to retain control over their incomes and their traditional status are being increasingly threatened by some of the following factors:

- Alcoholism. With increasing marginalization and alienation, excessive alcohol consumption has become widespread among tribal men. Not only do the men's incomes decline but they start snatching even the women's earnings. Resistance invites domestic violence and abuse. Household food security becomes a major casualty.
- Migration and bigamy. In areas with high male migration, the men tend to bring other women back with them, throwing out their wives. With traditional institutions for regulating such behaviour at the weakest in such areas, the issue of women's land and inheritance rights is acquiring a new dimension. Tribal women's land rights are also becoming an important issue with

a minority of educated women gaining geographical and social mobility. A number of NGOs are working on the issue.

- Stereotype assumptions governing development interventions. As the majority of government programmes continue to target only men as the presumed 'heads' of households, traditional gender relations, characterized by greater balance and complementarity, are being affected.

MP is one of the few Indian states which has framed a state policy for women. Among other things, the policy advocates women's empowerment through increasing their access, ownership and control over productive assets, skills and resources and increasing their presence and participation in institutions at managerial and decision-making levels. Due to the important role of forests in local livelihood systems, the policy has a specific section on women and forests. This advocates ensuring that payment for NTFPs such as tendu leaf must be made directly to the women collectors, and that their membership of primary Tendu Leaf Cooperative Societies and representation in their managing committees should be increased and the proportion of women *phad munshis* increased to 50% by the turn of the century. New 'community' institutions also promoted by government have had some beneficial impact on creating space for women's participation in community affairs.

HOUSEHOLD TYPOLOGY, PERCEPTIONS AND PRIORITIES

For this study, households were subdivided into four socio-economic strata:

- the poorest of the poor: nearly all the Primitive Tribal Groups, the landless households and the female headed/supported households with young children;
- the very poor: nearly all the remote forest dependent villages practicing upland farming systems, all the other female headed households, all the marginal farmers independently of the production system,

and some of the small farmers not having access to any lowland;

- the poor: most villages practicing mixed production systems and small farmer households having some fields in lowlands;
- the less poor: small farmer households and other farmers, especially those having access to lowland with an assured source of irrigation.

During the PRA exercise, an attempt was made to understand, from the perspectives of tribal women and men, the dimensions of poverty and well being. Independently of the tribe, caste or gender, landlessness (or very small holdings), followed by dependency on wage labour emerged as the main indicators of poverty. Subsidiary ones, in descending order, were lack of (or few) livestock, not enough food from the farm, no access to drinking water and low levels of literacy.

Indicators of well being for men from settled tribes were: (i) assured source of water though construction of tanks, water management, and/or lift irrigation (ii) access to good supply of improved seeds, (iii) regular monthly income and (iv) having a school in the village. Settled women's perception of well being were: (i) food self-sufficiency, (ii) access to health and education, and (iii) having a large number of livestock.

Indicators of well being of men from PTG's were: (i) permanent rights to land, (ii) protection of crops from wild animals and (iii) easy access to NTFPs. For PTG women (i) having access to food throughout the year, (ii) good housing conditions and (iii) no consumption of alcohol by men emerged as indicators of well being.

Priorities at Village and Household Level

According to the PRA exercise, water management (construction/rehabilitation of tanks and construction of check dams and other forms of community irrigation), emerged as the overwhelming priority of all sample villages. Land development support for the uplands and better roads were the other priority for males of settled tribes. Priorities for women were: (i) availability and proximity of fuelwood and water, (ii) availability of good quality seeds, (iii) education and (iv) proximity of a public distribution shop.

Priorities for men from PTGs were: (i) permanent title to land; (ii) license to collect NTFP, (iii) availability of good quality seeds and (iv) bullocks for ploughing. For women from PTG tribes, priorities were: (i) local employment opportunities; (ii) education for children; (iii) access to a public distribution shop; (iv) availability of seeds, and (v) construction of a causeway on the stream to allow passage of people during the rainy season.

- In a Birhor village in Angara block for example, the majority of households were found dependent on seasonal migration for several months each year.
- The relatively higher literacy rates among the ST population in Raigarh/Jaspur districts compared to those in Surguja district are attributed to the work of Christian missionary organizations.
- All information on health and nutrition is based on the 1992-93 NFHS (National Family Health Survey).
- Underweight prevalence among pre-school children in Kerala is 28.5 % compared to 62.6 % in Bihar.
- Poor nutrition, excessive alcohol consumption and the lack of safe drinking water and health facilities in their settlements due to their small, scattered and remote nature, makes the situation grave for the PTGs if they become afflicted by an infectious disease.
- By tradition, the Pahari Korwas also abandon the house in which a death has taken place.
- In the interior Mutu village in Manora block, the tradition of both the women and the men getting together to discuss village affairs was found to be intact. In addition, groups of neighbours were continuing to work collectively on each others' private lands for agricultural operations.
- In a Ho village in Tonto block, a number of younger men, not related to the traditional leadership, had heard about the movement for tribal self rule (TSR) and had

taken the initiative to form a village association to organize the villagers. 2 of the 9 members of the managing committee they had formed were women.

- In a mixed tribal and caste village in Bagicha block, although the community spirit was still alive, considerable socio-economic stratification had developed within the village. Ghasi Scheduled Caste members of the community were landless and the poorest while four Muslim traders were engaged in money lending and an Oraon teacher had accumulated 50 acres of land.
- In Dharamjaigarh block of Raigarh district, a 'Samaj Panchayat' of 23 villages of the Rathia Kanwar community was being held. The woman chairperson of a village forest committee (VFC) had gone there to raise the issue of her daughter, married into another village, being made to do what she considered an unreasonably high amount of work by her in-laws.
- The decision about the Lo Bir Sendra (annual hunt) among the Santhals, about transplanting and wage rates among the Hos and seasonal management of cattle grazing among most communities, continue to be taken in *Gram Sabha* meetings.
- One NGO working in the study area in Bihar, has been facilitating the development of such village women's associations which take up cases related to women's land rights, promote collective action against alcoholism and domestic violence, support income generation through NTFP processing and increase awareness among women about the legislation related to tribal self rule. Interestingly, initially they encountered strong resistance from traditional male leaders to women's active participation in the *Gram Sabha*s on grounds of its being against tribal 'cultural traditions'.
- *Ragi* (finger millet), *Marua* (*Eleusine*), *Gundli* (*Panicum milare*), pearl millet, other minor millets.
- In the four villages within or near forests where PRAs were done in Bihar, as many as 91% of the total households were found dependent on collection and sale

of firewood from the forests, an activity primarily done by women.

- The mission came across only a couple of cases where the local wage rate for women and men was the same.
- In Raigarh district, the only women beneficiaries were the minuscule minority of female landowners. The participation of women even in village-based training programmes was 1-5%. Only 3.5% of the beneficiaries of tank leases for fisheries in Raigarh district were women.
- In the case of maize, however, the woman sows the seed walking behind the man on the plough. Women can also sow vegetables possibly due to vegetable cultivation being a recent introduction to the local cropping pattern.
- Leaves of the *Tendu* tree, primarily collected by women and used for rolling cheap Indian cigarettes called *Bidis* are one of the economically most important NTFP in the study area. The annual turnover of the trade runs into many Rupees.
- Local agents appointed for collecting tendu leaves on a commission basis.

VOCATIONAL TRAINING CENTRES IN TRIBAL AREAS

The Ministry of Tribal Affairs was constituted in October 1999 with the objective of providing more focused attention on the integrated socio-economic development of the most under-privileged sections of the Indian society namely, the Scheduled Tribes (STs), in a coordinated and planned manner. The Ministry of Tribal Affairs is the nodal Ministry for the overall policy, planning and coordination of programmes for development of STs. To this end, the Ministry of Tribal Affairs undertakes activities that flow from the subjects allocated under the Government of India(Allocation of Buisness)Rules,1961. These include:

1) Social security and social insurance to the Scheduled Tribes.
2) Tribal Welfare: Tribal welfare planning, project formulation, research, evaluation, statistics and training.

3) Promotion and development of voluntary efforts on tribal welfare
4) Scheduled Tribes, including scholarship to students belonging to such tribes
5) Development of Scheduled Tribes 5(a) All matters including legislation relating to the rights of forest dwelling Scheduled Tribes on forest lands

Note: The Ministry of Tribal Affairs shall be the nodal Ministry for overall policy, planning and coordination of programmes of development for the Scheduled Tribes. In regard to sectoral programmes and schemes development of these communities policy planning, monitring, evaluation etc. as also their coordination will be responsibility of the concerned Central Ministries/Departments, State Governments and Union Territory Administrations. Each Central Ministry/Department will be the nodal Ministry or.Department concerning its sector

6(a) Scheduled Areas; (b) Matter relating to autonomous districts of Assam excluding roads and bridge works and ferries thereon; and,d (c)Reglations framed by the Governors of States for Scheduled Areas and for Tribal Areas specified in Part'A' of the Table appended to paragraph 20 of the Sixth Schedule to the Constitution.

7(a) Commission to report on the administration of Scheduled Areas and the welfare of the Scheduled Tribes; and (b) Issue of directions regarding the drawing up and execution of schemes essential for the welfare of the Scheduled Tribes in any State.

8 The National. Commission for Scheduled Tribes. Commission for Scheduled Tribes.

9 Implementation of the Protection of Civil Rights Act, 1955 (22 of 1955) and the Scheduled Castes and the Scheduled Tribes (Prevention of Atrocities) Act, 1989 (33 of 1989), excluding administration of criminal justice in regard to offences in so. far as they relate to Scheduled Tribes.

The Role

It needs to be emphasized that the programmes and schemes of the Ministry are intended to support and supplement, through financial assistance, the efforts of other Central Ministries, the State Government and voluntary organizations, and to fill critical gaps taking into account the situation of STs. The primary responsibility for promoting the interests of Scheduled Tribes thus rests with all the Central Ministries. The Ministry compliments their efforts by way of various developmental interventions in critical sectors through specially tailored schemes. These, comprising schemes for economic, educational and social development, are administered by the Ministry of Tribal Affairs and implemented through the State Governments/ Union Territory Administrations and voluntary organizations.

Organization

The Ministry of Tribal affairs is functioning under the overall guidance of the Union Minister Shri Kanti Lal Bhuria, Minister of State Sh. Mahadeo Singh Khandela and the Secretary Sh. Arvind Kumar Chugh The Secretary is assisted by Sh. Prabhu Dayal Meena, Joint Secretary, Dr. Bachittar Singh, Joint Secretary, Shri S.K. Gupta, Deputy Director General (Stat.) and ...., Economic Adviser. Shri S.K. Ray, Addl Secretary & Financial Adviser, Shri A.N Bokshi, CCA are assisting the Secretary, Ministry of Tribal Affairs.

The Ministry is organized into Divisions, Sections and Unit. Each division is headed by a Deputy Secretary/Director. The Ministry of Tribal Affairs has a sanctioned strength of 131 employees (including 5 posts of PAO) and a working strength of 110. There are 33 group "A" posts, 51 group "B" posts, 31 group "C" posts and 16 group "D" posts. The organizational chart of the Ministry is at Annex-I.

Administration

The establishment and general administration of the proper Ministry and the National Commission for Scheduled Tribes (NCST) are handled in the Administration Division. In addition, establishment matters of officers appointed under Central Staffing Scheme for the Department proper and ex-cadre posts, i.e. Economic Advisor, various Statistical Cadre, etc., are being administered in this Division. Ministry of Tribal Affairs had been facing severe crunch of space since its inception. To mitigate the problem, with the permission of Ministry of Urban Development, office space measuring 3593.62 sq.ft in August Kranti Bhawan at Bhikaji Cama Place, New Delhi has been hired and some Divisions viz. Research & Media, Monitoring & Evolution, Statistics and Cooperative Marketing & Regulation Divisions have been located there.

Computer Centre (NIC)

NIC has established a Computer Centre for the Ministry of Tribal Affairs in Shastri Bhawan for IT. Coapplications, development and operation. The Technical Director (NIC) heads the centre. NIC provided WAN connectivity through NICNET Gateway with Optical Fiber Cable (OFC) of 34 mbps connectivity and with a back up of 54 mbps RF (full duplex) and 4 mbps of Leased Line for Shastri Bhawan. NIC has established a LAN (Local Area Network).having 140 nodes at Shastri Bhawan. To make it virus free and to ensure smooth LAN and WAN functioning, an anti-virus server and patch management server has been installed at Shastri Bhawan for on-line updation of windows & antivirus software.

Web-based portal development work on monitoring system for implementation of Forest Right Act has also been started. Training on File Tracking System (FTS) is being imparted to the staff of Ministry. Data Entry work on Composite Payroll System (CPS) is functioning. The System Studies for monitoring of various schemes of NGO division and the schemes of all divisions is being attempted. such as the *Scheduled Tribes and Other Traditional Forest Dwellers (Recognition of Forest Rights) Act,2006,* Notifications, Rules, News, Schemes of Education Divisions, Research and Media are being uploaded in the website from time to time.

Budget Allocation

The Budget allocation for various schemes/programmes of Ministry for 2007-08 was Rs.1,719.71 crore. This was retained at the same level even at the RE stage. The total releases made by the Ministry during the year 2007-08 (upto 31.12.2007) are Rs.l 194.53 crore, which is 69.46% of the revised estimates. In comparison to this, the total releases made atiduring the corresponding period of 2006-07 were Rs. 1282.91 crore which was 77.43 % of orrespongind R.E. The Budget. Coallocation forthe year 2008-09 is Rs.2121 crore.

The scheme-wise budget allocation and expenditure during the Tenth Plan is at Annex -II and Budget Estimates, Revised Estimates and scheme-wise expenditure during 2007-08 upto 31.12.2007.

Progressive Use of Hindi

Hindi is the official language of the Government of India and, therefore, the Ministry is actively involved in promoting its use in official work. A Hindi Section, assisted by an Assistant Director (OL), one Senior Translator, two Junior Translators and one Hindi Stenographer looks after the work of translation and the Official Language Policy and Act. It also monitors the progressive use of Hindi in official work in organizations under the Ministry. The Ministry has a working strength of 104 officers and staff, most of whom either have proficiency or working knowledge of Hindi.

Continuous efforts are being made made to achieve the targets fixed by the Department of Official Language in the Annual Program for the year 2006-07, for correspondence in Hindi with various offices/regions etc. All the letters received in Hindi are being replied to in Hindi only. During the period of this Report, most of the original letters to 'A' and 'B' regions were sent in Hindi. All administrative and other reports are being made bilingually. All rubber stamps and printed stationary have also been made in Hindi and English. Section 3(3) of the Official Language Act is being complied with by the Ministry.

Implementation of the programme is being regularly monitored/reviewed in the meetings of the Official Language Implementation Committee.

Hindi Salahkar Samiti

The meeting of the Hindi Salahkar Samiti was held on 5th December 2007 atiunder the Chairmanship of Shri P.R. Kyndiah, Hon'ble Union Minister of Tribal Affairs. During the discussions, suggestions were given by the members of the Samiti to encourage the use of Hindi in offices.

Inspection of Parliamentary Committee

Inspection of Parliamentary Committee on official language was held on 2nd July 2007. During the meeting, some suggestions were given by the members of the Committee at improving the usage of Hind official work

Vigilance Activities

Dr. Bachittar Singh, Joint Secretary was designated as the Chief Vigilance Officer (CVO) in the Ministry with effect from 28.03.2007. The CVO provides assistance to the Secretary of the Ministry in all matters pertaining to vigilance and acts as a link between the Ministry and the Central Vigilance Commission (CVC). The CVO looks after the vigilance work in addition to his normal duties as Joint Secretary in the Ministry. One Director (Vigilance) in the Ministry assists the CVO in discharging his functions. Standard Notice Boards were displayed in the office premises for attention of public.

Pursuant to the instruction from the the Central Vigilance Commission, the Ministry celebrated 'Vigilance Awareness Week from 12.11.2007 to 16.11.2007. Secretary, Ministry of Tribal Affairs administered the pledge to the officers and staff of the Ministry on 12.11.2007.

Public Grievance Redressal Mechanism

Dr. Bachittar Singh, Joint Secretary, has been designated as Director of Grievances in the Ministry w.e.f. 16.1.2007. Contact details of Dr. Singh such as room number, telephone number, etc. have also been widely circulated. The Director of Grievances also held regular meetings with officers/staff and sometimes, with their to representatives to hear their problem and grievances.

SCHEDULED TRIBES

The Constitution of India does not define Scheduled Tribes as such. Article 366(25) refers to scheduled tribes as those communities who are scheduled in accordance with Article 342 of the Constitution. According to Article 342 of the Constitution, the Scheduled Tribes are the tribes or tribal communities or part of or groups within these tribes and tribal communities which have been declared as such by the President through a public notification. As per the 1991 Census, the Scheduled Tribes account for 67.76 million representing 8.08 percent of the country's population. Scheduled Tribes are spread across the country mainly in forest and hilly regions.

The 1991 Census figures reveal that 42.02 percent of the Scheduled Tribes populations were main workers of whom 54.50 percent were cultivators and 32.69 per cent agricultural labourers. Thus, about 87 percent of the main workers from these communities were engaged in primary sector activities. The literacy rate of Scheduled Tribes is around 29.60 percent, as against the national average of 52 percent. More than three-quarters of Scheduled Tribes women are illiterate. These disparities are compounded by higher dropout rates in formal education resulting in disproportionately low representation in higher education. Not surprisingly, the cumulative effect has been that the proportion of Scheduled Tribes below the poverty line is substantially higher than the national average. The estimate of poverty made by Planning Commission for the year 1993-94 shows that 51.92 percent rural and 41.4 percent urban Scheduled Tribes were still living below the poverty line.

The Constitution of India incorporates several special provisions for the promotion of educational and economic interest of Scheduled Tribes and their protection from social injustice and all forms of exploitation. These objectives are sought to be achieved through a strategy known as the Tribal Sub-Plan strategy, which was adopted at the beginning of the Fifth Five Year Plan.

The strategy seeks to ensure adequate flow of funds for tribal development form the State Plan allocations, schemes/programmes of Central Ministries/Departments, financial and Developmental Institutions. The cornerstone of this strategy has been to ensure earmarking of funds for TSP by States/UTs in proportion to the ST population in those State/Uts. Besides the efforts of the States/UTs and the Central Ministries/Departments to formulate and implement Tribal Sub-Plan for achieving socio-economic development of STs, the Ministry of Tribal Affairs is implementing several schemes and programmes for the benefits of STs.

The progress over the years on the literacy front may be seen from the following :-

	1961	*1971*	*1981*	*1991*	*2001*
Total literate population	24 %	29.4 %	36.2 %	52.2 %	64.84%
Scheduled Tribes (STs) population	8.5 %	11.3 %	16.3 %	29.6 %	47.10%
Total female population	12.9 %	18.6 %	29.8 %	39.3 %	53.67%
Total Scheduled Tribes (STs) female population	3.2 %	4.8 %	8.0 %	18.2 %	34.76%

There are now 194 Integrated Tribal Development Projects (ITDPs) in the country, where the ST population is more than 50% of the total population of the blocks or groups of block. During the Sixth Plan, pockets outside ITDP areas, having a total population of 10,000 with at least 5,000 scheduled tribes were covered under the Tribal Sub-Plan under Modified Area Development Approach (MADA). So far 252 MADA pockets have been identified in the country. In addition, 79 clusters with a total population of 5,000 of which 50 per cent are schedule tribes have been identified.

In order to give more focussed attention to the development of Scheduled Tribes, a separate Ministry, known as the Ministry of Tribal Affairs was constituted in October 1999. The new Ministry carved out of the Ministry of Social Justice and Empowerment, is the nodal Ministry for overall policy, planning and coordination of programmes and schemes for the development of Scheduled Tribes.

The mandate of the Ministry includes social security and social insurance with respect to the Scheduled Tribes, tribal welfare planning, project formulation research and training, promotion and development of voluntary efforts on tribal welfare and certain matters relating to administration of the Scheduled Areas. In regard to sectoral programmes and development of these communities, the policy, planning, monitoring, evaluation as also their coordination is the responsibility of the concerned central Ministries/Departments, State Governments and UT Administrations. Each Central Ministry/Department will be the nodal Ministry of Department concerning its sector. Ministry of Tribal Affairs supports and supplements the efforts of State

Governments/U.T. Administrations and the various Central Ministries/Departments for the holistic development of these communities.

INTEGRATED TRIBAL DEVELOPMENT PROJECTS/ AGENCIES (ITDPS/ITDAS)

The ITDPs are generally contiguous areas of the size of a Tehsil or Block or more in which the ST population is 50% or more of the total. On account of demographic reasons, however ITDPs. in Assam, Karnataka, Tamil Nadu, West Bengal may be smaller or not contiguous. Andhra Pradesh and Orissa have opted for an Agency model under the Registration of Societies Act and the ITDPs there are known as ITD Agencies(ITDAs). So far 194 ITDPs/ITDAs have been delineated in the country in the states of Andhra Pradesh, Assam, Bihar, Gujarat, Himachal Pradesh, Karnataka, Kerela, Madhya Pradesh, Maharashtra, Manipur, Orissa, Rajasthan, Sikkim, Tamil Nadu, Tripura, Uttar Pradesh, West Bengal and Union Territories of Andaman & Nicobar Island and daman & Diu. In Jammu and Kashmir though no ITDP has been delineated yet the areas having ST Population in the State are treated as covered under the TSP strategy. In eight states having scheduled areas the ITDPs/ITDAs are generally co terminus with TSP areas. The ITDPs/ITDAs are headed by Project Officer though they may be designated Project Administrators or Project Directors.

Modified Area Development Approach (MADA) pockets

These are identified pockets of concentration of ST population containing 50% or more ST population within a total population of minimum of 10,000. The total number of MADAs identified so far in the various TSP States is 259. Generally, MADA pockets do not have separate administrative structures to implement development programmes. The line Departments of the State Govt. are expected to implement development programmes in MADA pockets under the overall control of the District authorities.

These are identified pockets of tribal concentration containing 50% or more ST population within a total population of about 5,000 or more. As in the case of MADA pockets, there are no separate administrative structures for Clusters. So far 82 Clusters have been identified in various T.S.P. states.

Primitive tribal groups are tribal communities among the STs who live in near isolation in inaccessible habitats. They are characterised by a low rate of growth of population, pre-agrcultural level of technology and extremely low levels of literacy. So far 75 PTGs have been identified.

Definition

The tribal situation in the country presents a varied picture. Some areas have high Tribal concentration while in other areas, the tribals form only a small portion of the total population. There are some tribal groups, which are still at the food gathering stage, some others practice shifting cultivation, yet other may be pursuing primitive forms of agriculture.

The Constitution of India provides for a comprehensive framework for the socio-economic development of Scheduled Tribes and for preventing their exploitation by other groups of society. A detailed and comprehensive review of the tribal problem was taken on the eve of the Fifth Five Year Plan and the Tribal sub-Plan strategy took note of the fact that an integrated approach to the tribal problems was necessary in terms of their geographic and demographic concentration. If a faster development of this community is to take place. Accordingly, the tribal areas in the country were classified under three broad categories:

States and Union Territories having a majority scheduled tribes population. States and Union Territories having substantial tribal population but majority tribal population in particular administrative units, such as block and tehsils. States and Union Territories having dispersed tribal population.

In the light of the above approach, it was decided that tribal majority States like Arunachal Pradesh, Meghalaya, Mizoram, Nagaland and U.Ts. of Lakshadweep and Dadra & Nagar Haveli may not need a Tribal sub-Plan, as the entire plan of these States/Union Territories was primarily meant for the S.T. population constitutioning the majority. For the second category of States and Union Territories, tribal sub-Plan approach was adopted after delineating areas of tribal concentration. A similar approach was also adopted in case of States and Union Territories having dispersed tribal population by paying special attention to pockets of tribal concentrations, keeping in view their tenor of dispersal. To look after the tribal population coming within the new tribal sub-Plan strategy in a coordinated manner, Integrated Tribal Development Projects ere conceived during Fifth Five Year Plan and these have been continued since them. During the Sixth Plan, Modified Area Development Approach (MADA) was adopted to cover smaller areas of tribal concentration and during the Seventh Plan, the TSP strategy was extended further to cover even more smaller areas of tribal concentration and thus cluster of tribal concentration were identified.

At the time of delineation of project areas under the Tribal sub-Plan strategy, it was observed that the ITDPs/ITDAs are not co-terminus. Areas declared under Fifth Schedule of the Constitution. The Scheduled Areas as per the Constitutional orders have been declared in eight States viz A.P., Bihar, Gujarat, H.P., Maharashtra, M.P., Orissa and Rajasthan, As per the provisions contained in the Fifth Schedule of the Constitution, various enactment in the forms of Acts and Regulations have been promulgated in the above states for the welfare of scheduled tribes and their protection from exploitation

Since TSP strategy also has twin objectives namely Socio-economic development of Schedule tribes and protection of tribal against exploitation, the Govt. of India in Aug., 1976 had decided to make the boundaries of Scheduled Areas co-terminus with TSP areas (ITDP/ITDA only) so that the protective measure available to Sch. Tribes in Sch. Areas could be uniformly applied to TSP areas for effective implementation of the development programmes in these areas. Accordingly, the TSP areas have been made co-terminus with Sch. Areas in the State of Bihar, Gujarat, H.P., Maharashtra, Madhya Pradesh, Orissa and Rajasthan. The State of A.P. where the TSP areas are not co-terminus with sch. Areas has also furnished a proposal to this effect which is under examination.

EVALUATION

The total ST population comprise today of 8.08%. Even after 50 years of independence and in spite of various meas ures taken to improve the level of education in the country, literacy levels among tribal communities irrespective of the gender continues to be extremely low. The gap in the literacy level between the general population and the socially disadvantaged sections is persisting and even widening in some cases.

However, the difference between the literacy rate of STs and that of the general population is quite large; even the SCs have about 11% higher literacy rate than that of the STs. The status needs to be improved and for this serious efforts and focus is required on raising the level of literacy of the Scheduled Tribes population both males and females. There are historical and socio-economic reasons for having this wide gap between one section of society and the rest.

However, it is seen that where educational facilities are provided they are not accessible in the real sense of the term to the targeted group. So far as Scheduled Tribes population and in particular the ST Girls are concerned, it is fret that lack of residential facilities in educational institutions both of general and of quality education deters, scheduled tribe families to send their children to such institutions. Considering the important role of women in shaping the size of the family and outlook of its members, and also as an active agent of economic and social development, investment in providing education to the women of these communities will not only improve their social and economic status, but will also help in accelerating the pace of development of these communities and the nation as a whole. Similarly, male literacy also needs special attention amongst the tribal population to raise the overall standard/ quality f if, they being on the last ladder of development even with reference to the other down trodden categories like SCs.

CENTRALLY SPONSORED SCHEME OF HOSTELS FOR ST BOYS AND ST GIRLS

Article 16 of the Constitution enables the Central government to make special provisions for the socio-economic development of the deprived sections of the society to enable them to share the facilities at par with the rest of the society. Education is the foundation for any kind of socio-economic development. Education of Scheduled Tribes assumes added importance in the sense that it elevates their social status and equips them with the acumen to take advantage of the emerging opportunities both in employment and other economic activities. While illiteracy is a general problem for the country cutting across caste, religion, region and such other barriers, its total effect on the life and status of the Scheduled Tribes stands out prominently as an area of national focus. The women among the Scheduled Tribe groups suffer from triple jeopardy in as much as that they suffer from social barriers as STs, then as females and then also as the least literate segment of the society.

Thus, there is a felt need for making a proactive discrimination in favor of ST girls while modifying the present scheme of hostel constructions so as to facilitate preferred proliferation of the educational infrastructure for them through, State Governments/UTs and Universities. The existing scheme of construction of hostels aims to supplement the efforts of the State Governments for creating a congenial study atmosphere free from the shackles of domestic shores, so as to encourage students belonging to the target groups to purse their education career without dropping out. Such hostels are immensely beneficial to the students of ST community hailing from rural and remote areas.

While the Scheme of Hostels for ST Girls is in operation since the 3rd Five Year Plan, the Scheme for of ST Boys was started with effect from the year 1989-90.During the 10th Five Year Plan both the schemes have been merged into a single scheme.

Scheme and Objectives of the Modification

The scheme is for ST boys and girls (including Primitive Tribal Groups). The primary objective of the modification is to attract the implementing agencies for undertaking hostel construction programme for ST Girls studying in middle schools, higher secondary schools, colleges and universities towards the broader vision of containment and reduction of their drop out rate.

Implementing Agencies and Eligibility

The Scheme will be implemented through the State Governments/Union Territory Administrations and the Central/ other Universities. The hostels under the Scheme should be constructed at a place where the educational institutions concerned are situated, keeping in view the concentration of ST population in a particular area or place. Further, the hostels under the scheme would be sanctioned as far as possible as a part of the established educational institutions or in close vicinity of such institutions. The hostels for Vocational Training Centres (VTCs) can be constructed only in those tribal areas where State Governments/UT Administrations take initiative to run these centres efficiently. The hostels under the Scheme can be constructed for middle, secondary, college and university level of education and also for Vocational Training Centres. The construction of boundary walls, two rooms set for hostel warden, a kitchen, a toilet, a common room and one room set for Chowkidar would be an integral part of the hostel scheme. The expenditure on maintenance of the hostels will be borne by the implementing agencies concerned from their own funds.

Strength of the Hostels

Generally, the number of inmates for whom the accommodation can be provided in a hostel under the Scheme should not exceed 100 but may exceed if there is a requirement of additional seats.

Hostels for ST Girls

For construction/extension of hostels for ST Girls under the Scheme, 100% central assistance would be provided to the State Governments/UT Administrations and the Central/other Universities.

Hostels for ST Boys

For construction/extension of hostels for ST Boys, the central assistance to the implementing agencies would be provided as detailed below:-

(a) The State Governments will be eligible to receive central assistance on 50:50 matching basis. However naxal-affected states (specified districts as identified by Ministry of Home Affairs from time to time-list of specified districts annexed) will be eligible for 100% central assistance. Also 100% financial assistance would be provided to the UT Administrations;

(b) The Central Universities would be eligible for 90% financial assistance;

(c) Other Universities would be eligible on the basis of 45% central share, 45% State share and the remaining 10% to be borne by the Universities concerned themselves;

(d) In case the State Governments concerned do not contribute their share of 45% to the Universities as prescribed in (c) above, the share of the former will also have to be borne by the Universities concerned, thereby raising their contribution to 55%.

The hostels for Vocational Training Centres (VTCs) for ST Girls and Boys will be funded on the same criteria as other hostels for (girls and boys) schools/colleges.

Manner of Release of Central Assistance

The grants-in-aid shall be released after ensuring physical release of requisite matching share by the State Government/ UT Administration/University concerned.

General Provisions:

(a) The central assistance will be limited only to the cost of construction/extension of the Hostels for ST Girls and Boys (including Primitive Tribal Groups) as indicated above.

(b) Unencumbered land will be made available free of cost by concerned State Government/UT Admn./University for construction of the hostel.

(c) The application for the grant shall be supported by the utilization certificate as well as details of physical and financial progress in respect of hostels sanctioned earlier by the Ministry of Tribal Affairs along with details of location of proposed hostel and number of seats in each hostel.

(d) Plan of the Hostel duly approved by the competent authority in the State Govt./UT Administration/ University.

(e) A certificate to the effect that matching provision wherever necessary exists in the State Budget for the Scheme.

(f) The hostels shall be completed within a period of 2 years from the date of release of the central assistance. However the period for completion of the extension of existing hostels shall be 12 months.

(g) A few rooms/blocks of the hostels should be constructed barrier free and facilities like ramps etc. should be included in the design of the construction for the convenience of the ST students with disabilities.

(h) The cost of construction of hostels will be worked out on the basis of State/UT PWD/CPWD schedule of rates prescribed for such type of construction.

(i) In case, any State Government is unable to provide the required matching share from its budget, any MP/MLA can provide the State's share from his/her MPLADS/ MLALADS fund.

(j) Preference will be given to State Governments who commit annual maintenance expenditure, as per reasonable norms.

Monitoring and Evaluation

The implementing agencies shall closely supervise the construction of hostels regularly and shall submit quarterly progress reports, both physical add financial, to the Ministry of Tribal Affairs, New Delhi till the completion of the hostels. For the purpose of effective monitoring, the ministry may itself conduct or cause field visits to be conducted by appropriate agencies/authorities to inspect the projects. The expenditure on evaluation/monitoring and administration of the scheme shall be met out of the funds provided for this scheme.

5

Health Care Practices Among the Tribal People of India

Anthropology as an integrated science of man deals with biological and cultural aspects of man. Presently anthropologists are more involved in applying their knowledge and techniques for human welfare. Ethno-medicine is a sub-field of medical anthropology and deals with the study of traditional medicines: not only those that have relevant written sources (e.g. Traditional Chinese Medicine, Ayurveda), but especially those, whose knowledge and practices have been orally transmitted over the centuries. In the scientific arena, ethno-medical studies are generally characterized by a strong anthropological approach, more than a bio-medical one. The focus of these studies is then the perception and context of use of traditional medicines, and not their bio-evaluation.

TRIBES IN INDIA

The Indian sub-continent is inhabited by 88.2 million tribal populations belonging to over 577 tribal communities that come under 227 linguistic groups. They inhibit varied geographic and climatic Zones of the country. Their vocation ranges from hunting, gathering, cave dwelling nomadic to societies with settled culture living incomplete harmony with nature.

Forests have been their dear home and totally submitted themselves to forest settings. Their relationship with the forest was symbolic in nature. They have been utilizing the resources without disturbing the delicate balance of the eco-system. Tribal thus mostly remained as stable societies and were unaffected by the social, cultural, material and economic evolutions that were taking place with the so called civilized societies. But this peaceful co-existence of the tribal has been disturbed in recent years by the interference in their habitats. Traditional communities living close to nature have, over the years acquired unique knowledge about the use of living biological resources. Modernisation, especially industrialization and urbanization has endangered the rich heritage of knowledge and expertise of age old wisdom of the traditional communities.

A study on the utilization of local tribal revealed that they hold precious knowledge on the specific use of a large number of agents of wild plant and animal origins, the use of many are hitherto unknown to the outside world.

HERBAL HISTORY AND TRADITION IN INDIAN CONTEXT

The Rigveda, the oldest document of human knowledge mentions the use of medicinal plants in the treatment of man and animals. Ayurveda gives the account of actual beginning of the ancient medical science of India, which according to western scholars was written between 2500 to 600 B.C. Charaka and Susruta wrote around 1000 B.C. Charaka concentrates more on medicine while Susruta deals with surgery in details along with therapeutics.

TRIBES AND ETHNO-MEDICINE

Ethno-medicine refers to "those beliefs and practices relating to disease which are the products of indigenous cultural development and are not explicitly derived from the conceptual frame work of modern medicine" (Hughes, 1968, cited from Misra et al, 2003). Various institutions are now concerned with the traditional health care system and means of traditional treatment.

The tribal people are the real custodians of the medicinal plants. Out of 45,000 species of wild plants, 7500 species are used for medicinal purposes. The World Health Organization (WHO) has been promoting a movement for 'Saving plants for saving lives'. This is because of the growing understanding of the pivotal role medicinal plants play in providing herbal remedies to health maladies.

India is the home of several important traditional system of health care like Ayurveda. This system depends heavily on herbal products. Several millions of Indian households have been using through the ages nearly 8000 species of medicinal plants for their health care needs. Over one and half million traditional healers use a wide range of medicinal plants for treating ailments of both humans and livestock across the length and breadth of the country. Over 800 medicinal plant species are currently in use by the Indian herbal industry.

In recent times with the increased knowledge of life and culture of the tribal communities, the social scientists are taking interest in ethno-medicinal studies. Many works have been reported especially from among the rural and tribal communities of India. Ray and Sharma (2005) have given a description of ethno-medicinal beliefs and practices prevalent among the Savaras, a tribal community of Andhra Pradesh.

Kumari (2006) gave an account on the concept of illness and disease and the application of folk medicine among the Saureas of Jharkhand. However, ethno-medicinal studies are relatively less in Northeast India. Guha (1986) has reported from among the Boro-Kachari tribe of Assam. A glimpse of indigenous health practices among the plain tribes of Assam is given by Sharma Thakur (1999). The socio-economic condition of some of the tribes of Arunachal Pradesh and their problems of health and indigenous methods of treatment has been reported by Choudhury (2000), Duarah andPathak (1997), Kohli (1999), Bhasin (1997, 1999,2002, 2003, 2005).

ETHNO-MEDICINE AND HEALTH CARE PRACTICES AMONG SONOWAL KACHARIS IN ASSAM (INDIA)

The Sonowal Kacharis is an endogamous group of Kachari tribe and a popular plain scheduled tribe population of Assam. Various types of locally available herbs and leaves of wild plants are used by them as medicine. Like many other communities of the region, there are few herbal specialists among the Sonowal Kachari. These specialists or medicine-men have considerable knowledge about the herbs and its medicinal use. Normally they learn about these medicinal plants and its uses from their ancestor. These medicine-men are referred by different term according to the cultural norms. Among the Sonowal Kachari's they are called as Bez (Barua and Phukan, 1958: 334). Of course in rural Assam, they are mainly known by this term.

It has been observed in the villages that use of herbal medicine for curing certain diseases are quite known to the people and besides medicine-men, many elderly persons known about the use of herbal medicines. Some of the diseases and their indigenous methods of treatment are given below:

Fever: Lime (Citrus auran tifolia) juice mixed with sugar is applied on the forehead of the patient to get relief from fever.

Diarrhoea: Dry goose berry (Emblica officinalis) powder and black salt mixed with cold water is taken. Bark of Long Pepper (Pipoli tree) mixed with Misiri water is also used to cure the disease.

Dysentery: Lime (Citrus auran tifolia) juicewith hot water and little salt is used in dysentery. The juice of black Tulsi leaves (Ocimum sanctum) and Sirata (Swertiachirata) is also used for the purpose. The juice of tender leaves (three numbers) of mango (Mangifera indica), black berry (S.cuminii) and goose berry (Emblica officinalis) (equal proportions) together with honey are mixed with goat milk and is taken to cure blood dysentery. Honey together with the juice of Dubari grass (Family-Gramineae) can cure blood dysentery and need to be taken for three/four days. They also use a kind of wild herb, locally called Manimuni (Centila asiatica). The juice of this herb mixed with sugar or honey should be taken continuously for a month to cure the disease. They also use limewater (chun pani) mixed with juice of turmeric (Purcuma domestica) leave to get relief from blood dysentery and mucous.

Blood Vomiting: A table spoon of carrot (Dancus carota) juice mixed with honey can cure blood vomiting.

Liver Disease: Two to three raw or ripe Papayas (Carica papaya) daily can cure liver disease. A curry prepared from the bud of banana (Musa paradisiaca) and the meat of pigeon is also used as a medicine for the purpose.

Jaundice: The medicine is prepared by pounding five or six number of Silikha (Myroballum) mixing with jaggery and it can cure jaundice. A glass of sugarcane (Saccharum officinarum) juice twice daily prescribed for the purpose. Boiled raw papaya (Carica papaya) is said to be good for curing the disease. Kardoi (Averrhoa carambola), Goose Berry (Emblica officinalis), Sugar cane (Saccharun officinarum), Neem leave (Azadirachta indica), a wild herb known as Duran ban (Lecas aspera), Brahmi sak (Herpestis monnieria), Purakol (Musa sapientum) are prescribed edibles for the patient.

Nose Bleeding: Flower of Pomegranate (Punica granatum Linn) is crushed and 3-4 drops of juice is poured inside the nose to give immediate relief.

Tonsilities: Juice is prepared by mixing one Amara seed (Sponolias mangifera), one Silikha seed (Mysoballum) and a piece of Turmeric (Purcuma domestica) and advice the patient gargles for a week regularly.

Worms: Paste of five lemon seeds (Citrus aurantifolia) mixed with water and is prescribed to eat in empty stomach for a few days. The twigs of Chirata (Swertia chirata) are soaked in the water overnight and the water is prescribed to drink in empty stomach in the morning for one week regularly.

Scabies: Lemon juice (Citrus aurantifolia) mixed with coconut oil is massaged for curing scabies. To remove scabies they take bath with hot water in which leaves of Neem (Azadirachta officinarum) were boiled. Twigs of Chirata (Swertia chirata) arecrushed into paste with water to be used as an ointment and applied on the skin. Chirata water is prescribed to drink in the morning in empty stomach.

Pain in the Ear: Juice of Tulsi (Ocimum sanctum) is boiled and put it in the ears to heal earache.

The patient is treated with available herbs, flora and minerals. Some of these are home remedies and some are specially prescribed by herbalist or folk medicine man available in the community. The practice of ethno-medicine is a complex multi-disciplinary system constituting the use of plants, spirituality and the natural environment and has been the source of healing for people for millennia. The spiritual aspects of health and sickness have been an integral component of the ethno-medicinal practice for centuries.

PRESENT POSITION OF TRIBES

The tribal health care practices and system of treating diseases are based on their deep observation and belief in nature. But with the development of education and their awareness towards importance of health and health care and also with the advent of modern health care facilities, Government health measures these people are becoming more interested in taking modern medicine instead of traditional herbal medicine.

According to the text of Vishnu Samhita, causing any harm to the plants/animals is a sin. Even purloining of parts/products of any of these living beings is a crime. The sinner/criminals are liable to chastisement in this life and also after death. The punishments are of diverse nature:-pecuniary, corporal, expiatory and donation of specific articles to Brahmins.

The growing disinterest in the use of the ethno-medicinal plants and its significance among the younger generation of the tribes will lead to the disappearance of this practice. Educated younger generation of the tribes should be encouraged by the Government to protect and cultivate these valuable herbal plants before they get lost due to the impact of modernization and urbanization and also due to deforestation.

The role of Anthropology is also very important in the field of saving herbal plants. By educating tribal people we can preserve all these things for future generation. It is the Government duty to take necessary steps to preserve all these things.

INDIGENOUS HEALTH AND SOCIOECONOMIC STATUS IN INDIA

Indigenous groups in India were found to have excess mortality rates compared with non-indigenous groups. A socioeconomic gradient within indigenous populations was also found. Systematic evidence on the patterns of health deprivation among indigenous peoples remains scant in developing countries. We investigate the inequalities in mortality and substance use between indigenous and non-indigenous, and within indigenous, groups in India, with an aim to establishing the relative contribution of socioeconomic status in generating health inequalities.

Methods and Findings

Cross-sectional population-based data were obtained from the 1998–1999 Indian National Family Health Survey. Mortality, smoking, chewing tobacco use, and alcohol use were four separate binary outcomes in our analysis. Indigenous status in the context of India was operationalized through the Indian government category of scheduled tribes, or Adivasis, which refers to people living in tribal communities characterized by distinctive social, cultural, historical, and geographical circumstances.

Indigenous groups experience excess mortality compared to non-indigenous groups, even after adjusting for economic standard of living (odds ratio 1.22; 95% confidence interval 1.13–1.30). They are also more likely to smoke and (especially) drink alcohol, but the prevalence of chewing tobacco is not substantially different between indigenous and non-indigenous groups. There are substantial health variations within indigenous groups, such that indigenous peoples in the bottom quintile of the indigenous-peoples-specific standard of living index have an odds ratio for mortality of 1.61 (95% confidence interval 1.33–1.95) compared to indigenous peoples in the top fifth of the wealth distribution. Smoking, drinking alcohol, and chewing tobacco also show graded associations with socioeconomic status within indigenous groups. Socioeconomic status differentials substantially account for the health inequalities between indigenous and non-indigenous groups in India. However, a strong socioeconomic gradient in health is also evident *within* indigenous populations, reiterating the overall importance of socioeconomic status for reducing population-level health disparities, regardless of indigeneity.

OVERCOMING PROBLEMS IN THE PRACTICE OF PUBLIC HEALTH AMONG TRIBALS

India is home to almost half the tribal population of the

world. Tribals are characterized by a distinctive culture, primitive traits, and socio-economic backwardness. The tribals of India, constituting 8.2% of the total population (84 million), belong to around 698 communities or clans. Around 75 of these groups are called primitive tribal groups due to pre-agricultural level of knowledge, extreme backwardness, and a dwindling population. However, the exact number of tribal groups may be lesser than 500 due to group-overlapping in more than one state.

Though the Indian tribals are a heterogeneous group, most of them remain at the lowest stratum of the society due to various factors like geographical and cultural isolation, low levels of literacy, primitive occupations, and extreme levels of poverty. Although scheduled tribes are accorded special status under the fifth/sixth schedules of the Indian Constitution, their status on the whole, especially their health still remains unsatisfactory. This book explores the problems in delivering public health services to the tribal population of India and suggests solutions.

DEMOGRAPHY OF THE INDIAN SCHEDULED TRIBES

Scheduled tribes are distributed throughout the country except Pondicherry, Haryana, Punjab, Chandigarh, and Delhi. Almost 25% of the Indian tribals live in Madhya Pradesh and Chattisgarh.

The total population of scheduled tribes according to the 2001 Census is 84.3 million and has increased from 67.8 million in 1991, showing a decadal growth rate of 24.3%. The rate of growth has shown a declining trend (from 25.7% in 1981-1991) similar to that seen in the general population, but remains still higher than the national average of 21.3%. This declining trend in growth is seen in all tribal regions except the Southern states.

The sex ratio of tribals is more favorable to females than the general population (972/1000 males vs. 927/1000). However, there is a wide variation among the different groups and states (1002 in Orissa to 889 in Goa). The geriatric population (above 60 years of age) among tribals is 6.1%. Though this is actually an increase from 5.6% in 1981 in comparison to the general population (7.9%), the proportion is less. The dependency ratio among tribals is 83.9% and in the general population is 69%. Literacy is increasing (47% in 2001 from 29.6% in 1991) but still lower than the general population (65%) and the gap between the literacy rates of STs and the general population continues almost at the same level of 17-18% for the last three decades. Almost 65% women are illiterate against the national figure of 46%. High drop-out rates of 79% from formal education are a major problem.

Around 91% of the tribal population still lives in rural area as against 72% for the whole nation. The percentage of tribals living below poverty line is 47.3% in rural and 33.3% in urban areas, which is higher than the corresponding national figures of 28.3% and 25.7%, respectively. The average tribal household size is 5.2 and is comparable to the national average of 5.3. 81.6% of the total ST workers, both rural and urban, are engaged in the primary sector, essentially agriculture.

Maternal and Child Health Indicators

There are vast differences in the health status of mothers and children between tribal and non-tribal populations. The indicators comparing the maternal and child health, highlighting the under-achievements among the tribals. Compared to the NFHS 2 survey, the infant mortality, under-five mortality, and neonatal mortality have decreased, the proportion of home deliveries is at a standstill. There was a fall in the median months of exclusive breastfeeding, while it had shown improvement among others from 1.3 months to 1.9 months. The total fertility rate had shown a slight increase compared to the NFHS 2 survey.

Other Public Health Problems Among Tribals

Malnutrition, as expected, is the most common health problem among tribals. In addition, communicable diseases such as tuberculosis, malaria, and STDs are major public health problems. Some tribal groups are also at high risk for sickle cell anemia. Generally tribal diets are seen to be deficient in protein, iron, iodine, and vitamins. A comparative analysis of the nutritional status of tribals and non-tribals. According to the NFHS-3 survey, 47% of tribal women are having chronic energy deficiency (CED) compared to 35% among the general population.

The most common diseases seen among tribals are respiratory tract infections and diarrheal disorders. 21% of children suffer at least two bouts of diarrhea every year and 22% suffer from at least two attacks of respiratory infections. Tribals account for 25% of all malaria cases occurring in India and 15% of all falciparum cases. Intestinal helminthiasis is widely prevalent among tribal children (up to 50% in Orissa and 75% in MP). Skin infections such as tinea and scabies are seen among tribals due to poor personal hygiene. Sexually transmitted diseases are relatively more common (7.2% prevalence of syphilis among Kolli hills tribals of Tamil Nadu). The prevalence of tuberculosis is high, especially in Orissa. Sickle cell trait prevalence varies from 0.5% to 45%, disease prevalence is around 10%. It is mostly seen among the tribals of central and southern India, not reported in North-East, The prevalence of tobacco use is 44.9% among tribal men and 24% among tribal women.

Public Health Infrastructure

Although in tribal areas the government has provided for the establishment of primary health centers for every 20,000 population and sub-centers for every 3000 population, health care is not available to the majority of the tribals. This is due to several factors:

Lack of accessibility to health facilities: As of the year 1999, 20,770 sub-centers, 3289 primary health centers, and 514 community health centers were available in the tribal areas. This leaves almost 25% of the tribal population without adequate access to health services even with the existing norms under the minimum need program. Non-availability of health staff in the health centers: Almost 20% of the PHCs in tribal areas are not staffed with doctors (15% in non-tribal areas) and 15% of the posts of paramedical workers is vacant.

Quality of services: Non-availability of essential drugs and equipments, lack of proper building facilities, difficult terrain and constraints of distance and time (one ANM may typically be entrusted with 15-20 scattered villages), and lack of transport and communication facilities hinder the provision of health care. Traditional practices and superstitions: Local beliefs, customs, and practices have obstructed health care delivery to the tribals. However, acceptance toward modern medicine is found to be increasing among tribals in the recent years.

HUMAN RESOURCES DEVELOPMENT APPROACH

One of the major problems in delivering health care to the tribals is shortage of manpower. Doctors and paramedical workers from the general population are reluctant to work in backward tribal areas. Further, there are not sufficient medical personnel hailing from the tribal communities, who will have a better understanding about the needs of their people and who may be more willing to work in such areas. Out of the available 26,509 doctors who pass out of medical colleges every year, there are not more than 1050, who belong to the ST group. This is approximately 3.9%, whereas the proportion of tribals is 8.2% and this scenario has not changed in 2004. Thus, there is a need to more than double the number of doctors qualified from among tribals (1875 admissions every year). Though there is a statutory provision of 7.5% reservation for tribals in medical education, apparently either the enforcement of this policy is not strictly done or there are not enough takers from the tribals for these seats. It is proposed that the proportion of distribution of these 1875 seats be worked out according to the proportion of the individual clans of tribals. The local clan communities may sponsor the requisite number of candidates for graduate medical education through the Ministry of Tribal Affairs at the state/central levels. In order to support this system, a parallel sponsorship at the middle and higher secondary school levels has to be actively undertaken, so that sufficient numbers of feeder-candidates are available. Though this is a long-term strategy, it will certainly help achieving the required results to a large extent - even granting that some proportion of such qualified doctors may tend to stay back in the developed urban areas.

Estimates on the public costs of providing graduate medical education are not available. A study done in Kerala during

1999 estimated that the total spending of the government for the whole MBBS course amounted to around Rs. 500,000. It is believed that the present graduate medical education may cost between Rupees 10 and 15 lakhs. This entails a total cost of Rs. 1.8-2.8 billions (187-282 crores) for 1875 candidates from the ST community to the government. This expenditure is mainly borne by the Ministries of Health and Family Welfare at the central and state governments.

A similar ladder-like approach of sponsorship is recommended for postgraduate medical education, which should be need based particularly in the fields of tuberculosis and malaria (for example, one tuberculosis specialist, one senior tuberculosis laboratory supervisor, and one senior treatment supervisor per million tribals).

The situation is worse among other cadres of health workers. On the one hand, as such, the number of available paramedical education institutions is very less compared to the needs of the country. Only 13,000 ANMs are graduating every year. A phenomenal increase is required in this area, which is the purview of general policy. Within this area, a parallel sponsorship cum educational opportunities has to be developed to cater for the needs of the tribal population.

The existing policies on reservation of medical seats do not meet the demands. If all the tribal areas in the country are to be covered by sub-centers and primary health centers with doctors and health staff from the tribal communities, a total of 4200 doctors, an equal number of pharmacists and laboratory technicians, 29,400 female health workers, 25,200 male health workers, and 4200 male and female health assistants are needed. If the primary health centers and sub-centers in the tribal areas are to cater for 5000 and 1000, respectively a total of 16,800 doctors and 84,000 female health workers would be needed.

Though health is a state subject, the Centre has been given the authority of giving directions to the State Governments (Article 339(2), of the Fifth Schedule in the interest of the tribal population), which should be used to direct the State Governments to ensure provision of separate Tribal Sub Plans based on the percentage of tribals as recommended by the Ministry of Tribal Affairs.

Empowerment and Missionaries Approach

It is the authors' opinion that detailed quantitative and qualitative assessments of the agricultural and forest produce of the tribals are made. It is also suggested that the government should come forward with realistic procurement prices and arrange for timely procurement as well as redistribution of their agricultural/forest products. These measures will lead to not only a sustained and regular income, but also would encourage them to further their agricultural activities. The recent Tribal Cooperative Marketing and Development Federation of India Ltd. (TRIFED) is a welcome sign as provides marketing assistance and remunerative prices to STs for collection of minor forest produce (MFP) and surplus agricultural produce to protect them from exploitative private traders and middlemen. Irrigational and power support, along with modern communication and transport facilities are to be concentrated upon, on the lines of the Minimum Needs Program, and the special provision of funds under grant-in-aid under Article 275(1) of the Constitution has to be utilized for these developmental projects.

In those of the tribals where the system is matriarchal, it is envisaged to strengthen the system. However, among patriarchal tribals, measures like women's Self-Help Groups (particularly with economic yield) have to be introduced. A liberal financial policy of loans/grants must be evolved.

Nutrition and education are basic accessories needed to modernize any community. A closely knit, Public Distribution System has to be developed, covering every interior pocket of the tribal areas, with a well-supported supply network. It is the authors' opinion that free distribution of both raw and fresh rations has to be implemented on a time frame, say for two generations; subsequently, this can be upgraded to the subsidized and later the fully paid strategy. The positive food fads of any given tribal community have to be addressed in this type of the public distribution system. For example, a targeted PDS scheme similar to Anthyodaya Anna has to be devised, covering all tribal households. The food grain distribution has to be totally free and this must take care of their energy and protein needs. The present monthly per capita spending on food in the rural areas is Rs 299 (90% of the monthly per capita income), which has been shown to cover only 77% of energy needs. Hence, at least Rs.390 is to be spent in providing rations to each tribal individual. This would entail a total cost of Rs. 327 crores. The Village Grain bank Scheme provides funds for building storage facility, procurement of weights and measures and for the purchase of initial stock of one quintal of food grain of local variety for each family should be further strengthened by providing the rations as per the authors' recommendations given above.

On similar lines, schooling and education have to be developed fully utilizing the help of anthropologists and non-governmental organizations to inculcate the habit of universal education at the primary, middle, and higher secondary levels. Free distribution of educational and related items like books, uniforms, footwear, raincoats, sweaters, and bicycles along with supplementary nutrition has also been found successful in states like Tamil Nadu. The areas that need to be addressed are the inadequacy of the school buildings, both in number and in facilities, the lack of education in the mother language or dialect in primary classes, ignorance of non-tribals teachers about tribal languages and ethos, and the delay in the distribution of scholarships, textbooks, and uniforms.

The authors consciously note that many methods suggested above are not entirely new ones and have been tried with success in vast sections of non-tribal areas. Hence, it is more of the administrative skills and organizational capabilities that need to be tuned up according to the tribal needs. This aspect is dealt within the section on administrative reforms.

As noted in the earlier discussion, the setting of the official machinery is of prime importance. On the medical/health side, it is suggested that the population covered by the primary health centers and the sub-centers should be slashed down to 5000 and 1000, respectively, from the present norms of 20,000 and 3000. This is imperative given the difficult terrain and environment of the tribal topography. However, demanding this may appear to be in the initial stages, in the long run it would be possible to amalgamate these formations and upgrade them according to the needs of the times.

Similar administrative reforms in connection with Public Distribution System, School education, and establishment of women's Self help Groups have been highlighted earlier. The positive points from earlier research works in the demography and behavior of tribals - such as the favorable sex ratio, intercommunity marriages, non-consanguineous marriages, and positive acculturation behavior can be exploited and extended into other sections of tribals. For reasons of ensuring optimal attention for such developmental activities, the authors suggest the designation of the coming decade as the *Decade of Tribals* for appropriate raising, grouping, and redistribution of resources.

6

PRIs Model for Participatory Local Development in India

The Andhra Pradesh *Panchayat Raj* Act, framed in the light of the Constitution's 73rd Amendment, came into effect in May 1994, setting up a three-tier PRI structure with a *Zilla Parishad* at the district, *Mandal Praja Parishad* at the intermediate and *Gram Panchayat* at the village level. It also provides for the constitution of village *Gram Sabhas* made up of all registered voters in the village. The state government has satisfactorily conducted elections to constitute the PRIs and has devolved functions, powers, and resources to these bodies. Election, tenure and composition of members at the three Panchayati Raj levels. The PRIs have a five-year term. Members are to be directly elected on the basis of Wards of the *Gram Panchayat* and Territorial Constituencies in the case of *Mandal Parishad* and *Zilla Parishad*, with reservations for Scheduled Castes and Scheduled Tribes in proportion to their population. One-third of the total number of directly elected seats in each of these bodies is reserved for the backward classes and another one-third for women. The *Mandal* and *Zilla Parishad* have one or two members co-opted from the minority communities.

The Head of the *Gram Panchayat* is elected directly by the electorate in the village whereas the *Mandal Parishad* President and the *Zilla Parishad* Chairperson are elected from among the directly elected members of these bodies. One-third of the top PRI posts are reserved for Scheduled Castes/Tribes and another one-third for women. There is an organic linkage among the three PRI tiers with the elected heads of the lower levels being permanent invitees to the meetings of the next higher tier. Thus, all *Gram Panchayat* Heads in a *Mandal* participate in *Mandal Parishad* meetings and *Mandal Parishad* Presidents within a district attend the *Zilla Parishad* meetings. The District Collector (top district administration official) is also a permanent invitee to the meetings of the *Mandal* and *Zilla Parishad* Standing Committees. Permanent invitees can join the discussions but without the right to vote.

Powers, Functions and Resources at Each Panchayati Raj Level

Ten out of 29 subjects in the Eleventh Schedule of the Constitution of India have been transferred to *Gram Panchayats*. These include minor irrigation, water management, watershed development, drinking water, roads, culverts and bridges. The *Gram Sabha* is expected to meet at least twice a year to consider matters placed before it by the *Gram Panchayat*. These generally include the annual statement of accounts and the audit report on the administration of the preceding year; programmes of works for the current year; proposals for fresh taxation or for increasing existing taxes; and selection of schemes, beneficiaries and locations. While implementing programmes, the *Gram Panchayat* gives due consideration to suggestions made during the *Gram Sabha* meetings. There is provision for seven Standing Committees at the *Zilla Parishad* level, dealing with planning and finance, rural development, agriculture, education and medical services, women's welfare, social welfare, communications, rural water supply and power. Each Standing Committee has the *Zilla Parishad* Chairman as ex-officio member and others nominated by him or her according to prescribed rules. The Standing Committee is the decision-making body in its respective field, subject to the ratification of the general body of the *Zilla Parishad.*

PANCHAYATI RAJ LEVEL

Gram Panchayat

- Implementing land reform measures, including consolidation of land holdings and cooperative management of community lands.

- Implementing programmes related to agriculture, animal husbandry, cottage industry, pre-primary and primary education, health and sanitation, women, children, destitute people and people with disabilities.
- Resource planning by preparing an inventory of human and natural resources and other assets at the village level.
- Preparing and prioritizing plans/programmes to harness these resources to meet local needs and aspirations.
- Disseminating technology to increase farm and related production; expanding services like health, veterinary and sanitation services in their jurisdiction.

Mandal Parishad

- Co-ordinating rural development activities within their jurisdiction and consolidating *panchayat* plans into a *Mandal Parishad* plan.

Zilla Parishad

- Organizing data collection and consolidation of *Mandal Parishad* plans, allocation of funds and approval of *Mandal Parishads* budgets.

MOBILIZATION OF RESOURCES & RESPONSIBILITIES

Gram Panchayat

Only the *Gram Panchayat* can levy taxes. This includes a house tax, a tax on the produce sold in the villages (*Kolagaram* or *Katarusum*) a tax on agricultural land and a land cess at the rate of two *paise* to a rupee (2 percent) on the annual rental value of occupied land.

It can also charge fees such as for the use of land and for the occupation of public buildings such as shelter homes, and duty on land in the form of a surcharge at a rate not exceeding twenty-five *paise* to the rupee (25 percent). The state government also shares with local governments the revenue collected under certain items by way of land/local cess, surcharges on stamp duty, taxes on minor minerals and entertainment taxes. The government also provides a variety of grants to PRIs.

Mandal Parishad

The main sources of income are funds relating to institutions and schemes transferred by the government, or heads of departments funds relating to different development programmes. Other sources include funds or aid from central, state and other national bodies promoting *khadi*, silk, coir and handicraft; contributions from *Gram Panchayat / Zilla Parishad*; shares of land revenue; and annual grants at the rate of five rupees per person residing in the *Mandal*. A *Mandal Parishad's* own resources account for only five percent of the total income.

Zilla Parishad

It derives 5 percent of its income from rents on buildings and commercial complexes, market/industrial fees, etc. The *Zilla Parishad* (ZP) is paid a per capita grant of two rupees per person residing in its jurisdiction. An important grant is for salaries of *ZP* staff and school teachers, which accounts for 50 percent of the receipts.

The Janmabhoomi Programme

The programme shows how the administrative machinery can be made more responsive to local needs and to facilitate participation by rural poor in local governance.

PANCHAYATI RAJ IN KARNATAKA

The Karnataka *Panchayati Raj* Act of 1993 incorporates the institutional structure set out by the 73rd Amendment. It has established the *Gram Panchayat* at the village, *Taluka Panchayat* at the intermediate and *Zilla Panchayat* at the district levels.

Local Development Planning

The PRIs are responsible, among other things, for development planning at the district, *taluk* (intermediate) and village level. This involves identification of local needs and resources for formulating local development projects, determining resource allocation priorities and locating projects within the integrated area development framework.

Although the *Gram Sabha* is expected to prepare and

promote village development schemes during its open meetings, in practice, such meetings produce a list of demands, such as for school facilities, drinking water supply, a primary health centre, veterinary dispensary or a market link road. The demands are considered by the *Gram Panchayat* (GP), which prepares a GP sub-plan to accommodate the needs of individual villages as far as possible. The GP plans are incorporated into the *Taluka Panchayat* (TP) plans, which form part of the *Zilla Panchayat* (ZP) Plan. This process is designed to ensure that every local aspiration is taken note of. To promote regional balance, the State Finance Commission (SFC), set up by the Karnataka Government in 1996, recommended criteria for distribution of resources among the PRIs, giving a relatively higher share to backward areas/regions. Moreover, an untied grant of Rs 100 000 is being given to every GP as additional financial assistance, which should not be adjusted against the funds recommended for devolution by the SFC.

The GPs are also empowered to levy taxes on buildings and lands, which are not subject to agricultural assessment within the limits of the *panchayat* area. The GP can fix the rate for supply of water for drinking and other purposes and levy charges such as tax on entertainment, market fee, pilgrim fee, etc. However, there is insufficient resource mobilization at GP level. This has continued their reliance on the transfer of state resources on the basis of SFC recommendations, which is limiting the realization of the objective of promoting more autonomous planning and administration by local elected bodies within *Panchayati Raj*.

PARTICIPATORY LOCAL DEVELOPMENT

The recognition of the benefits of participatory local development planning has engendered changes in the needs, concepts, approaches, techniques, the general conduct of and ways of measuring the effectiveness of training. This has led to a number of innovations, including a shift from instructional to interactive to the greater use of a participatory approach in training.

The conventional approach of 'giving' in a training situation is being gradually replaced by 'sharing', 'learning together' or acting as a 'facilitator'. The role of a facilitator is to encourage participation without being judgmental and by listening with interest and empathy to help the trainees (participants) to tap into the reservoir of their own abilities gained through their experiences. This is known as the 'participatory approach' having a strong content of interaction.

Training that aspires to promote stakeholder participation in local development planning must use participatory methods in its design, context and conduct. It should

1. bring about changes in attitudes, behaviour and functioning of various governmental and non-governmental development functionaries and elected representatives through a change in their perception of the abilities and needs of rural people;
2. change attitudes and behaviour of rural people through empowerment by a) arming them with the information to take right decisions, and b) equipping them with the skills/means to implement these;
3. be need-based, a continuous process, an integral part of any development strategy and include institutional development; and
4. be able to measure progress against identified key indicators and goals.

The trainer should judiciously assume the role of a facilitator/catalyst; facilitating the trainees/participants to effectively use their knowledge/skills and experience for solving development problems. This is also in keeping with the changing perceptions of rural development as reflected in the Eighth and Ninth Five Year Plans as well as the 73rd Constitutional Amendment and innovative decentralization of rural development efforts such as *Janmabhoomi* in Andhra Pradesh.

Training Needs Assessment (TNA)

An assessment of training needs for participatory local development must take into account rural development programmes and strategies, organizational culture and functioning of the decision-making process, in particular the attitudes, behaviour and local livelihood conditions and needs of rural people concerned. TNA provides answers to the following:

- where training is needed?
- who needs training?
- who will organize the training?
- where will it be organized?
- what will be the content of training?
- what skills and knowledge are needed?
- will it be institutional or non-institutional?
- are requisite training facilities available?
- are resource persons of requisite calibre available?
- who will finance the training?
- what are the likely outcomes of training?

Identification of Stakeholders

The stakeholders to be trained at district, sub-district, block (or *Mandal* or *Taluk*) and village levels are:

1. senior state government officials responsible for local development planning;
2. PRI members, including *Gram Panchayat* elected officials and the *Sarpanch* at village level;
3. new entrants, especially women and those from weaker sections elected under the one-third quota provided by the 73rd Constitution Amendment;
4. functionaries of government line departments; and
5. representatives of NGOs/CBOs/SHGs/media..

The training can be to upgrade skills and refresher courses; pre-posting and refresher courses for higher level central and state officials; specially for certain implementing staff of various rural development programmes; refresher courses for new entrants to political parties; special courses run by different government agencies/institutions for women and functionaries from other weaker social sections; or run by NGOs for their staff, representatives of other NGOs and for self-help groups of women, other weaker sections and youth. Training of PRI officials is a big challenge because of the vast and varied nature of local needs and situations. Training courses can be i) pre-service training; ii) orientation training; iii) induction training, iv) in-service training; v) on-the-job training; and vi) refresher training/orientation. These can be residential programmes in training institutions or on-the-job, conducted by mobile training units. Women who are unable to leave family responsibilities need training within the home environment. Adult/non-formal education, health, nutrition and hygiene programmes for women, are examples of mobile training where training facilities go to the trainees instead of the other way round.

Spatial-specific Training

Residential training programmes on theory and practice have the advantage of giving the trainees confidence and time for self-assessment in terms of peer values and help in attitude-building and behavioural change.

Target Group-specific Training

This training is geared to the needs of marginalized social groups who need special attention for mainstream integration, e.g. Scheduled Castes and Scheduled Tribes in India.

Gender-specific Training

Women in most developing countries are now recognized as an important part of decision making in society and are being mobilized to participate in development. This has given them newer roles and functions, generating the need for new capacity-building programmes. Women are also actively involved in political administration and need to be specially trained for their new roles and responsibilities. For instance, a large number of women, on being elected as *Panchayati Raj* representatives, have a crucial role in the grassroots decision-making process. Gender-specific training is essential to develop and nurture potential skills in women for their successful integration into the development process.

Capacity-building Areas for Training

Capacity-building areas for training of trainers on participatory local development, which have been identified on the basis of the assessment of training needs of PRI council members, government officials, NGOs and CBOs are: i) advocacy/promotion/learning; ii) social mobilization/ participation; iii) local leadership; iv) social development/gender issues; v) technical/professional/managerial skills development; and vi) thematic topics.

THE AUTHORITY OF THE CENTRE AND THE STATES IN TRIBAL AFFAIRS

The term "Scheduled Areas" denotes the tribal regions to which either the Fifth Schedule or the Sixth Schedule applies. The two Schedules have very different mechanisms for governing their jurisdictional areas. The Fifth Schedule was, until PESA was legislated, an entirely centralized system where the communities—the majority being tribal—were directed in their affairs by provincial governors. The Schedule permitted the states to extend their executive power to the Scheduled Areas, and granted the Governor of each state the authority to "make regulations for the peace and good government of any area in a State which is for the time being a Scheduled Area." The Governor was thus the "sole legislature for the Scheduled Areas and the Scheduled Tribes," competent to make laws on all subjects enumerated in the Constitution's Union, State, and Concurrent Lists.

The Governor could also preclude the application of any federal or state law in the Fifth Schedule areas. Gubernatorial authority was "of a very wide nature" and subject to only two restrictions: (i) that the Governor would consult a Tribes Advisory Council "before making any regulation"; and, (ii) that all regulations would receive Presidential assent before taking effect. In contrast, the Sixth Schedule has always given the tribes considerable autonomy. This Schedule divides the tribal areas in India's northeastern states into "autonomous" regions, each allocated to a particular tribe. The elected councils in the Sixth Schedule areas are vested with administrative authority, make laws with respect to a variety of subjects, and even exercise judicial authority through traditional legal systems embedded with certain features of federal law. The councils are also financially independent and do not labour under the executive authority of the states. Though the Sixth Schedule's scheme renders all exercise of executive and legislative authority by the councils subject to the approval of the provincial Governor, the superior courts have interpreted the Governor's authority to be considerably restricted. The Indian Supreme Court's decision in Pu Myllai Hlychho clarified that even though the Sixth Schedule is not a "self-contained code" or a "Constitution within the Constitution," the courts must nevertheless defer to the legislative, administrative and judicial independence that the Schedule grants District and Regional Councils.

There were two reasons for the different treatment that the tribes received. First, the tribes in Fifth Schedule areas were considered incapable of self-government. Second, unlike the Sixth Schedule areas, some tribal communities in peninsular India coexisted with a minority non-tribal population, and autonomy for the tribes in such a case seemed impractical. These were considerations that had been settled well before independence, so that by voting on the inclusion of the Fifth Schedule in the Constitution the founding fathers were, in a sense, continuing the colonial typecast that the tribes' contentment depended not so much on "rapid political advance as on experienced and sympathetic handling, and on protection from economic subjugation by the [non-tribal] neighbours." Even the Supreme Court of India later endorsed this paternalism justification when it said that "[t]he tribals ... need to be taken care of by the protective arm of the law, ... so that they may prosper and by an evolutionary process join the mainstream of the society."

The Panchayat (Extension to Scheduled Areas) Act 1996

In 1996, however, Parliament exercised its reserved legislative authority to extend the provisions of the Constitution's Part IX exclusively to the Fifth Schedule areas. As a result, any habitation or hamlet "comprising a community and managing its affairs in accordance with traditions and customs" could now exercise limited self-government.

After PESA was enacted, communities in the Fifth Schedule areas (the majority of whom were tribal) were directed to follow democratic elections, conform to the hierarchical Panchayat system stipulated in Part IX, and exercise the powers thought "necessary to enable them to function as institutions of self-government." On the other hand, while devolving power to the local communities the states were to ensure that (i) their laws comported "with the customary law, social and religious practices and traditional management practices of community resources," and (ii) the Gram Sabhas (bodies "consisting of persons whose names are included in the electoral rolls for the Panchayat at the village level" were "competent to safeguard and preserve the traditions and customs of the people, their cultural identity, community resources and the customary mode of dispute resolution."

PESA is therefore considered by many as a "logical extension of [both] the Fifth Schedule" and Part IX of the Constitution. But, as innocuous as it may seem, this—top-down—model has in the last 10 years progressively denied tribal communities self-government and rights to their community's natural resources.

A REVIEW OF PESA: THE IMPAIRMENT OF TRIBAL RIGHTS IN A DECENTRALIZED GOVERNMENT

Even though PESA is projected as legislation transforming tribal representation in Fifth Schedule areas, the tribes feel as much "culturally deprived and economically robbed" as under colonial rule. Neither PESA in the last decade, nor the Fifth Schedule before it, has helped the tribal communities "acquire the status and dignity of viable and responsive people's bodies," as Parliament had intended.

Tribal local governments are often ignored in development plans and the benefits of any actual development "rarely percolate down to the local tribes," which are "subordinated to outsiders, both economically and culturally." PESA and the Fifth Schedule have also not prevented large corporations from gaining "control over the natural resources which constituted the life-support systems of the tribal communities;" neither have they made the tribes prosperous from the mineral-rich land on which they live. In fact, the tribes have "gradually lost control over community resources such as forests" to both settlers and the State; and one author would go so far as to equate non-tribal acquisitions with tribal displacement. Deceit and the active connivance of state employees with non-tribal communities is another debilitating factor reversing, in this case, the benefits of land reform legislation. Shankar's study of tribal lands in the northern state of Uttar Pradesh revealed a nexus between traditionally influential non-tribal landowners and corrupt government officials.

The latter exercised their discretionary powers to favour non-tribals by transferring lands over which tribal communities may have had a valid claim. Even in a tribal majority state like Jharkhand in the north, the tribes are the worst affected in the population since the state government's mining operations and hydro-electric power projects exploit natural resources in the resource-rich tribal areas, thus making the tribes "outsider[s] in [their] own land." Faced with this onslaught, many tribes have resisted settlers, the government and private enterprises, and sought to reassert their identity. For instance, in the Bengal region the Kamatapur tribal movement has cited neglect, exploitation, and discrimination, and demanded a separate state. Tribes in the neighbouring state of Orissa have demanded a prohibition on private consortiums that intend to mine bauxite from one of the most richly endowed regions in India.

Similarly, in the south, Kerala's tribal population has recently begun to defend its rights by banding together in various political groups at the state and local community levels in order to compel the administration to review land alienation, poverty, and exploitation by private enterprises. It is far too easy to dismiss these incidents as mere consequences of "misplaced development strategies" and lack of interest among state administrations. The critics of tribal governance in India see the dangers in an extremely narrow compass, criticizing provisions in PESA as "impracticable" or the states as legislatively ignorant. In sum, they believe that good civil administration alone will assuage tribal woes.

The Anathema of State Legislative Incompetence

To begin, PESA only marginally altered the power balance between state governments and the tribes because of ineffectual participation by the former, and the "general tendency at the state level to monopolize power rather than share power with people at large." This apathetic attitude has manifested itself in two forms. First, the majority of the states with tribal populations procrastinated in their decentralization programs. Although all states with Scheduled Areas have now enforced PESA, their past dilatory performance has led to the risk of delays in future amendments necessary to reflect changed circumstances.

Second, when they did legislate, the states either ignored tribal "customary law, social and religious practices and traditional management practices of community resources" or enacted incomplete laws. Samal gives one such example: though PESA stipulates a community as the basic unit of governance, the Orissa Gram Panchayat (Amendment) Act of 1997 conferred authority on the larger Gram Sabha comprising all communities in a de-marcated territory. As a result, the Orissa legislation disregarded the "distinct socio-cultural practices and different interests" of the individual communities within that territory.

The unenthusiastic response of the states appears to be a product of policies advocated by the first national commission on Scheduled Areas and Scheduled Tribes established in 1960. The Dhebar Commission, as it was known, allegedly did not favour the creation of more Scheduled Areas in the country, and is said to have considered the Fifth Schedule "as a temporary expedient" until the tribes were brought on par with the rest of society. The Commission's 1961 report thus gave "State Governments, which had 'openly' or 'subtly' practised the art of rebalancing demographic equations in tribal areas ... an alibi to stall demands for 'tribal republics'." The later realization that assimilation alone could not be the solution to tribal underdevelopment caused Parliament and the federal executive to change tack, but the damage had already been done.

The states which exercised actual authority in the Scheduled Areas had settled into a mode of governance predicated on the belief that programmatic state-supervised development was the only solution to primitive tribal societies. Attempts to devolve decision-making powers upon tribal communities have since been largely unsuccessful because the primary responsibility for implementing PESA remains the prerogative of those very states. This reinforces the view that self-government is, in many ways, a privilege granted to the tribal communities rather than an inherent right.

The Fading Tribal Rights in Natural Resources

In 10 years PESA has facilitated the gradual evisceration of tribal rights in the natural resources of the Scheduled Areas. The complication arises because PESA delegates the management of natural resources to tribal communities, without divesting control or ownership by the State. My objective here is to provide support for this claim in the context of tribal rights in land, forest and water resources.

The Continuous Erosion of Tribal Land Rights

One of the most basic rights that inures to the benefit of a community is a right in the commons. Therefore, property rights have become a natural rallying point for modern Indigenous peoples' movements around the world; 87 and nations have been seen to have a duty to recognize "people's proprietorship of the land they occupy and to which they have long had a sense of belonging" as a "principle of human justice."

Yet, the tribes in India are regularly deprived of their property rights predicated on the low (and ambiguous) thresholds of 'consultation' and 'recommendation'. While some states have individually sought to protect tribal rights through laws prohibiting private non-tribal purchases of land, there is no legislation restricting acquisitions by the State in the "public interest". Instead, appropriations are legislatively backed by the Land Acquisition Act of 1894 in order to justify the government taking personal property for numerous purposes.

The root of the problem is that the tribes cannot exercise a fundamental right to property under Indian law. Fundamental rights are given much greater deference and have a special status in the Constitution. In contrast, the tribes can only invoke a legal right to property under Article 300A of the Constitution ("no person shall be deprived of his property save by authority of law").

Since the tribes' right to property is merely a legal right, and not a fundamental right, the State can acquire their property with just compensation if it can establish that such appropriations are by "authority of law". That "authority of law" is found in section 4(i) of PESA which explicitly authorizes the acquisition of land in Scheduled Areas. What is also evident is that the categorization of tribal property rights as legal rights reinforces PESA's low and ambiguous thresholds mentioned earlier. Because the bur-den of establishing a violation of the legal right to property lies with the tribes, they face a formidable task disproving that the State did not properly 'consult' or seek 'recommendations'.

Moreover, the Indian Supreme Court has ruled that the government is the "best judge" to determine if a public purpose is served by an acquisition.

This substantially eases the burden on central and state governments to defend a particular acquisition, and, with later Supreme Court decisions opining that the Land Acquisition Act is "a complete Code by itself," the central and state governments' powers of appropriation have been strengthened because government agencies are no longer obligated to refer to any other legislation for determining the propriety of their actions. It also means that the Land Acquisition Act, which does not provide special protective rights in tribal land, can be incidentally applied to prevail over any proprietary rights otherwise guaranteed to the tribal communities in either PESA or the Fifth Schedule. Against this background, it appears illogical that the maximum protection provided in PESA against usurpation of tribal land is the obligation that state agencies should consult the local governments "before making the acquisition of land in the Scheduled Areas." PESA does not stipulate the precise manner in which those consultations should take place, and the ambiguity lowers the standard for ensuring procedural safeguards since the courts are unlikely to assail an acquisition for a public purpose unless that action was shown to be egregious or patently illegal. Consequently, administrations conveniently refrain from investing any more time and effort than that required to satisfy the requirement for a consultation as mandated by PESA.

The inconsistency regarding the true nature of the rights in land that Parliament afforded tribal communities when it enacted PESA has become a source of discord between the judicial and executive branches of the State. The controversy can be traced back to the Supreme Court's Samatha decision in 1997, where the court had ruled that the Fifth Schedule enjoined governors to make regulations preventing the purchase and exploitation of tribal land for mining activities by any entity that was not state-owned or a tribal enterprise. The judgment had prompted an opposite reaction from the federal Ministry of Mines, which proposed a constitutional amendment that granted governors unfettered authority in the "transfer of land by members of the schedule[d] tribe[s] to the Government or allotment by Government of its land to a non-tribal for undertaking any non-agricultural operations." The Ministry also believed that Samatha had altered the balance of power stipulated in the Fifth Schedule by "tak[ing] away the sovereign right of the government to transfer its land in any manner." Although the Constitution was ultimately not amended, the controversy has since encouraged various states to express similar views on their competence to permit exploitation of natural resources in the Scheduled Areas by private, non-tribal enterprises.

Insufficient Protection for Tribal Forest Rights

Forest laws in India classify forests into three categories: reserve forests (which should be left untouched); protected forests (where exploitation is allowed unless specifically prohibited); and village forests (that are assigned to local communities for management and use). The ability of a tribal community to exploit a forested region for consumption would thus depend on its classification. So, for instance, even though PESA grants tribal communities "the ownership of minor forest produce," the right is almost sterile unless state governments ensure that forested areas near tribal communities are denoted village forests and not reserve forests. Despite such clear federal restrictions on forest use, PESA does not provide any guidance on the manner in which the states should protect tribal rights to forestlands. Interestingly, even a program that encourages cooperation between the state forest departments and village communities for conservation has proved counterproductive.

The Joint Forest Management (JFM) program is the preferred national policy for forest conservation under which a state can constitute separate village committees supervised by that state's forest department, alongside local governments and empowered under PESA.

Although such committees would ideally be staffed entirely by members of the tribal community in Fifth Schedule areas, they are for all intents and purposes separate institutions controlled by the state administration. The lack of interoperability between village committees constituted under PESA and those formed under the JFM program is evident from the fact that the JFM guidelines released in 2000 (and revised in 2002) by the federal Ministry of Environment and Forests does not so much as mention PESA. State conservation agencies have also frequently asserted that PESA should not be interpreted as securing tribal rights over protected forestlands, irrespective of whether the communities have traditionally exploited those resources. Sarin et al. therefore conclude that "devolution policies [such as JFM] have largely reinforced state control over forest users, giving the relationship new form rather than changing its balance of power or reducing the conflict between state and local interests."

Tribal Rights to Water Resources Remain Ambiguous

PESA provides that local communities in Scheduled Areas should be entitled to manage "minor water bodies"—a statutorily undefined term. While states would typically follow administrative guidelines setting out the rules for managing such water bodies, the difficulty is that the directives identify a "minor water body" based on acreage rather than territorial jurisdiction and traditional use patterns of the tribal communities. The problems are compounded when some states either devolve management responsibilities without ascertaining community needs or neglect to pass new laws. The contrasting actions taken by the states of Madhya Pradesh and Maharashtra are noteworthy: while the state of Madhya Pradesh in central India swiftly and properly delineated rules for the use of minor water bodies in Scheduled Areas, the Maharashtra legislature entrusted management of minor water bodies to local governments, but left the actual determination of authority amongst the tiers of local government to the absolute discretion of the state executive. The lack of community participation in policies to manage water resources in Scheduled Areas is also an issue that the federal government has been unable to resolve. Though the National Water Policy released in 2002 recommends "special efforts ... to investigate and formulate projects either in, or for the benefit of, areas inhabited by tribal or other specially disadvantaged groups," the policy fails to identify the rights and responsibilities of tribal local governments.

The Tribal Struggle to Cope with Imposed Laws

Contrary to PESA's guarantees that state laws would respect tribal customs and traditions, the Act has debased the tribal traditions of self-governance. The propensity to violate tribal norms is not only a product of subnational apathy, but also the outcome of a statutory scheme that compels the tribes to adopt non-tribal concepts. By promoting the system of local government prescribed for non-tribal communities in Part IX of the Constitution, the Indian Parliament has instantly abolished centuries-old systems of Indigenous governance.

The abrupt shift from traditional institutions to alien concepts of elected representatives and Panchayats has resulted in "very low" tribal participation and an underutilization of the institutions. Thus, for example, the Lanjia Saoras, a tribe in the state of Orissa, have been unable to adopt the electoral system of government mandated by Part IX of the Constitution, as have the Santals. Similarly, the tribes in Madhya Pradesh that were asked to adopt the Panchayat form of government have not seen "the importance of panchayat.....for their own welfare [or] society development," while in Gond and Bhil societies the Panchayat system eroded the significance of traditional councils and strained ties within the community.

A more subtle reason for the tension between the customary and the received is the entrenched perception in India that the tribes are primitive communities with little or no order in society. Of course, such a view can only be seen as a product of the dominant culture's prejudice against, and ignorance of, the culture of both settled and nomadic tribal peoples, particularly those deemed 'primitive', since each of these groups, of course, has its own customs, traditions and laws.

The Manki-Munda system in the state of Jharkhand, for instance, competes with state laws enacted to enforce PESA because the tribes prefer their traditional law's emphasis on collective and consensual decision-making.

PESA's drafters mistakenly believed that an ambiguous directive to the states to design their laws in consonance with such "customary law, social and religious practices and traditional management practices of community resources" would resolve the dichotomy. What they overlooked was the inevitable displacement of indigenous laws and institutions that accompanies the imposition of a non-native system of governance.

PANCHAYATI RAJ IN THE SCHEDULED AREAS IN INDIA AND MADHYA PRADESH

The local self-government has been in existence in India for a long time. The prevalence of *Gramsabhas* or rural communities is found in the *Vedas*, in *Ramayan*, in the *Sabhaparva* of *Mahabharat*, in the *Arthshastra* of *Kautilya* and in the Buddhist and Jain literature. The Mughals interfered very little with the villages and incorporated them into its administration as a unit for revenue and police purpose. The establishment of British in India resulted in altogether a different kind of change as Lord Rippon's famous Resolution of 1882 recommended the starting of local self-government (Sharma, Shakuntla, 1994:89-90). Through the Government of India Acts of 1919 and 1935, village panchayats came to be established more systematically with defined powers and functions. The Constitution of India further dealt with the issue of taking steps to organize village panchayat and this became more firmly entrenched with the creation of Panchayati Raj in India in 1959 when the authority and responsibility for rural development was entrusted on the people.

A large part of tribal India under British rule remained unexplored and untouched though, various Acts, particularly related to land and forests were promulgated. The British economic policies favouring individual titles to property and creating a market for land and forest products escalated the exploitation of the tribals at the hands of moneylenders, contractors and other subordinate officials. The repercussions of this could be seen in various tribal revolts that took place in British India between 1820 an 1890 and even later which were crushed by the Britishers and gave them the reason to introduce laws and regulations to isolate tribals to the restricted area at the pretext of their special protection. (Furer-haimendorf, 1992 : 36-37). *The Government of India Act 1919* provided that the Governor-General in Council may declare any territory in British India to 'Backward Tract' and that any Act of the Indian legislature should apply to such tracts only if the Governor-General so directed. *The Government of India Act 1935* further classified the areas into two the 'excluded' (north-east region) and the 'partially excluded' areas. These areas were to be insulated from the control of the Indian legislature and ministries, and left in direct charge of the Governor of the Province who was always a British and usually an ICS officer.

What were known as 'excluded' and 'partially excluded' areas during the British rule came to be known as the 'Sixth' and the 'Fifth' Scheduled Areas in the Constitution that came to force (1950) in India after independence (1947). The Fifth Schedule [244 (1)] contains provisions regarding the administration and control of the Scheduled Areas and Scheduled Tribes. In the Constitution the 'expression "Scheduled Areas" means such areas as the President may by order declare to be Scheduled Areas'. In reference to the Scheduled Tribes, the Constitution says that, 'the president may with respect to any State or Union Territory and where it is State, after consultation with the Governor thereof, by public notification specify the Tribes or tribal communities or parts of or groups within tribes or tribal communities shall for the purpose of their constitution be deemed to be scheduled tribes in relation to that state or union territory, as the case may be'. (Article 342).

The tribals were spread over in most parts of the different sub-divisions of what became the state of Madhya Pradesh in 1956 (these were – Madhya Bharat, Bhopal, Vindhya Pradesh and Sironj Sub-division). Of all these sub-divisions, most of the tribal areas were found in the Central Provinces and Berar regions where the beginning of panchayat system was made in 1920 through the *local-Self Government Act.*

The Central Provinces and Berar Panchayat Act of 1946 had taken note of the special needs of tribal areas and section 156 of this Act stipulated that if the state government was of the opinion that if the standard 3-tier panchayat structure was unsuitable for any tribal majority area, the Act which provided for setting up Tribal and Pargana Panchayats in the predominantly tribal areas. The State used this provision by the notification of 21st January 1955, when 57 tribal panchayats and 17 *pargana* panchayats were established in Bastar and Jashpur sub-division of Raigarh district and were notified for a special tribal panchayat structure in 1956.. The Act of 1962 followed the similar provisions for the panchayats in the tribal majority areas. Even panchayat elections held in 1965 and 1970, were not held in these areas of tribal concentration. Later this provision was reversed and those prevalent in other regions were made applicable in 1972 in tribal areas as well.

Incidentally, *The State Panchayat Acts of 1981,1990 and 1993* (as originally enacted) in Madhya Pradesh made no exception for tribal areas or retain the possibility of such exception. While on the one hand, the state did not made any special provision for the panchayat structure in the scheduled Areas as provided in the 73 Amendment Act, it made a move simultaneously on the other hand, for inclusion of certain Schedule V areas of the State in Schedule VI recommending the need for different autonomous self-government institutions in these areas. The government also applied pressure on the Union Government to frame a law to facilitate the setting up of District Councils in the four tribal dominated areas of 17 other districts under the Sixth Schedule.

A large number of people mostly non-tribals, but also tribals expressed their disapproval of the Schedule VI structure in the tribal areas of M.P., mainly for their own interest but also because of the vast magnitude of change that has come in these areas over the years creating diversity and heterogeneity. But opposition to the provision of application of the 73rd Amendment Act to the Schedule Areas of Madhya Pradesh came from very few quarters and similar provisions were applied throughout in the whole of the State. The panchayat elections were also held uniformly throughout Madhya Pradesh in June 1994. The state law was finally mended in 1997 to conform to *The provisions of the Panchayat (Extension to the Scheduled Areas) Act, 1996* by which the 73rd Constitutional Amendment was extended to these areas with some modifications. The Panchayati raj Act (73rd Amendment to the Constitution), 1992 and its Extension to the Scheduled Areas – With Special reference to Madhya Pradesh.

Article 243 M of the Panchayati Raj Act, 1992 questions the uniform applicability of the Act and calls for special measures for the governance for Scheduled Areas. The Article, 243 M (1) states that 'nothing in this part shall apply to the Scheduled Areas referred to in clause (1), and the tribal areas referred to in clause (2) of Article 244'. However, according to Article 243M4 (b), 'parliament may, by law extend the provisions of this part to the scheduled areas and the tribal areas referred to in clause (1) subject to such exceptions and modifications as may be specified in such law. But, in most of the states with scheduled Areas, including Madhya Pradesh, panchayat elections were held uniformly. In some states like in Andhra Pradesh, Orissa and Maharashtra holding elections were withheld as they were challenged in the various High Courts. (Mukul, EPW, 3-9 may 1997: 928). The courts viewed the extension as unlawful and according to them the Panchayati raj could be extended to the scheduled Areas only through an Act of Parliament. Consequently, to look into these matters and making recommendations for extending the provisions of the 73rd Amendment to the Scheduled Areas, a Committee under the Chairmanship of Dileep Singh Bhuria (then the Member of Parliament) was constituted in June 1994.

The Bhuria Committee submitted its report in February 1995 with far reaching recommendations on the law to extend the provisions of Part IX of the Constitution to the Scheduled Areas. It dealt with the issues of village governance and participatory democracy, effectiveness of customary laws, community control over resources and appropriate administrative framework for Scheduled Areas. The Committee felt that while sharing the new panchayati raj structure in tribal areas, it is desirable to blend the traditional with the modern by treating the traditional institutions as the foundation on which the modern super structure should be built and taking cognizance of their indigenous institutions and ethos while considering democratic decentralization in tribal areas. The important recommendations of the Bhuria Committee included wide-ranging powers to the gram sabha, reservation of seats as members and chairpersons and the formation of district and sub-district councils in tribal districts with powers (administrative and legislative) identical with those in the Sixth Schedule Areas.

There were some criticisms of the Bhuria Committee Report. The recommendation (para 1) of the report suggests that all tribal sub-plan areas and other smaller tribal concentrations, not already notified as Scheduled Areas, should be done so under the Fifth Schedule of the Constitution. According to B.K. Roy Burman, the relevance of this recommendation for framing legislation for operationalizing the 73rd Amendment of the constitution in the existing Scheduled Areas is not clear. It will pose two problems according to him. One while it will strengthen the upper layer of the bureaucracy, it will cause misgivings among the non-tribal peoples in those areas and sour tribal and non-tribal relations; and second, the people in this area would be vulnerable to be ruled by regulation promulgated by the Governor as the Fifth Schedule does not stipulate any devolution of power at the local level but provides for its centralization.

The recommendation in fact ignores the ground reality and diverts attention from the real reason for not very satisfactory functioning of the tribal Sub-plan approach as admitted in the Seventh and Eighth-plan. If the tribal Sub-plan has anything to do with the Fifth Schedule, the report should have explained, says Burman, why the condition is equally bad in the States like Orissa, Madhya Pradesh and Maharashtra where bulk of the tribal predominant areas of a State like West Bengal, which are not covered by the Fifth Schedule, the conditions are more or less the same if not slightly better in some cases. Apart from the criticism of the paternalistic design of the Fifth Schedule, other points of debate focused on – the reorganization of the administrative boundaries based on ethnic and demographic considerations, composition of the four tier structure and the relationship between each, the role of the MPs and MLAs in the panchayat bodies and the replication of the Sixth Schedule provisions to the Fifth Schedule Areas which would invite a non-tribal political backlash.

Finally, after some delay on the part of the Government and protest by certain individuals and organizations, the Act namely *The Provisions of the Panchayats (Extension to the Scheduled Areas) Act, 1996* came into force on 24th December, 1996. The objectives of this Act were to extend the provisions of Part IX to the Scheduled Areas with certain modifications, to provide self-rule to the tribals, to ensure participatory democracy, to evolve a suitable administrative framework, to safeguard and preserve the traditions and customs of tribal communities and to prevent outside interference and exploitation of the tribal people.. This Act is to be applicable in the Scheduled Areas referred to in clause (1) of Article 244 of the constitution. The States in the Scheduled Areas were required to amend their own Panchayat State Acts before the expiry of one year, i.e. by December 23, 1997. All States except Bihar and Rajasthan (which did later through an Ordinance) amended their Panchayat Acts to give effect to the provision contained in the Extension Act, 1996.

The Act directs the legislature of a state not to make any law, which is inconsistent with the customary law, social and religious practices and traditional management practices of community resources. The Act also recognizes the important role of village community and give wide-ranging power to the gram sabha for safeguarding and preserving traditions and customs of the people, approve the plans, programmes and projects for social and economic development of the village and several other powers to protect and regulate the natural resources as well as its misuse by the outsiders.

Besides these, the other important points the Act envisages are-the reservation of one half of the total seats for the scheduled tribes in the Scheduled Areas and the post of Chairperson at all levels of panchayat and the pattern of the Sixth Schedule of the Constitution to be maintained while designing the administrative arrangements for the district level panchayat. Thus the Extension Act, 1996 though diluted some of the recommendations of the Bhuria Committee Report, has accepted most of them, particularly the provisions relating to the power of the Gram Sabha. B.K. Roy Burman while appreciating these points is critical of some of these. According to him as the Act is for extension of the provisions of part IX of the Constitution in the Scheduled Areas, it is presumed that where it does not make specific provision on any matter the relevant provision in IX will operate. He raises problems regarding the use of certain concepts in the Act like 'community' or 'customary law', which would pose confusion and ambiguity at the operational level. There is a need as envisages in the Act, to extend the sixth Schedule to all tribal dominate areas of the country and later to even non-tribal areas, according to B.K. Roy Burman.

B.D. Sharma (also the member of Bhuria Committee) considers the 1996 Act as an important step in the direction of tribal self-rule. He however, feels that the agenda must include – areas totally left out from consideration like the Sixth Schedule areas, Urban Areas in Scheduled Areas not covered, some States with substantial tribal population totally left out like West Bengal, Kerala, Tamilnadu and Karnataka; and Tribal Areas in the Fifth Scheduled states but outside these areas. Some people feel that the positive aspects of the Act are meant to ensure an easy access to land for industry.

Given the fact that 80-85 percent natural resources are found in the tribal areas, it is going to affect them the most. With the processes of economic liberalization and globalization gaining strength, a destructive development is likely to be initiated legitimized by public interest. This would be at the cost of tribal way of life and culture, of their knowledge, resources and production skills, in fact at the cost of the human survival and the preservation of environmental and ecological balance. Besides these some important points are related to the customary laws and practices of the tribals, which vary among and within all tribes in different states. It may not be possible to have different laws for each tribe within a district or state. And, the customary laws are not properly codified and documented. The 'village' as described in the Act, which may be a 'hamlet', will pose a situation in which the revenue village may not be coterminous with the social village.

The term 'community' is not defined in the Act clearly, and therefore, it would be difficult to delimit a village. The reservation, especially for all chairpersons to be members of scheduled tribes, especially at the block and zilla levels will create problems, particularly in those districts where tribals do not constitute more than 50 percent of the total population of the district. In such places there will be a general resentment. Then there will be structural and administrative complications in the scheme. In Madhya Pradesh, a special section has been added to the *Madhya Pradesh Panchayati Raj Adhiniyam, 1993* by way of an amendment known as *'Special Provision for Panchayats in Schedule Area'*, Madhya Pradesh. This came into force on 5th December 1997 and provide for the extension of the provisions of part IX of the Constitution relating to the Panchayats in the Scheduled Areas of the State. It has incorporated most of the provisions of the extension Act, 1996.

These provisions ensure ample and significant representation of the tribals in the Scheduled Areas of Madhya Pradesh. The implementation of the provisions of the Extension Act, 1996 in Madhya Pradesh started with the amendment of certain other important laws, like the Excise Act, the Land Revenue Code, the Mining and Mineral Rules, the *Gram Nyayalaya Adhiniyam* and the Panchayt Act itself. As far as the acquisition of land is concerned, the M.P. Amendment Act made a provision with the Extension Act that before making the acquisition of land in the Scheduled Areas for development of projects and before rehabilitating persons affected by such projects in the Scheduled Areas, the gram sabha or the panchayat at the appropriate level shall be consulted.

The actual planning and implementation of the projects in the scheduled Areas shall be co-ordinated at the state level. Similar is the case with the grant of prospecting license or mining lease for minor minerals or for grant of concession for the exploitation of minor minerals by auction. The powers have been devolved to the gram sabha in matters of planning and management of water bodies, enforcement of prohibition or regulation or restriction of the sale and consumption or manufacture of any intoxicant, and management of village markets. The issue of Minor Forest Produce and that dealing with the move against money lending are however, still to be taken care of. But, in actual practice not all of them are implemented and there are still gaps and problems in their execution.

RESERVATION AND ELECTION - MADHYA PRADESH

The 1962 Act as well as 1981 Act provided for cooption by the elected members, of up to two women as members of gram panchayats and janpad panchayats if they did not figure, or were less than two, amongst the elected members. In the zilla panchayats it included co-option of one woman member. An Amendment in 1988 introduced 20 percent of seats for gram panchayat and janpad panchayat, as well as 10 percent for the posts of sarpanchs of gram panchayats, and members of janpad panchayat and zilla panchayat. The 1990 Act followed the same provision but included a reservation of 10 percent for the first time, in the district panchayat pradhans with at least one each for a member of these posts to be reserved for SC and ST women in the total parts for each category. The reservation of a particular seat was to be made by draw of lots and by rotation.

As far as reservation of seats for SC/ST is concerned, in Madhya Pradesh (as created in 1956) the *Panchayat Act of 1962* included through an amendment in 1973 for reservation of seats in Gram panchayats for SC/ST in proportion to their population in the Gram Sabha area. If no reservation was possible due to their small population co-option was to be made of SC or ST member as the case may be.

The Madhya Pradesh Panchayat Act of 1981, section 1 (4) provided for reservation for SC/ST in each village Panchayat proportionate to their population in the Gram Panchayat and for co-option in case no SC/ST member was elected. Section 15 stipulated that in a Gram panchayat where more than 50 percent seats are reserved for SC/ST or both together, the Sarpanch or Up-sarpanch, if Sarpanch was not found had to be from these categories. In the Janpad panchayat also, section 19 provided for co-option of a SC/ST member if no such member was elected to the Janpad panchayat. Under section 23, reservation was provided for SC/ST in the posts of Janpad Panchayat presidents in proportion to their respective population in the State. In addition, if more than 50 percent members of a Janpad Panchayat were SC/ST, the President or the vice-President as the case may be, was to be elected from amongst SC/ST. In the zilla panchayat, section 26 stipulated co-option of a member of the Scheduled Caste or Scheduled Tribe or one each from both if the elected members in the zilla panchayat did not include SC, ST or both of them. Where more than 50 percent members belonged to the SC or ST, the President has to be elected from amongst them as per section 27 of the Act. If the President was not an SC or ST, the Vice-President had to be SC or ST.

Madhya Pradesh Act of 1990 include section 13 (4) for reservation for SC/ST in gram panchayat seats proportionate to their population in the gram panchayat area. Section 17 provide for reservation of posts of Sarpanch for SC and ST in proportion to their population in the block. If the gram panchayat sarpanch was not a SC or ST the Up-sarpanch had to be elected from SC/ST members. In the Janpad Panchayats, section 22 provide for reservation of posts of Chairpersons of Janpad Panchayat for SC and ST proportionate to their population in the district. If the Chairman of the Janpad panchayat was not from SC/ST, the vice-chairman had to be from SC/ST in proportion for their respective population in the State. If the Pradhan of zilla parishad was not SC/ST, the Up-Pradhan had to be SC or ST.

The Constitutional 73rd Amendment provided for members to be elected and co-opted or nominated as ex-officio members. The reservation of one-third seats for women (including those of SC/ST), and for SC/ST according to the proportion of their population has been provided. This has enabled a large number of women to be in panchayat bodies. The reservation as finally provided at the time of the 1994 panchayat elections for the seats of chairpersons and members in the panchayats at three levels, show that 14.86 percent was reserved for scheduled castes, 29.88 percent for scheduled tribes and 17.03 percent for other backward classes.

A little over 33.87 percent seats were reserved for women, of which 14.84 percent were for women of scheduled castes, 28.86 percent for women from scheduled tribes and 17.51 percent women from OBCs leaving 37.79 percent for women in general category.

The Panchayat (Extension to the Scheduled Areas) Act, 1996, has further extended the reservation for the scheduled tribes in the Scheduled Areas. The reservations made in 1999 for the second panchayat elections in Madhya Pradesh saw an increase for S.T category, i.e. 31.83 percent, but a marginal decrease in other categories like 14.51 percent (S.C.), 16.84 percent (OBC) and 33.71 percent (women). For the reservations made for total women, 14. 52 percent were for S.C. women, 32.61 percent for S.T. women and 17.23 percent were for OBC women. The increase in the reservation in percentage of S.T. category as well as women belonging to Scheduled Tribe category is the reflection of the reservation for scheduled tribes in Fifth Scheduled Areas being of all chairpersons and not less than 50 percent of members besides being proportionate to their population.

The above data show enhanced increase in the participation of tribal women in the panchayats in the Vth Scheduled Areas since the passing of Panchayat Extension to the Scheduled Areas Act, 1996.

The state government constituted the State Election Commission in February 1994. The constitution of 30,922 gram panchayats, 459 panchayats at the block level and 45 zilla panchayats at the district level was notified in March 1994. The delimitation of wards/constituencies was completed in April and the elections were held in May-June 1994.

Of the total members of gram panchayats 63.12 percent were elected without contest and 8.38 percent sarpanches of gram panchayats, 13.60 percent janpad panchayat members, and 7.50 percent zilla panchayat members were elected unopposed. There were also cases of women and reserved category candidates contesting and getting elected on unreserved seats. Seventeen women became presidents of zilla panchayats against 15 posts reserved for them and 23 women were elected as presidents of janpad panchayats on unreserved positions.

RELATIONS BETWEEN TRIBES AND GOVERNMENT

The co-existence of established states and independent tribal communities living according to their own rules and customs dates back to the earliest times of recorded Indian history. In an age when the subcontinent was sparsely' populated and beyond the limits of centres of higher civilisation there were vast tracts covered in forests and difficult of access, populations on very different levels of material and cultural development could live side by side without impinging to any great extent on each others' resources and territories. Even at times of the greatest efflorescence of Hindu culture there were no organised attempts to draw aboriginal tribes into the orbit of caste society. The idea of missionary activity was then foreign to Hindu thinking. A social philosophy based on the idea of the permanence and invitability of caste distinctions saw nothing incongruous in the persistence of primitive life-styles on the periphery of sophisticated civilisations. No doubt, there were areas where the infiltration of advanced populations into tribal territory resulted in a closer interaction between aboriginals and Hindus.

In such regions, cultural distinctions were blurred, and tribal communities became gradually absorbed into the caste system, though usually into its lowest strata. Thus the untouchable castes of Cheruman and Panyer of Kerala were probably at one time independent tribes, and in their physical characteristics they still resemble neighbouring tribal groups which have remained outside the caste system. Aboriginals who retained their tribal identity and resisted inclusion within the Hindu fold fared better on the whole than the assimilated groups and were not treated as untouchables, even if they indulged in practices, such as the eating of beef, which Hindus considered polluting. Thus the Raj Gonds, some of whose rulers vied in power with Rajput princes, used to sacrifice and eat cows without debasing thereby their status in the eyes of their Hindu neighbours. The Hindus recognised the tribes' social and cultural separateness and did not insist on conformity to Hindu patterns of behaviour, and this respect for the tribal way of life prevailed as long as contacts between the two communities were of a casual nature. The tribal people, though considered strange and dangerous, were taken for granted as part of the world of hills and forests, and a more or less frictionless coexistence was possible because there was no population pressure, and hence no incentive to deprive the aboriginals of their land.

This position persisted during the whole of the Mughal period. Now and then the campaign of a Mughal army extending for a short spell into the wilds of tribal country would bring the inhabitants briefly to the notice of princes and chroniclers, but for long periods the hillmen and forest dwellers were left undisturbed. Under British rule, however, a new situation arose. The extension of a centralised administration over areas which had previously lain outside the effective control of princely rulers deprived many of the aboriginal tribes of their autonomy, and though most British administrators had no intention of interfering with the tribesmen's rights and traditional manner of living, the establishment of "law and order" in outlying areas exposed the aboriginals to the pressure of more advanced populations. In areas which had previously been virtually unadministered, and hence unsafe for outsiders who did not enjoy the confidence and goodwill of the aboriginal inhabitants, traders and moneylenders could now establish themselves under the protection of the British administration. Often they were followed by settlers, who succeeded in acquiring large tracts of the aboriginals' land. The process of land alienation will be illustrated by concrete examples, and it will become apparent that by imposing on tribal populations systems of land tenure and revenue collection developed in advanced areas the government unintentionally facilitated the transfer of tribal land to members of other ethnic groups. The deterioration of the aboriginals' position, which in many parts of Peninsular India began as early as the middle of the nineteenth century and continued into the twentieth century, occurred despite the fact that many British officials sympathised with the tribesmen and some of the most fervent advocates of tribal rights were found among the officers of the Indian Civil Service. Yet, the recommendations for reforms contained in numerous reports were seldom implemented in full, and even where they were incorporated in legislation they did not always prove effective.

Unable to resist the gradual alienation of their ancestral land, the aboriginals of many regions either gave way by withdrawing further into hills and tracts of marginal land or, if no such refuge areas were left, had no other choice than to accept the economic status of tenants, sharecroppers, or agricultural labourers on the very land their forefathers had owned.

There was only one part of British India where a policy of non-interference and protection enabled the tribal populations to retain their land and their traditional life-style. In the hill regions of Northeast India which enclose the Brahmaputra Valley in the shape of an enormous horseshoe tribes such as Nagas, Mishmis, Adis, Miris, Apa Tanis, and Nishis were the sole inhabitants of a vast region of rugged mountains and narrow valleys into which the peoples settled in the plains of Assam had never penetrated. A small volume of barter trade between hills and plains was carried on by tribesmen from the foothills, but most of the hill people never set foot in the Brahmaputra Valley. When in the second half of the nineteenth century and during the first decades of the twentieth century the British extended their administrative control over part of the hill regions, they did not encourage the entry of plainsmen, but devised a system of administration which allowed the hillmen to run their affairs along traditional lines. As late as the 1930s the entire administration of the Naga Hills District, for instance, was in the hands of one deputy commissioner stationed at Kohima and one subdivisional officer, whose headquarters was Mokokchung. With the help of a few clerks and a small force of Assam Rifles, these two officers maintained peace and order in a large hill region where bridle paths were the only means of communications. No plainsman was allowed to acquire land in the hills, and the indigenous system of land tenure was retained virtually unchanged. This policy protected the hill people from exploitation and land alienation. It is not surprising that the introduction of a much more elaborate and less flexible system of administration in the years following 1947 sparked off a great deal of unrest, for tribesmen used to running their own affairs reacted violently to interference from a host of minor officials lacking in understanding of local customs. This is not the place to discuss the cause of the rebellions of Nagas and Mizos, which at the time of writing have by no means completely ended, but no analysis of the relations between aboriginal tribes and the governments in power can be complete without consideration of at least some of the rebellions by which tribal populations tried to shake off the yoke of those who had invaded their habitat, usurped their ancestral land, and mercilessly robbed them of the fruits of their labours.

Anyone familiar with the oppression and exploitation aboriginals of regions such as the Telengana districts of Andhra Pradesh have suffered at the hands of landgrabbers, landlords, unscrupulous traders and moneylanders, and, regrettably, many minor officials must be surprised not by the fact that now and then tribal groups rose against their oppressors in violent outbursts but that organised rebellions were so few and so short-lived. If any of the tribes of Arunachal Pradesh or even of such settled hill regions as the Garo or Mikir hills had been exposed to injustices as severe as those suffered by Gonds, Kolams, Koyas, and Reddis, murder and violence would have been the order of the day, but most of the tribes of the Deccan are on the whole so gentle and inoffensive that extreme provocation is necessary before they take the law into their own hands.

Rebellions of aboriginal tribesmen against the authority of the government are among the most tragic conflicts between ruler and ruled. Whatever course the clash may take, it is always a hopeless struggle of the weak against the strong, the illiterate and uninformed against the organised power of a sophisticated system. There may be loss of life on both sides, but it is always the aboriginals who court ruin and economic distress. I do not refer here to the past risings of martial frontier tribes whose aims were basically political, but to the rebellions of primitive aboriginal tribes of Peninsular India, such as the Santal Rebellion in Bihar, the Bhil Rebellion in

Khandesh, and the Rampa Rebellion in the East Godavari District. All these uprisings were defensive movements; they were the last resort of tribesmen driven to despair by the encroachment of outsiders on their land and economic resources. As such they could all have been avoided had the authorities taken cognizance of the abonginals' grievances and set about to remedy them, not as it happened in most cases *after* the rising, but *before* the pressure on the tribesmen made an outbreak of violence unavoidable.

The Santal Rebellion of 1855—56, with which we are here only marginally concerned, was mainly an effort to undo the steady loss of land to non-tribal immigrants, but E.G. Mann, writing in 1867, listed also a number of specific grievances as having caused the Santals to rise against an inefficient and lethargic government, totally inexperienced in dealing with primitive tribes. Among the causes of the rising were: the grasping and rapacious manner of merchants and moneylenders in their transactions with the Santals, the misery caused by the iniquitous system of allowing personal and hereditary bondage for debt, the unparalleled corruption and extortion of the police in aiding and abetting the moneylenders, and the impossibility of the Santals obtaining redress from the courts. The causes of the Santals' uprising, one of the greatest rebellions in the annals of tribal India, were very similar to the circumstances which led to outbreaks of violence in other tribal areas. An insurrection which occurred in an area now part of Andhra Pradesh involved the Hill Reddis, a tribe whose present situation. This uprising occurred in 1879 and is commonly known as the Rampa Rebellion, after an area which now falls within the Chodavaram Taluk of the East Godavari District.

At the time of the cession of the Northern Circars by the Nizam to the East India Company, the Rampa country was in the possession of a ruler alternatively styled *zamindar, mansabdar,* or *raja.* This feudal lord was not a Reddi, but we do not know how he had originally gained possession of the country and by what means he controlled the independent and elusive hill people. He appears to have leased his villages to certain subordinate hill chiefs known as *muttadar,* and from these he received an annual income of Rs 8,750 per annum, an amount equal to at least Rs 800,000 according to the present value of money. This *mansabdar* was succeeded first *by* his daughter and subsequently by an illegitimate son. The latter's oppressive rule led to several minor insurrections, but the last straw was an excise regulation forbidding the drawing of palm wine for domestic purposes and leasing the toddy revenue to contractors entitled to collect taxes at their own discretion. Their illegal extortions and the oppressiveness of a corrupt police were the immediate causes of the Rampa Rebellion in 1879. The operation of the civil law of the country was an additional grievance of the tribesmen, whose trustfulness and ignorance of court proceedings enabled traders from the lowlands to make unfair contracts with them, and if these were not fulfilled according to the trader's own interpretation, to file suits against them, obtain ex parte decrees, and distrain as much property as they could lay hands on. The hill people laid the blame for all this injustice on government and government regulations and thought that their only remedy lay in rising against the authorities.

The rebellion started in March 1879 with attacks on policemen and police stations in Chodavaram Taluk, and it spread rapidly to the Golconda Hills of Vishakapatnam and to the Rekapalli country in the Bhadrachalam Taluk, which had recently been transferred from the Central Provinces to Madras Presidency. While under the previous administration shifting cultivation *(podu)* had been virtually unrestricted, the Madras government trebled the land revenue and excluded the tribal cultivators from certain areas. Because of these restrictions the Rampa leaders found adherents in the Rekapalli country, and soon five thousand square miles were affected by the rebellion. In the ensuing guerilla war the government forces comprised several hundred police drafted from neighbouring districts, six regiments of Madras infantry, two companies of sappers and miners, a squadron of cavalry, and a wing of infantry from the Hyderabad contingent. Despite these formidable forces the rebellion was not entirely suppressed until November 1880.

In this context the history of the Rampa Rebellion is relevant for two reasons. It shows first that aboriginal tribes, even if inherently not of a warlike character, are capable of considerable efforts if driven to extremities, and second that the grievances which had led to the rebellion were basically similar to the injustices and the exploitation under which tribal populations of Andhra Pradesh labour up to this day.

In the East Godavari Agency of Madras Presidency the conditions of the tribal populations were considerably improved as a result of the Rampa Rebellion. The necessity of instituting special methods of administering primitive populations had been forcefully brought before the eyes of the authorities, and steps were taken to protect the aboriginals from the encroachment of outsiders.

The various orders passed from time to time with the view of ameliorating the conditions of the tribal population of the East Godavari Agency were ultimately consolidated in legislation known as The Agency Tracts Interest and Land Transfer Act, 1917. The regulations of this act formed a model for similar legislation in other tribal areas, and I shall therefore quote some of its main sections. In order to save the tribals from the exploitation of moneylenders, the act laid down that "a) interest on any debt or liability shall not as against a member of a hill-tribe be allowed or decreed at a higher rate than 24% per annum nor shall any compound interest or any collateral advantage be allowed against him; b) the total interest allowed or decreed on any debt or liability as against a member of a hill-tribe shall not exceed the principal amount."

Even more important were the sections restricting the transfer of land from tribals to outsiders. The relevant section (4) contained the following provisions:

1. Notwithstanding any rule of law or enactment to the contrary any transfer of immovable property situated within the Agency tract by a member of a hill-tribe shall be absolutely null and void unless made in favor of another member of a hill-tribe or with the previous consent in writing of the Agent or of any other prescribed officer. [Agent was the revenue officer comparable to the collector of a normal district.]
2. Where a transfer of property is made in contravention of sub-section (1) the Agent.... may on application by

anyone interested decree ejectment against any person in possession of the property claiming under the transfer and may restore it to the transferor or his heirs.

These sections of the Act of 1917 should, if fully implemented, have put a stop to all alienation of tribal land, and it is a sobering thought that sixty-one years later large areas in what was the Godavari Agency' are no longer in the possession of their previous tribal owners, even though the provisions of the Act of 1917 remained in force till the promulgation of the Andhra Pradesh Scheduled Areas Land Transfer Regulation, 1959.

It is only fair to admit, however, that in the period 1917-47 the condition of the tribal populations in the East Godavari Agency Tract was relatively favourable, and that the massive invasion of tribal land by outsiders occurred after 1947.

The need for special protection of aboriginal tribes was not confined to the areas notified as Agencies, and in 1919 an act known as the Government of India Act, 1919, provided "that the Governor-General in Council may declare any territory in British India to be a 'Backward Tract' and that any act of the Indian Legislature should apply to such Backward Tracts only if the Governor-General so directed."

The legislation of 1919 was a forerunner of the Government of India Act, 1935, and the Government of India (excluded and partially excluded areas) Order, 1936. "Excluded areas" were backward regions inhabited by tribal populations to which acts of the Dominion Legislature or of the provincial legislatures were to apply only with the consent of the governor of the province. The intention of this provision was to prevent the extension of legislation designed for advanced areas to backward areas where primitive tribes may be adversely affected by laws unsuitable to their special conditions. Though at the time Indian nationalists saw in it a device to retain British control over selected areas, after the attainment of independence the government of India adopted a somewhat similar policy in regard to several territories on the North East Frontier.

The Indian Constitution of 1950 also provided for the notification of "scheduled tribes" and their protection by special legislation. Regarding the administration of the scheduled areas the governor of each state which includes a scheduled area is bound to submit a report to the president annually or whenever required. The states periodically prepare lists of scheduled tribes, and these have to be confirmed by parliament. As scheduled tribes are in receipt of various benefits, there has been considerable pressure from backward classes for inclusion in this list, and as late as 1977 new additions were proposed by various states and confirmed by parliament.

As this volume is largely concerned with the changing fortunes of tribal populations in parts of Andhra Pradesh which used to be part of H.E.H. the Nizam's Dominions, we will now turn to the situation as it prevailed in Hyderabad State, both in the days of the Nizam's rule and after the incorporation of the state in the Republic of India in 1948.

In contrast to the administration of adjoining provinces of British India, the government of Hyderabad State had not provided for any special privileges for tribal communities. Indeed it was not until the 1940s that the condition of the aboriginal tribes received serious attention from government. In his foreword to my book *The Chenchus* (vol. 1 of *The Aboriginal Tribes of Hyderabad)* the late Sir Wilfrid Grigson, then Revenue Minister of Hyderabad State, commented on the ignorance of the average Hyderabad official in regard to the tribal communities in the following words:

> *This ignorance tends to blind him to the suffering and the loss of land and economic freedom that results in the backward areas when Hindu, Rohilla or Arab cultivators, contractors, traders and moneylenders are allowed freely to exploit the aboriginals. In such records therefore as can be traced of dealings between the governing classes of Hyderabad and the aboriginal and backward tribes little will be found of deliberate oppression or of positive policy.* Laissez faire *has been the governing principle, but, as everywhere in India, and not least in Hyderabad,* laissez faire *more than anything else has mined the aboriginal and turned him into a landless drudge and serf.*

The plight of the aboriginals, be they Gonds, Koyas, or Konda Reddis, is as much the usual attitude of the dominant classes of Andhra Pradesh as it was that of the ruling classes of Hyderabad State. Yet today no one can claim the excuse of ignorance. Ethnographic accounts and published reports are found in libraries, and the files of government departments are crammed with reports on conditions in the tribal areas; moreover, administrative action taken during the last years of the Nizam's government pointed clearly to the type of policy which could have prevented the present decline in the aboriginals' fortunes.

But let us return to the situation in the early 1940s when I began the study of the tribal populations of Hyderabad State. At that time there were in the districts of Warangal (which then included the present Khammam District) and Adilabad large forest areas where tribal communities persisted in relative isolation from more advanced populations. However, these areas had already begun to shrink, and the alienation of tribal land by members of non-tribal communities was an on-going process. Moreover, the reservation of forests, often decreed with scant regard for the needs of the tribal forest dwellers, had begun to encroach on the traditional habitat of such tribes as Reddis, Kolams, Koyas, and Gonds.

There were at that time no officials specifically concerned with the welfare of the tribes and no legislation protecting tribal interests comparable to the Agency Tracts Interest and Land Transfer Act, 1917, of the neighbouring Madras Presidency. The position of the tribes of Hyderabad State was hence rapidly deteriorating. In the course of anthropological research, initially undertaken without any thought of providing data to be utilised in the planning of administrative reforms, I discovered a great many cases of exploitation and oppression of tribal communities and subsequently incorporated my findings in a series of reports submitted to the Nizam's government.

Several of these reports were published by the Revenue Department under the title *Tribal Hyderabad,* with a foreword by W.V. Grigson, who held the portfolios of Revenue, Police, and Forest, thus being in charge of the departments most vitally concerned with tribal problems. The very positive reaction of the government to these reports—a reaction one could hardly imagine coming in that form from any minister in 1979—can best be outlined by quoting some passages from Grigson's foreword:

> *The problems of the Hyderabad aboriginal areas are in kind exactly similar to the problems of aboriginal areas elsewhere in India.... Conditions in fact in the tribal areas of Hyderabad differ only from those in the Central Provinces in that in the Hyderabad areas till recently no determined effort had been made by district officials to keep their subordinates in check and prevent the extortion by them from the aboriginals of* mamul, begar, rasad *and bribes or to fight the exploitation (with their connivance) of the aboriginals by cleverer immigrants, such as the Banjara, the Maratha, the Brahman, the Muslim, the* sahukar *and the* vakil, *the less scrupulous among whom have long found in the tribal areas a happy hunting ground.... The lessons [of these reports] should also be felt in non-tribal areas elsewhere in the State where villagers suffer from the unchecked oppression of that bad minority of the* deshmuks, watandars *and* sahukars *who thereby bring discredit on their order as a whole. The press and political bodies have in recent months drawn attention to such tyrannies in various parts of Telingana. But the tribal areas, where the local bully has the freest scope, are less in the public eye and have less news-value, and the offender there is perhaps more often a subordinate official than a* watandar *or a* sahukar.... *In backward forest tracts where men are poor and ignorant and distances great, justice delayed or justice that is not cheap is justice denied. What are needed are touring officers combining executive and judicial powers, able to punish the tyrant or the exploiter on the spot.*

Reading these comments thirty-five years after they were written, one cannot help feeling that the problem of the exploitation and oppression of tribals exists today as much as it existed then and that neither *sahukars* nor minor government officials have mended their ways to any great extent.

As a result of the interest shown by Grigson in the conditions in the tribal areas of Hyderabad State a number of ameliorative measures were taken which in a short time transformed the atmosphere, at least in Adilabad District, where as recently as 1940 ten Gonds had been killed in a bloody clash between tribals and policemen. A detailed account of this mini-rebellion is given elsewhere; here it suffices to say that the measures instituted by government soon changed the tribesmen's mood of gloom and despair to one of hope and confidence in the future.

A beginning was made in 1943 when a scheme for the training of Gond teachers and the establishment of special schools for Gonds indicated a new concern by government for the welfare of the tribesmen. This was followed by the appointment of a special officer for the tribal area of Adilabad and the allotment of land on permanent tenure *(patta)* to numerous aboriginals, both Gonds and Kolams who until then had no legal titles to the land they and their forefathers had been cultivating, and who therefore had always been liable to eviction on various pretexts. These administrative measures were followed by the preparation of comprehensive legislation designed to afford protection to tribal populations. It was recognised that rights to land were of crucial importance. Only by placing aboriginals in a position in which they were safe in the possession of their land was it possible to free them once and for all from the threat of economic enslavement by moneylenders and landlords. Even before legislation recognised the aboriginals' prior rights to land, administrative measures and the instructions given to the officers entrusted with the task of looking after the tribals' welfare brought about a change in the whole attitude to the aboriginals. The extortion of illegal fees which minor government servants, such as forest guards or police constables, used to collect from the villagers was stopped or at least greatly reduced simply by the enforcement of stricter discipline, and, while it was clearly impracticable to eradicate all cases of corruption, a great improvement in the situation was soon noticeable. By 1946 the conditions of the Gonds in most parts of Adilabad District had changed out of all recognition, and a community which used to be seriously underprivileged became suddenly the "most favoured" ethnic group in the region.

In recognition of the need for the creation of a special agency for the implementation of the new policy vis-a-vis the tribals of the state, the Nizam's government established a new department known as the Social Service Department, attached to the Revenue Department and headed by the adviser for tribes and backward classes. This department consisted of a number of gazetted officers, as well as of social service inspectors and organisers, all of whom were posted in tribal areas. Existing special tribes officers, who were in the rank of deputy collector and had been drawn from the Revenue Department, were incorporated in the cadre of the Social Service Department, whereas the more junior posts of inspectors and organisers were filled by graduates with qualifications in social anthropology or sociology. After gaining experience in administration many of these directly recruited graduates were promoted to gazetted posts and ultimately replaced the special tribes officers drawn from the Revenue Department.

The culmination of the entire tribal policy of Hyderabad State was the promulgation of an act known as the Tribal Areas Regulation 1356 Fasli (1946 A.D.). This regulation empowered the government to "make such rules as appear to them to be necessary or expedient for the better administration of any notified tribal area in respect of tribals and of their relations with non-tribals." The substance of this regulation was incorporated in the Tribal Areas Regulation 1359 Fasli (1949 A.D) and the rules giving effect to its provisions were issued by the Revenue Department under the title Notified Tribal Areas Rules 1359 Fasli on 16 November 1949. A schedule annexed to the Tribal Areas Regulation notified as "tribal" 384 specified villages in Adilabad District plus all the 169 villages of Utnur Taluk, and 156 specified villages in Warangal District plus all the villages of Yellandu Taluk minus 3 named villages and all the villages of the Taluk and Samasthan of Paloncha minus 6 named villages. The schedule described the area to which the Notified Tribal Areas Rules were to apply.

The establishment of tribal *panchayat* backed by the authority of government gave the tribesmen confidence that they could run their own affairs without outside interference. Some of these *panchayat,* whose proceedings I was able to observe when revisiting Adilabad District in the early 1950s, worked extraordinarily well, and though the rules did not prescribe the keeping of records, cases and decisions were carefully recorded. In one village of Utnur Taluk, Mankapur, which had a powerful and greatly respected headman, such a *panchayat,* attended by members from several villages, was still functioning in 1980, even though the Tribal Areas Regulation which had invested it with authority had long been repealed.

The Gonds of Adilabad District still speak with nostalgia of the time when the Tribal Areas Regulation was in force and officers of the Social Service Department worked among them, for at that time they were secure in the possession of their land, and exploitation by outsiders had been greatly reduced. The presence of officers of the Social Service Department acted as a check even on the high-handedness of forest guards and *patwari,* who knew that corrupt practices and the extortion of illegal fees would be reported to their superiors.

Even after the partition of Hyderabad State in 1956 and the merging of the Telengana districts with the Andhra districts in the new State of Andhra Pradesh, the Hyderabad Tribal Areas Regulation of 1949 remained in force for seven more years. Unfortunately for the aboriginals of the Telengana districts, this regulation was repealed in 1963 and replaced by the Andhra Pradesh Scheduled Areas Land Transfer Regulation, 1959. While the latter regulation also protected the land of tribals, prohibiting any transfer to non-tribals, it did not contain any provision for the maintenance of tribal *panchayat,* and more importantly stripped the social service officers of the authority and judicial powers with which the Hyderabad regulation and rules had invested them.

The enforcement of the laws prohibiting the transfer of tribal land to non-tribals was now left to the ordinary revenue officials, who had neither the inclination nor the time to concern themselves with the welfare of the tribals. They were also much more exposed to the pressure of vested interest than the officers of the Social Service Department had been. Moreover, the authority of the civil courts, which the Hyderabad Tribal Areas Regulation had set aside in all cases involving tribal land, was now fully restored, and any non-tribal whose occupation of tribal land was challenged by a revenue official could, and still can, lodge an appeal in a civil court. The immediate consequence of all these changes was the alienation of large areas of tribal land in several of the taluks of Adilabad District.

Some relief to the tribals threatened by non-tribal landgrabbers was subsequently provided by amendments of the Land Transfer Regulation. 1959, enacted in 1970 and 1971, which prohibit all transfer of land in scheduled areas, not only from tribal to non-tribal but even from non-tribal to non-tribal, by providing for conducting *suo moto* enquiries into non-tribal occupations of lands in tribal areas and for the restoration of such land to the tribal owner if the non-tribal is an illegal occupant, and by prohibiting attachment of tribal land in execution of money decrees. The absolute ban on transfer of immovable property in scheduled areas to non-tribals from a tribal or non-tribal except in the case of partition or devolution by succession, large areas of tribal land were in fact illegally occupied by non-tribals in the years 1970 to 1979.

Protection of the tribesmen against the alienation of their land, which in Hyderabad State was the cornerstone of tribal policy, seems to have taken second place in the thinking of planners as soon as tribal development was merged with the multisided activities of programmes known as Community Development and extending throughout India as part of the first Five Year Plan, which commenced in 1952. Community projects were not particularly geared to tribal needs, and in Andhra Pradesh only one out of four pilot projects covered tribal areas. In the second Five Year Plan there was a greater concentration on specific tribal areas, and the projects were now renamed Multipurpose Projects. In Andhra Pradesh four such projects covered predominantly tribal areas: one in Utnur Taluk of Adilabad District, one in Narsampet Taluk of Warangal District, and two in Vishakhapatnam District.

The effectiveness of these projects was assessed in the Government of India Report of the Committee on Special Multipurpose Tribal Blocks, 1960, in which Verrier Elwin played a leading role. This committee found that the programmes lacked a specific tribal bias, with the result that non-tribals residing within the project areas benefited from the funds expended more than the tribals. Officials in charge of the projects were more concerned about spending the allocated funds, often on inessential and elaborate buildings, than on meeting the urgent needs of the tribals. The committee recommended a change of priorities and emphasised that officials in charge of projects in tribal areas should not be transferred for a minimum of three years.

In the third Five Year Plan period, Multipurpose Projects were renamed Tribal Development Blocks, and twenty-four of these were located in Andhra Pradesh, coveting most areas of tribal concentration. There was no major change in strategy during the fourth Five Year Plan, but it was during this period that in several tribal areas, notably that of Srikakulam District, the eruption of politically motivated violence reflected the shortcomings of the state's tribal policy. While these eruptions were undoubtedly sparked by a widespread revolutionary movement commonly known as Naxalite, their initial impact and support by large numbers of tribesmen showed very clearly the latter's resentment of the unrelenting pressure which advanced populations exerted on their resources.

The response of the government to the Naxalite-led tribal unrest was a repetition of official reaction to earlier rebellions. Ruthless suppression by police freely using automatic arms against tribesmen wielding bows and arrows and the occasional outdated gun was followed by remedial measures, long overdue but never implemented as long as the tribals were docile and law-abiding. Enactment of debt relief, restoration of tribal land, and various welfare measures such as nutritional aid for children were intended to placate the restive tribals.

With the commencement of the fifth Five Year Plan in 1977 an administrative setup known as the Integrated Tribal Development Agency was inaugurated. In this, high priority is being given to agricultural development, largely by provision of minor irrigation schemes. At the same time communications are to be improved and electricity brought even to backward areas. In order to provide employment for landless tribals, the establishment of minor industries is envisaged, and the Girijan Cooperative Corporation is supposed to provide improved marketing facilities for minor forest produce and to supply to tribals many of their basic needs. In pursuance of these aims Integrated Tribal Development Projects were prepared for specific areas of tribal concentration, or in some cases for individual tribal groups.

The successes and failures of the integrated approach, but anticipating such an analysis it may be stated that many of the plans under the Integrated Tribal Development Agency are admirable on paper, but have suffered from grave deficiencies in their implementation.

The administrative machinery designed to carry out the various development schemes consists in each of the districts containing tribal blocks of a project officer and a tribal welfare officer, both of whom are usually posted at the district headquarters. There are no officers of the Tribal Welfare Department at taluk or block level, and the implementation of most of the development schemes falls thus to the block development officers and the village development officers, neither of whom have been trained in the treatment of specifically tribal problems. The attitude of many of them ranges therefore from conscientious but unimaginative application to outright lethargy. Many good schemes break down because of the disinterest of local officials, while, on the other hand, an active and dedicated project officer can inspire officials at block level to evince commitment and real efficiency. Yet frequent transfers among the officials at all levels have proved damaging to programmes however well funded and well-thought-out they may have been.

It is inherent in any plan for the protection and support of tribal minorities that whatever benefits are envisaged for tribesmen must adversely affect the interests of some more advanced sections of the population. Alienation of tribal land cannot be prevented without depriving non-tribal landowners of the chance to enlarge their holdings, a curb on exploitation by moneylenders interferes with the activities of local businessmen, and any attempt to eradicate corrupt practices of minor officials diminishes the income such persons are accustomed to derive from dealings with ignorant and illiterate tribals. Thus any policy of tribal rehabilitation arouses the opposition of vested interests. When the Nizam's government embarked on schemes for the betterment of tribals, there arose a good deal of resentment among members of the landlord and business community in districts such as Adilabad, and this resentment led to attacks on the policy in the press. But a system of benevolent autocracy could easily dismiss such attacks by vested interests, whereas nowadays similar vested interests can affluence members of the Legislative Assembly and through them even ministers, with the result that measures designed to benefit tribal minorities tend to be watered down or abandoned altogether. In such situations officers sympathetic to tribals and assiduous in the protection of their interests are likely to be transferred and replaced by officers more pliable to the wishes of locally powerful pressure groups. It is therefore no exaggeration to say that only an administration of high integrity can successfully implement a policy of tribal development, and it would seem that the failure of many plans for tribal betterment is due to the lack of such integrity in high places and not to any inherent fault in the plans worked out by civil servants.

A few quotations from a report prepared in 1975 by D. Bandyopadhyaya, Joint Secretary, Ministry of Labour, Government of India, and B.N. Yugandhar, Special Assistant to the Deputy Chairman, Planning Commission, will indicate that government officials are fully aware of the reasons for the justified sense of grievance felt by so many tribal populations. The two civil servants visited the Parvathipuram Agency of Srikakulam District at a time when the activities of Naxalite rebels had passed their climax. After several meetings with groups of local tribes they wrote:

The Girijans came in touch with the administration only in a state of confrontation when they were tackled for infringement or infraction of one or the other regulation which in fact abridged, annulled or tinkered with their customary rights and privileges. Thus the Girijans of the Parvathipuram agency tract found themselves totally alienated from the administrative machinery and newly set up self-governing institutions and were denied opportunities of gainful economic activities. They suffered not only from poverty but also from a deep sense of insecurity. They found themselves deprived at each point and at each front. A deep sense of grievance and injustice enveloped the entire tribal population through decades of neglect by the local administration. The indifference and the neglect was so much that when the agency tracts were redefined large areas of hill tracts inhabited by the tribal Girijans were left outside the agency through an administrative mistake.... Later attempts by some energetic district officials to bring them within the fold of the agency tracts have not met with any success.... The Girijan is suspicious of every move of the administration. He cannot rely on it. Today after the experience he had of [the Naxalite] movement and its consequences, he is slightly confounded but not cowed down. He has a sullen look and defiance is apparent.

When I visited Srikakulam in 1979 the atmosphere had greatly changed. By the restoration of thousands of acres to their erstwhile tribal owners and the expenditure of large amounts of money on various welfare measures the government had gained the confidence of the majority of the tribals, while the former exploiters, intimidated by the violence of the Naxalite movement, had not dared to resume their domineering role. Thus the Naxalite rebels had in a way achieved their aim by stimulating the government to tackle the tribal problem and by breaking the power of those who used to exploit and oppress the tribals.

In other districts of Andhra Pradesh, where there has been no spontaneous uprising against the tyranny of landlords, moneylenders, and oppressive petty officials, the position of the tribal populations is far less happy.

7

Tribal Traditions, Society and Culture in India

There can be little dispute that the socio-cultural norms, practices, and rituals in the mainstream Hindu tradition subsume a deep ideological repugnance towards gender equality. But this contrasts with the country's overall tribal culture and society. Indeed, the latter, which has for long been exterior to the patently patriarchal and caste-hierarchical Hindu socio-cultural orbit, is traditionally characterised by a high degree of gender equity with its many admirable demographic concomitants (for example, lower infant and child mortality and fertility). However, India's tribal peoples have not exactly been insulated from the mainstream society and culture, and they have indeed been absorbing since long many of the mainstream socio-cultural features and values, particularly kinship patterns including gender inequities and biases. None can possibly doubt that this is a disturbing trend contrary to the oft-proclaimed goal of effacing India's 'infamous' distinction of being a land of deep-rooted anti-female biases and discriminations. Ironically enough, as I argue here, it is some of the basic values and ideology imbibed in the traditional tribal socio-cultural milieus that should have been emulated and promoted amongst the non-tribal mainstream, not, as has been going on, the other way round.

The term 'tribe', as is widely known, subsumes enormous complexities—both anthropological and historical. However, the British India Censuses used to enumerate tribes as Animists until the 1931 Census, in which they were categorised as those practicing 'Tribal Religion'. Thus, up to the 1941 Census, the criterion of primitive or tribal religion enabled the British census authorities to bypass many complex anthropological issues surrounding the notion of 'tribe' or 'tribal'.

Kingsley Davis, a celebrated authority on India's demography, who pioneered the imaginative and meticulous use of British India's Census information, calculated the number of children aged 0-4 years per 1000 women (this is called child-woman ratio, CWR for short) as a rough measure of human fertility, which turned to be the highest for the aggregate tribal people amongst all major religious groups in the early twentieth century. In explaining the fertility of overall tribes, whom Davis called 'most prolific', he invokes a notion of 'aboriginals' naturally high fertility', coupled with the Indian tribes' permissiveness of widow remarriage not permitted amongst the Hindus.

However, whether the fertility of the 'aboriginal' people is (and/or had been historically) particularly high in the global context is far from conclusive. For example, there have been for long some fertility-suppressing features of the traditional tribal marriage system. Indeed India's tribal females used to get married traditionally much later than their Hindu counterparts, apart from the former's higher rate of celibacy. Besides, a higher CWR in a section of the population could also obtain if the relative mortality of children vis-à-vis adults was comparatively low in comparison with other section of the population and/or if vice versa. For instance, if the tribal maternal mortality were sufficiently high, a higher CWR in the tribal population could go hand in hand with a lower average number of children born per tribal woman. Indeed, the Report of the Census of 1911 on Central Provinces and Berar reported 'more than proportionate death-rate of women in child-birth'. In the same vein, the Census of 1931 information shows that 'while the proportion of aged people is comparatively small among the tribal people, that of children 0-5 years is decidedly higher than it is among the higher castes; among Hindus it is 15 per cent but among the tribal it is 19 per cent'. This is what researchers have sometimes called 'phenomenal absence of aged people among the tribal people'. Thus, the relatively low infant and child mortality (vis-à-vis adults) in the tribal population, if true, could provide a clue simultaneously to their relatively high CWR on the one hand and a stability of their relative population size vis-à-vis a secular decline for the Hindus over the first half of the twentieth century on the other. In fact our own demographic estimates (based on an 'indirect demographic technique') show lower levels of both mortality and fertility among aggregate tribal people than those of the Hindus in the early last century India, reinforcing further doubts on Davis' hypothesis of highest tribal fertility. A brief overall portrayal of an admirable demographic regime (that is, relatively low fertility and mortality) among India's tribes sounds pretty vivid in the following remarks made as late as 1985 by C. von Fürer-Haimendorf, a celebrated authority on Indian tribes over the large part of the last century:

> ....only one or two generations ago many tribal communities enjoyed the advantages of a well-balanced ecology fully in tune with the natural resources of their environment and boast an overall quality of life superior in many ways to that of large sections of the Indian rural population. Adequate food-supplies, non-exploitative social structure, freedom from indebtedness and other forms of dependence on non-tribal outsiders, equality of the sexes and a remarkable tolerance in all interpersonal relations were outstanding characteristics of such tribal societies. Moreover there seems to be no reason to assume that their way of life could not have continued for the foreseeable future without requiring any aid from outside sources, particularly as in most tribal areas there was no excessive population growth threatening the ecological balance.

First, some leading anthropologists of British India reported about the (relatively) low fertility and also about their use of indigenous methods of birth control (including abortion) in some major tribal communities such as the Baiga, the Gonds of central India. Also, the traditional tribal custom of relatively late entry into marital union (vis-à-vis the Hindus) should also have been a contributory factor towards a lower tribal fertility. In the early twentieth century India, about fifty per cent Hindu females aged 10-14 years were found 'married' as against the corresponding tribal proportion of only twenty per cent. While ninety per cent of Hindu females in 15-19 year age group got married (in the Madras Presidency in 1921), about half of the tribal counterparts were found in the 'never-married' state (for example, in Central Provinces and Berar). The proportion of 'unmarried' women aged 20-24 years used to be about three times as large in overall tribal population as compared to that of their Hindu counterparts. For example, the average age of marriage of tribal females in Mysore was found to be 18.1 years in the 1901 Census, as against only 14 years among their Hindu counterparts. A typical tribal girl has traditionally been far more 'liberated' than her Hindu counterpart so as to choose the prospective groom through, as it were, pre-marital love affairs and somewhat free mixing with the prospective spouses.

H.H. Risley, India's Census Commissioner in the early twentieth century, wrote about Santhali girls getting 'married as adults mostly to men of their own choice.. [while] high-caste Hindus marry their daughters between the ages eight and twelve'. Even in case of some tribes like Bondos, 'girls prefer to marry younger boys'. Added to this was a much higher celibacy rate among the tribal females too. According to the Census information for 1911 and 1921 in such locations as Bihar, Orissa, Bombay, the proportion of never-married tribal women in their forties—though it was smaller than in historical Europe—has been much larger than (for example, three-four times) the figures for their Hindu counter-parts. This presumably has exerted a negative influence on the fertility of the tribal population (vis-a-vis that of the Hindus). However, the proportion of widowed women (who are outside the realm of conceptions) has generally been much less among tribals—a fact which, as was much emphasised by Davis, should have put an upward pressure on the tribal fertility (vis-a-vis that of Hindus).

However, the fertility-suppressing effects of the traditional tribal nuptial features (for example, relatively late marriage and high celibacy) seem to have been, on balance, no less—indeed somewhat greater—than those resulting from the Hindus' social sanction against widow remarriage. This—in the absence of direct information on past fertility levels by social group—provides (at least) some indirect evidence of a lower—or (at least) not higher—tribal fertility than that of the Hindus as far back as the early last century.

Tribal customs of relatively delayed female marriage resemble some of the typical European marriage patterns, wherein an adult male has to work and wait for marriage until he has accumulated enough savings for setting up his independent household (and in addition in case of tribal males, for often paying a bride price—albeit nominal and/or rather symbolic). It was not really rare among the Hos of Chhotanagpur for a tribal girl to wait till her mid-thirties before her prospective/chosen groom could save at least as much as to pay for the bride-price. Thus like large parts of historical Europe where fertility had been comparatively low owing to delayed marriage and high incidence of spinster-hood, Indian tribes, too, historically used to marry late with the result of their relatively low fertility. Even in the more recent past researchers have found (comparatively) low tribal fertility in various Indian locations, which is largely attributable to their traditional marriage patterns resembling those of historical Europe (that is, relatively delayed marriage and high proportion of never married).

IT can be argued that above-noted traditional tribal features of marriage reflect, and/or partly stem from, a greater female autonomy and status that have historically been the hallmarks of overall tribal culture and society in India. For example, the Report of the Census of India 1901 wrote about Santhali girls that 'they generally married men of their own choice [and] sexual intercourse before marriage is tacitly recognised'. Indeed, the evidence—albeit scattered—of higher female status/autonomy in almost all walks of life (for example, decision-making, freedom of movement) in tribal societies abounds in the Indian anthropological literature. These traditional tribal features of marriage, consistent with and/or founded on a high degree of female autonomy and gender equity, reflect in turn a socio-cultural framework/structure which is conducive to producing (relatively) 'superior' demographic outcomes (for example, low fertility and infant and child mortality). The above argument is reaffirmed by a considerable contemporary evidence for the mainstream population showing a close inverse association between various indicators of female status/ autonomy and major demographic outcomes such as fertility and infant and child mortality.

Historically, the more patriarchal Hindu society—pretty distinct from the overall tribal traditional kinship features—has had inherent fertility-raising forces. First, in the former the control over fertility decisions typically rests with the older members, who can often derive disproportionately large benefits from a large family. Second, woman's insecurity arising from her economic and social dependence on men, breeds a strong desire in her to produce as many sons as, and as soon as, possible as an insurance against the risk of events which threaten her wellbeing (such as loss of husband's support). Various restrictions on female autonomy are often likely to suppress innovative behaviours favourable to reproductive regulation and control. Since a large part of the cost of child-bearing/rearing is borne by women (for example, captivity during pregnancy, risk of maternal complications and death), women's inherent disincentives against frequent childbirth remain greatly suppressed by stark patriarchal subjugation.

Higher levels of population sex-ratio [that is, the number of females per 1000 males] and women's participation in directly productive work are generally held to mirror higher degrees of gender equality and female autonomy. Historically, more balanced gender relations in the tribal communities (vis-a-vis the Hindu population) are amply testified by the former's far more balanced sex-ratio. For instance, the Report of the Census of India 1931 read as follows: '[t]he general conclusion as to the sex ratios of India proper is therefore that in the aboriginal tribes the numbers of two sexes are approximately equal, whereas in the rest of the community males exceed females.' (Government of India 1931: 200) Notwithstanding a certain degree of inter-regional and inter-tribal variations in sex-ratios, a higher level of gender equality among the overall tribal population has historically been borne out—albeit somewhat indirectly—by the latter's much higher proportion of females in the total population than ever found for the mainstream Hindu population.

Also, relatively high levels of productive participation of tribal females are widely known. In fact, post-independence Census data clearly testify to this, and there can hardly be any reason why this should not have been the case in the early last century and even before.

In fact, India's historical ethnography and other kinds of evidence provide distinct (though somewhat scattered) indications of a high degree of work participation (or sharing) of tribal females —a fact which reflects and perhaps reinforces comparatively high levels of autonomy, equality, and social position of tribal women. As noted already, the latter should have had bearings favourable to the relatively low fertility of tribal women as compared to their Hindu counterparts. Indeed, contemporary statistical exercises—though undertaken generally for communities belonging to the non-tribal mainstream—show a strong negative association between female labour force participation and fertility level.

Many overall tribal socio-cultural features have historically been favourable not only to relatively lower fertility, but to a comparatively lower mortality too, particularly among infants and children. First, the relatively long birth interval and low fertility—which are the traditionally known features of the tribal community —are conducive to better survival chances of infants and children. Second, lesser gender biases in tribal societies should also be partly instrumental to better survival outcomes, health, and wellbeing of infants and children. Moreover, tribal habitations generally have some healthy features such as less crowding and more intimate relationship with nature, apart from some of their traditional practices favourable to infant and child health, namely, prolonged breastfeeding and early food supplementation.

Even in the more recent period the evidence of relatively longer breastfeeding and lower risk of conception has often been found among tribal women (vis-a-vis their non-tribal counterparts), who give 'solid food to their infants after six months post-partum and most of them continue with breast feeding'. A relative mortality advantage of the tribal children is often discernible in more recent periods—albeit in an increasingly subdued form with time.

A few other good features of infant and childcare practices among tribes include holding infants and children vertically during most of waking time and a closer physical contact with mothers. In contrast, many mainstream (non-tribal) customs during childbirth and afterwards are often reported to be inimical to the survival chances of the infant. In this context an illuminating excerpt from the Bengal Report of the Census of 1881 on the mortality advantage of tribal children vis-a-vis Hindus is worth noting:

For the years of infant life from the beginning of the first to the end of the fourth complete year the percentage of living children to the whole population is higher among the aboriginal tribes [18.20] than among the followers of any other religion [14.03 for Hindus; 15.77 for Muslims]. ...and the fact affords a fresh illustration of the well-known law that the productive powers of man are in inverse proportion to the standard of luxury which has reached; and that given a sufficient quantity of food without excessive hardships of climate, the off-spring of the primitive tribes is more numerous and more healthy than that of their more civilised neighbours. More particularly is this case in India, for it is impossible to conceive customs more prejudicial to the chances of survival than those which prevail both among Hindus and Mohamedans at the birth of a child [for example, suffocating atmosphere created by closed windows, smoke and overcrowd. (Italics added)

Furthermore, the absence on the whole of the child (and/or early) marriage practice among the majority of tribes particularly in the past was probably instrumental (partly) in ensuring a mortality advantage in infancy, as the risk of death is often higher among infants of very young mothers. The lower tribal fertility itself—to the extent it results from longer birth spacing and prolonged breastfeeding—could contribute to a lower infant and childhood mortality. Relatedly, a somewhat better nutritional level of the tribal children could also arise—in line with recent empirical studies of poorer households—from a greater female autonomy/command over resources in tribal households.

Tribes, who generally inhabit relatively less crowded settlements and in close intimacy with natural environments, for example, forest and hill, are globally known to have fared better in mortality terms in the past. Insofar as this has have been particularly true prior to the age of mass scale use of antibiotics/antibodies and vaccines, this should have been a veritable scenario for the majority of Indian tribes too in the past, with indigenous healing methods and herbal medicines having been relatively effective in these societies ever more close to nature. Besides, the tribal people—partly because of these healthy aspects of their habitation, and partly due to their isolation from mainstream population—were probably relatively less inflicted by epidemics. Although evidence in support of this hypothesis in the Indian context is hard to find, there is some evidence elsewhere [for example, the mortality effect of the great Influenza Pandemic of 1918 being relatively less pronounced among pygmies and bushmen of the Kalahari desert]. Furthermore, the spread and transmission of disease and associated elevation of mortality among aggregate tribal population has often been viewed as one of the many negative fallouts of their increasing contact/assimilation with the mainstream (non-tribal) population.

A few more plausible hypotheses relating to a relative mortality advantage among India's tribal population in the past can also be adduced. For example, the malaria, which had remained almost the largest killer particularly during the period considered here, might have been less in tribal habitations in relatively high altitude and with greater dryness. Indeed the incidence of diarrhoeal and respiratory diseases might have been relatively less among the tribal people because of their greater dependence on spring waters and lesser density and crowding. As one eminent anthropologist, W. Handwerker, notes, 'foraging societies experience relatively low levels of infant and child mortality due to synergistic effects of nutritional patterns yielding adequate growing and maintenance requirements and a relatively low incidence of infectious disease'. Apart from historical advantage in the mortality of Indian tribes as a whole, there are other good reasons (relating to, for example, marriage, gender relations and social organisation) to expect tribal fertility to have been lower than that amongst the Hindus in the historical past. Also, as noted already, the tribal people were familiar with some indigenous medicines (for example, herbal) and methods of prevention of conceptions (including abortion), apart from prolonged breastfeeding, longer birth intervals, and perhaps somewhat greater incidence of sterility and infertility—both primary and secondary—in tribal communities.

The historic regime of comparatively low fertility and mortality among the overall tribal population continued to be echoed—albeit greatly subdued—in the contemporary periods. Alas, more lately much of this historic superiority in terms of demographic outcomes and the many commensurately admirable socio-cultural characteristics of the aggregate tribal world in India has withered away. This reversal, ironically, is not because the mainstream society has increasingly taken to admittedly admirable traditional socio-cultural/kinship/nuptial features of the tribes (for example, greater gender equity, female autonomy). On the contrary, increasing material benefits, ramifications, and socio-cultural spin-offs of the relentless flows of modern technology, comfort-enhancing commodities, and faster communications, which are over-whelmingly confined to the non-tribal mainstream, have placed the present tribal communities in a relatively stark material and demographic disadvantage. More damagingly, many tribes currently appear in an increasingly poor light in terms of their many socio-cultural parameters, which are otherwise just the metamorphosed outcomes of their longstanding infliction by the mainstream ideology, society, and culture. Thus, it is well-neigh a 'tragedy', surely one amongst many others in our 'land of tamashas', that 'tribals are identified by non-tribal caste-structured society as culturally inferior and are referred to by pejoratives such as junglee (rowdy, jungle-man) and karparaj (nigger)'.

TRIBAL CULTURES OF INDIA

One has to love tribal culture in India to understand the uniqueness of their culture. Warm hospitality, simple ways of living and sincere judgment of the opinions are some of the traits that mark the tribal cultures of India. Their custom depicts their belief in simplicity. Most of the tribes in India have their own gods and goddesses that reflects the dependence of Tribal people on nature. Except for the few most of the tribes in India is sociable, hospitable, and fun loving along with strong community bonds. Some of the tribes shares patriarchal cultural ties and some of the tribal societies are women oriented. They have their own festivals and celebrations. The tribal people are clinging to their identity despite of the external influences that threatened the tribal culture especially after their post independence turbulent period. However it is seen that Christianity has bought a change that can be termed as a total transformation in the tribal lifestyle and out look particularly in the North Eastern states of India. Of late it has been discovered that the efforts of the missionaries were not at directed in changing the basic customs of the tribal society.

ADIVASI CONTRIBUTIONS TO INDIAN CULTURE AND CIVILIZATION

Adivasi traditions and practices pervade all aspects of Indian culture and civilization, yet this awareness is often lacking in popular consciousness, and the extent and import of Adivasi contributions to Indian philosophy, language and custom have often gone unrecognized, or been underrated by historians and social scientists.

Although popular myths about Buddhism have obscured the original source and inspiration for it's humanist doctrine, it is to India's ancient tribal (or Adivasi) societies that Gautam Buddha looked for a model for the kind of society he wished to advocate. Repulsed by how greed for private property was instrumental in causing poverty, social exploitation and unending warfare-he saw hope for human society in the tribal republics that had not yet come under the sway of authoritarian rule and caste discrimination. The early Buddhist *Sanghas* were modelled on the tribal pattern of social interaction that stressed gender equality, and respect for all members. Members of the *Sanghas* sought to emulate their egalitarian outlook and democratic functioning.

At that time, the tribal republics retained many aspects of social equality that can still be found in some Adivasi societies that have somehow escaped the ill-effects of commercial plunder and exploitation. Adivasi society was built on a foundation of equality with respect for all life forms including plants and trees. There was a deep recognition of mutual dependence in nature and human society. People were given respect and status according to their contribution to social needs but only while they were performing that particular function. A priest could be treated with great respect during a religious ceremony or a doctor revered during a medical consultation, but once such duties had been performed, the priest or doctor became equal to everyone else. The possession of highly valued skills or knowledge did not lead to a permanent rise in status. This meant that no individual or small group could engage in overlordship of any kind, or enjoy hereditary rights.

Such a value-system was sustainable as long as the Adivasi community was non-acquisitive and all the products of society were shared. Although division of labour did take place, the work of society was performed on a cooperative and co-equal basis-without prejudice or disrespect for any form of work.

It was the simplicity, the love of nature, the absence of coveting the goods and wealth of others, and the social harmony of tribal society that attracted Gautam Buddha, and had a profound impact on the ethical core of his teachings.

Nevertheless, tribal societies were under constant pressure as the money economy grew and made traditional forms of barter less difficult to sustain. In matters of trade, the Adivasis followed a highly evolved system of honour. All agreements that they entered into were honoured, often the entire tribe chipping in to honour an agreement made by an individual member of the tribe. Individual dishonesty or deceit were punished severely by the tribe. An individual who acted in a manner that violated the honour of the tribe faced potential banishment and family members lost the right to participate in community events during the period of punishment. But often, tribal integrity was undermined because the non-tribals who traded with the Adivasis reneged on their promises and took advantage of the sincerity and honesty of most members of the tribe. Tribal societies came under stress due to several factors. The extension of commerce, military incursions on tribal land, and the resettling of Brahmins amidst tribal populations had an impact, as did ideological coercion or persuasion to attract key members of the tribe into "mainstream" Hindu society. This led to many tribal communities becoming integrated into Hindu society as *jatis* (or castes) while others who resisted were pushed into the hilly or forested areas, or remote tracks that had not yet been settled. In the worst case, defeated Adivasi tribes were pushed to the margins of settled society and became discriminated as outcastes and "untouchables". But spontaneous differentiation within tribal societies also took place over time, which propelled these now unequal tribal communities into integrating into Hindu society without external violence or coercion. In Central India, ruling dynasties emerged from within the ranks of tribal society.

In any case, the end result was that throughout India, tribal deities and customs, creation myths and a variety of religious rites and ceremonies came to absorbed into the broad stream of "Hindu" society. In the Adivasi traditions, ancestor worship, worship of fertility gods and goddesses (as well as male and female fertility symbols), totemic worship-all played a role. And they all found their way into the practice of what is now considered Hinduism. The widespread Indian practice of keeping *'vratas'*, i.e. fasting for wish-fulfilment or moral cleansing also has Adivasi origins.

Mahashweta Devi has shown that both Shiva and Kali have tribal origins as do Krishna and Ganesh. In the 8th century, the tribal forest goddess or harvest goddess was absorbed and adapted as Siva's wife. Ganesh owes it's origins to a powerful tribe of elephant trainers whose incorporation into Hindu society was achieved through the deification of their elephant totem. In his study of Brahmin lineages in Maharashtra, Kosambi points to how many Brahmin gotras (such as *Kashyapa)* arose from tribal totems such as *Kachhapa* (tortoise). In Rajasthan, Rajput rulers recognised the Adivasi *Bhil* chiefs as allies and *Bhils* acquired a central role in some Rajput coronation ceremonies.

India's regional languages such as Oriya, Marathi or Bengali developed as a result of the fusion of tribal languages with

Sanskrit or Pali and virtually all the Indian languages have incorporated words from the vocabulary of Adivasi languages.

Adivasis who developed an intimate knowledge of various plants and their medicinal uses played an invaluable role in the development of Ayurvedic medicines. In a recent study, the All India Coordinated Research Project credits Adivasi communities with the knowledge of 9000 plant species-7500 used for human healing and veterinary health care. Dental care products like *datun,* roots and condiments like *turmeric* used in cooking and ointments are also Adivasi discoveries, as are many fruit trees and vines. Ayurvedic cures for arthritis and night blindness owe their origin to Adivasi knowledge. Adivasis also played an important role in the development of agricultural practices-such as rotational cropping, fertility maintenance through alternating the cultivation of grains with leaving land fallow or using it for pasture. Adivasis of Orissa were instrumental in developing a variety of strains of rice.

Adivasi musical instruments such as the *bansuri* (flute) and *dhol* (drum), folk-tales, dances and seasonal celebrations also found their way into Indian traditions as did their art and metallurgical skills.

In India's central belt, Adivasi communities rose to considerable prominence and developed their own ruling clans. The earliest Gond kingdom appears to date from the 10th C and the Gond Rajas were able to maintain a relatively independent existence until the 18th C., although they were compelled to offer nominal allegiance to the Mughal empire. The Garha-Mandla kingdom in the north extended control over most of the upper Narmada valley and the adjacent forest areas. The Deogarh-Nagpur kingdom dominated much of the upper Wainganga valley, while Chanda-Sirpur in the south consisted of territory around Wardha and the confluences of the Wainganga with the Penganga.

Jabalpur was one of the major centers of the Garha-Mandla kingdom and like other major dynastic capitals had a large fort and palace. Temples and palaces with extremely fine carvings and erotic sculptures came up throughout the Gond kingdoms. The Gond ruling clans enjoyed close ties with the Chandella ruling clans and both dynasties attempted to maintain their independence from Mughal rule through tactical alliances. Rani Durgavati of Jabalpur (of Chandella-Gond heritage) acquired a reputation of legendary proportions when she died in battle defending against Mughal incursions. The city of Nagpur was founded by a Gond Raja in the early 18th century.

IDENTITY AND CULTURE

Globalisation can be defined as the increasing "interconnectedness of the world through new systems of communication" (Sacks, 2003), and affects all areas of life. This ever-increasing capacity to communicate worldwide has resulted in the increasing domination of American and European cultures, whose economics, and political institutions are most affluent and powerful. This process has had profound effects on less powerful cultures. Development planners seem uncomfortable with ethnic diversity because it challenges the homogenizing tendency of economists to reduce populations to quantifiable groups. Globalisation is more than just about economics. It is not only about the ratio of exports to Gross Domestic Product (GDP) but also about culture, society, politics and people.

Globalisation becomes a problem from the cultural identity perspective. In the global economy, culture has almost become only a one-way operating manner of business cultural goods and services produced by rich and powerful countries have invaded all of the world's markets, placing people and cultures in other countries, which are unable to complete, at a disadvantage. These other countries have difficulties in presenting the cultural goods and services, which they have produced to the world market and therefore are not able to stand up to competition the natural result is that these countries are unable to enter the areas of influence occupied by multinational companies of developed countries.

The most disturbing element in the process of Globalisation is its relentless drive towards cultural universalism of American/ European culture and associated ideological frameworks, and its implied disregard and disrespect for cultural and language diversity. There are some 350 million indigenous people in more than 70 countries around the globe, speaking autochthonous languages, and who are marginalized and frequently denied basic human rights, including their cultural rights.

Globalisation has led to democratization and identity politics in third world countries. Political identity and cultural identity have become part and driving forces of democratization.

Third world societies like South Africa, Nigeria and India too have discovered that identity and cultural dynamics are intrinsic forces. While global trends in economics and politics are converging, cultural, religious and social differences seem to be widening. Globalisation and the revolution in communications technology bring people together, but also cause fears about loss of cultural identity. Simultaneously, literature, film, theatre, art, and dance productions often create a sense of belonging to a specific national, regional or ethnic zone.

Under Globalisation there has been a great expansion of western culture. Accusations of cultural imposition and domination have been widely heard. English language has emerged to a predominant position of being the language of communication within and between global organizations and institutions. It has become the transmission belt for western goods and services.

Globalisation involves extensive migrations of people both within and across states. The communication networks make other cultures shape one's way of life very intimately. They strengthen the fabric of culture, which increasingly confronts tendencies for cultural domination.

GLOBALIZATION AND TRIBALS IN INDIA

India is a land with many cultures, faiths, and ways of life, dress, food habits, traditions and rituals, united like petals of one flower. Its political, economic and socio-cultural contexts occur under conditions of a multi-structural whole. The national movement and the exposure to the western culture mediated by the colonial rule made Indians very self-conscious of their cultural identity. The anxieties about the impact of Globalization and marketisation of economy, media and information systems, the leisure and style of life etc, have today generated anxious debate among the scholars, the people and political parties. Such policy has long been in the making, but today the process of Globalization and its impact on culture, both local and national, give it a new urgency (Singh, 1994).

The word 'tribe' is generally used for a socially cohesive unit, associated with a territory, the members of which regard them as politically autonomous. Different tribes have their own cultures-dialects, life styles, social structures, rituals, values, etc., differing some what from those of the dominant non-tribal peasant social groups. The forest occupies a central position in tribal culture and economy. The tribal way of life is very much dictated by the forest right from birth to death. It is ironical that the poorest people of India are living in the areas of richest natural resources. Historically, tribals have been pushed to corners owing to economic interests of various dominant groups.

Colonisers have always considered tribal and indigenous people as a race to be conquered. Individuals and groups who do not meet the racialised standard have their political and cultural rights questions and sometimes violated. International indigenous organising activities increasingly rely on similar beliefs about there being a global indigenous race that is monolithically in opposition to technology and globalization. At risk is respect for the political authority and distinct cultural practices of indigenous peoples. This realization of tribal and indigenous peoples inhibits decolonization and political self-determination. The scope of trade and market, which are accelerated by the process of Globalization, poses formidable cultural problems in both the developed and the developing societies. The economic policy of India up to the 1980's has been that of import-substitution and protectionism in trade and market. The full momentum of the Globalization of economy started from 1990's onwards but many checks and balances continue to persist. This historical change in policy has impacts upon local cultures deeply in addition to having an overall cultural impact on the society.

The new changes have been noticed in the lifestyle, consumption pattern, production of cultural objects and their circulation and usages, in the cultural ecology and habitat and the religious practices, etc.

The impact of Globalization on local culture and the changing role of the nation-state can be examined by observing the particularities of the social and cultural patterns and their local, national and transnational manifestations in India. These social and cultural realities have plural character in terms of language, geography, ethnicity, religion and culture. With partial exception of the tribal population, the caste system and its related kinship structures have shaped the profile of the culture, economy and power structures within the local communities and regions. The new institutional innovations that Globalization may bring about in society are market, trade and finance, communication and media, technology and science, migration and inter-cultural transactions. In social structural terms, Globalization is a historical process of transition from the agrarian-industrial, post-industrial and finally the stage of the information society (Dissanayake, 1988).

Indigenous people are on the cusp of the crisis in sustainable development. Their communities are concrete examples of sustainable societies, historically evolved in diverse ecosystems. Today, they face the challenges of extinction or survival and renewal in a globalised world. The impact of globalization is strongest on these populations and they have no voice, therefore, easily swept aside by the invisible hand of the market and its proponents. Globalization is not merely a question of marginalization for indigenous peoples it is a multi-pronged attack on the very foundation of their existence and livelihoods.

INDIGENOUS CULTURES

The indigenous and ethnic people of the world have learnt to live in most hostile environmental condition in this universe. The most interesting feature associated with these indigenous and ethnic has been found that, they live in localities which are immensely rich in biodiversity. It is estimated that about 300 million indigenous people are living in world, out of which nearly half i.e. 150 million are living in Asia, about 30 million of which are living in Central and South America and a significant number of them are living in Australia, Europe,

New Zealand, Africa, and Soviet Union. These ethnic and indigenous people have played a vital role in conservation of environmental management and development process as they posse's traditional knowledge which has been useful in Eco-restoration. It has been noticed that these people know how to live with harmony in nature.

Indigenous Tribes in India

In India, 68 million people belonging to 227 ethnic group and comprising of 573 tribal communities derived from six racial stocks namely-Negroid, Proto-Australoid, Mongoloid, Mediterranean, West Breachy and Nordic exists in different part of the country (Pushpgandhan 1). These ethnic people mostly the indigenous tribals live close in the vicinity of forests and have managed and conserved the biodiversity of their localities since long time. These tribals take shelter from forest and utilize wild edible plants both raw and cooked. The flower and fruits are generally eaten raw where as tubers, leaves and seeds are cooked. Tribals utilize forest produce, forest timber and fuelwood. These tribals are living in forest since ages and have developed a kind of affinity with forests.

India is a country with large ethnic society and has immense wealth due to which it is rich in biodiversity. There are 45,000 species of wild plant out of which 9,500 species are ethnobotanically important species. Of these 7,500 species are in medicinal use for indigenous health practices. About 3,900 plant species are used by tribals as food (out of which 145 species comprise of root and tubers, 521 species of leafy vegetables, 101 species of bulbs and flowers, 647 species of fruits), 525 species are used for fiber, 400 species are used as fodder, 300 species are used in preparation and extraction of chemicals which are used as naturally occurring insecticides and pesticides, 300 species are used for extraction of gum, resins, dyes and perfume.

Indigenous Culture and Religions

In addition to these a number of plants are used as timber, building material and about 700 species are culturally important from moral, cultural, religious, aesthetic and social point of view of. Indian sub-contient is one of the twelve mega-centres of biodiversity representing two of the eighteen hotspots of biological diversity one occurring in Western Ghat and another in North-Eastern Himalaya. Floristically 141 endemic genera belonging to over 47 families of higher plant occur in India In India 11.95% of the world's biodiversity has been conserved by ethnic people in many ways (Arora,4). Botanical survey of India has reported 46,214 plant species are found in India of global flora of these 17,500 represents flowering plants. Thirty seven of these are endemic and found in North-East of India.

Indigenous Human Rights

One Indigenous Perspective of Human Rights, Irene Watson, an Indigenous lawyer and academic, provides a uniquely Indigenous view of "rights" with particular reference to the Draft UN Declaration on the Rights of Indigenous Peoples and the stonewalling that surrounds acceptance by some member states of the meaning and intent of the term "self-determination" as proposed by Indigenous Peoples. An especially significant element of Watson's chapter is the movement backwards and forwards between her strong Indigenous voice and her articulation of the law in the international human rights arena. Perhaps most appealing to this writer is her frank discussion in a footnote of the misconstruction and misperception surrounding the term "Aboriginal leadership". This discussion should rightfully be developed as a chapter in its own right.

Cultural Human Rights

India is a pluralistic and multi-cultural society where many faiths and belief systems regulate the life of individuals. India is not a Hindu society even though Hinduism is the religion of the vast majority of the people. In this part of the globe many religious traditions, both indigenous and foreign, have been established over the years. We have Buddhism, Sikhism, Bhakti cult, Sufi tradition as well as Islam and Christianity. Many religious gurus, law-givers, social reformers and statesmen have come to guide and influence the life and culture of Indians. The Mahabharata, the Ramayana, the Bhagvat Gita as well as the Quran, the Bible, the Guru Bani, etc., have moulded the thinking pattern and consciousness of Indians. So also the

Hindu caste system and the joint family pattern have a decisive influence on the followers of other religions.

CIVILIZATIONS AND SETTLEMENT SOCIETIES

This book deals with an unstated premise of the twentieth century paradigm for cultural development. This premise is that civilizations are the legitimate teleology of cultural development and that settlement societies like the plantation societies formed from the eighteenth century onwards ought to be considered as resting on the peripheries of developmental process. On the face of it, there is nothing wrong in this premise: in our quest for authenticity and ennobling ideals of human development, we do of course look upon civilizations as the pinnacle. But the reality of the politicization of culture introduces a kind of historical distortion in the myth of civilization. I need not dwell at length on the nature of this distortion which is manifest in our own country at this time and historical conjuncture in the *Mandir-Masjid* dispute. In this dispute the civilizational myth of Ram has been hijacked for extremely parochial and violent ends. I plead, therefore, for a reversal of analytical perspectives between civilizations and settlement societies at the end of the twentieth century.

THE PROBLEMATIC OF CULTURE : INDIA AS A CIVILIZATION

It is best to locate the problematic of culture in India — 'Unity in diversity', to put it briefly — in the framework of the kind of plural society that obtains in this land. Here the Furnivallian concept of plural society, which is characterized by (a) culturally incongruous and mutually incompatible socio-cultural sections, (b) having inter-relationships only of the market place, and (c) all kept together as a functioning whole by the exercise of a superordinate power, is clearly inapplicable. We shall be wrong to postulate at the start that the Indian unity lacks a common will. It will be argued that the Furnivallian paradigm applies only to 'settlement societies' and not to civilizations.

The Civilizational Synthesis of Culture

Here we might take a lead from the anthropological

conceptualizations of unity in diversity in India, and posit the existence of a Great Tradition and several little traditions. The civilizational process in Indian history can then be traced as a continuous and sustained interaction between the Great Tradition and little traditions. Whereas this resolution to the problematic of culture takes us part of the way to understanding the dynamics of the Indian civilizational process, it has two shortcomings:

(a) There is a tendency to put greater value and hegemony on the centralizing classical traditions and a commensurate under-playing of the regional and local (decentralizing) significance of the little traditions.

(b) The civilizational process tends to marginalize the problems of culture that are encountered in building the Indian nation (especially in the last two hundred years) and the Indian state (especially during the post-Independence period of last forty to fifty years).

The Decentralized Paradigm of Unity in Diversity

Here we must recall, (a) the issues raised in the process of nation-building in India, especially during the nationalist struggle, and (b) the cultural problems in the functioning of a federal state structure in India. As soon as we focus on the dominant thrust of the above problem areas two cultural problems, namely, clash and diversity of religion with its twin faces of communalism and the partition of the country into India and Pakistan, and the formation of linguistic states in India as the solution to centralization/decentralization dilemma come to the fore. In other words the decentralized paradigm of unity in diversity forces us to look closely at religion and language as forces of present discord and potential unity in the problematic of the Indian culture.

Religion and Language

Crisis and creativity in Indian culture: As regards the potential of Indian religions not only for cultural diversity but for the potential unification of the heritage of the country, one type of solution was suggested by the Nehruvian secularism which, with some modification, was enshrined in our

Constitution as *Sarva-dharma-sambhava* or the coexistence of all religions in the eyes of the state. A glaring inadequacy in the implementation of this policy has been that the appearance (ritualism) rather than the reality (spiritualism) of religious diversity in India has been encouraged and sponsored by the state. This has led to the unhealthy phenomenon of a tie-up between religion and politics such that the *status quoist* and recondite aspects of religious tradition (cf. the *Mandir-Masjid* issue) have gained prominence and, in the name of religion and creed, vote banks have been created. What is needed for disentangling religion from politics is a:

(a) philosophical acceptance fundamentally of the individual rather than collective freedom of religious faith and worship.

(b) following from (a), the distinguishing of spiritual from the merely ritualistic aspects of religion, and

(c) following from (a) and (b) the recognition by both the state and the voluntary agencies that religion is not only a force for cultural persistence and *status quo* but also for change and liberation. An accent on mediaeval *bhakti* tradition of India which still powerfully influences the weaker sections of society and the incorporation and welcoming of such tendencies as liberation theology in Christianity are signs in this direction. It has been rightly pointed out that a fundamental tenet of all spiritual quest for change is the mutual respect between various religions.

This brings me to the second focal aspect of culture, namely language which is seen primarily as a factor for fissiparous rather than synthesising currents in Indian society. Here it must be emphasized that a diversity of mother tongues spoken by the Indian population is a source of tremendous strength rather than weakness. The preservation of mother tongues not only makes the problem of spreading literacy much easier (cf. in Kerala); as in the biological world the ecologists have come to value the diversity and preservation of multi-form species, as students of culture we should value the preservation of linguistic and cultural diversity. A culturally homogeneous world will be an unbearably boring place to live in. It only needs a moment's reflection to appreciate how richly the diverse written and unwritten languages of the country have contributed to our cultural heritage. The experiment carried out by the *Bharatiya Jnanapitha* is a point in that direction.

Finally, we shall try to show that diverse languages far from creating tendencies for disunity will merge into a common stream. Our argument rests on the fundamental cultural discovery that Indian languages, though they may be syntactically diverse, are semantically similar. They furnish an exciting proof of the unity in diversity that is the Indian culture.

I have often been asked as to what I think of 'national integration' — what is the import of what I have said for this acute problem? I think that the whole question of 'national integration' is abstruse, primarily because of its monopolization in a politicized universe of discourse. Not the least difficult is the fact — in that political perspective — that the very idea of nation is a Western import. I think in a decentralized framework, such as I am pleading for, one may strive for the 'culturalization' of the idea of national integration.

TRIBAL RELIGIONS HISTORY

Contemporary tribal communities have a great variety and complexity in their religious beliefs and practices. However, they share one characteristic which binds them "by common understanding as to the ultimate nature and purpose of life". This ultimate purpose is "the creation of a meaningful order through imitation of the celestial model, transmitted by myths and celebrated in rituals".

The Naga tribes live in the mountains of northeast India. They believe in an earthquake god who created the earth out of the waters by earthquakes. The sons of this god now watch over mankind and punish those who do wrong. Other deities without name or form live in the mountains, forests, rivers, and lakes, who need placating as they are hostile to men. Omens and dreams are generally believed in. Witchcraft is practised and some men are thought to be able to turn into tigers. Some groups sacrifice a dog or pig when making a wood carving, otherwise the carver will become ill or die. This most likely belongs to the older tradition of only allowing a man to carve a human figure in a morung (bachelors' dormitory) when he had taken a head. Head-hunting was an important practice, for fertile crops depended on a sprinkling of blood from a stranger over the fields. Reincarnation is believed by many Naga tribes, and the dead are buried in the direction from which their ancestors have come. The doctrine of genna (tabu) involves whole social groups-villages, clans, households, age groups, sex groups, in a series of rituals that may be regularly practised or be the result of an emergency such as an earthquake. The Bhil are one of the largest tribes of western India, living in parts of Rajasthan, Gujarat, and Maharashtra. Many Bhil are Hinduised. There is a myth of descent from a tiger ancestor. The Jhabua Bhil and others believe in Bhagavan or Bholo Iswor, who is a personal supreme god. They also believe in minor deities who have shrines on hills or under trees. Worship of Bhagavan is at the settlement's central sanctuary. There is a human-oriented cult of the dead, whose main ritual is called Nukto and is practised in front of the dead person's house. Nukto purifies the spirit of the dead and unites it with Bhagavan. Gothriz Purvez is the collective ancestor. The concept of a spirit rider is important in Nukto and Gothriz Purvez accompanies the spirit on part of its journey to the afterworld.

The Todas are a small pastoral community living on the 7,000 Nilgiri Hills in South India. They believe in 1600 or 1800 superior godlike beings, the two most important being On and Teikirzi. On is the male god of Amnodr, the realm of the dead, and he created the Todas and their buffaloes. He was himself a dairyman. Teikirzi is a female deity and more important with the people, whom she once ruled when she lived in the Nilgiris and established Toda social and ceremonial laws. Most other deities are hill-gods, each associated with a particular hill. There are also two river-gods belonging to the two main rivers. Toda religion is based on the buffaloes and their milk. The temples are the dairies.

Many tribes in India show considerable syncretism with Hinduism, such as the Kadugollas of Karnataka, who worship gods such as Junjappa, Yattappa, Patappa, and Cittappa, but in reality are more devoted to Siva, who dominates their festivals and religious observances. Local deities are still of importance, though, as with the Bedanayakas of Karnataka, who worship Papanayaka, a deity supposed to have lived 300-400 years ago as a holy man among them and who performed miracles.

There is a variety of archaeological evidence from the prehistoric period, but this tells us very little of early religion. By adding evidence from physical anthropology, philology, and other sources, we can say there were unified tribal communities. Some scholars go further and suggest that the prehistoric tribal community was a "religious universe" in which all living was a religious way of life. We must not assume that there are many similarities between prehistoric and contemporary tribal communities. The eminent anthropologist Evans-Pritchard wrote that tribal communities "have just as long a history as our own, and while they are less developed than our own society in some respects they are often more developed in others".

From the 2nd millenium BCE, the tribal peoples have been increasingly dominated by the majority population, with their lands encroached on by peasant farmers. In this century industry and social planning have made inroads into the tribal lands. The result is a loss of cultural identity and Hinduisation. Tribal peoples are becoming absorbed into Hindu society at the lowest caste levels. Even the most isolated tribes are affected by this process. Cultural exchange has long been important, as with the Bhil, the Santal, and the Toda.

The Nagas remember their genealogies with great care. Stone monuments are erected in the belief that as long as the stone stands, so the family will endure, through the propitiation and aid of the dead. Such beliefs may relate to elaborate stone circles of an earlier time.

The Bhils are believed to be the Dravidian Billa (meaning 'bowman'), one of the non-Aryan tribes of India. In early Sanskrit writings they are the Pulinda and Nishada, and have been identified with the Phyllitai of Ptolemy.

The origin of the Todas has been much speculated on and it has even been suggested that they came from ancient Sumer. There are many stone circles and other megalithic monuments on the Nilgiri Hills, of which the Todas now take little interest, though these may have been erected by the older Teivaliol strata of the people who have been superceded by the pastoral Tartharol.

In the Vijayanagara period (1336-1565) the eclectic attitude towards religion resulted in the growth of folk forms of religion, whose influence still continues today, especially in the Tamil south. Gods such as Aiyanar, Karappacami, Mariamman, and Murugan have expanded into Hinduism, as has the Kerala god Aiyyappa.

Among the Nagas status symbols are displayed at major festivals and ritual dance acts out oral tradition. Woven designs are mainly geometric with a limited colour range. Animal or human forms are rare except on the bags and sashes of the Khampti. Once certain tatoos showed the wearer had taken an enemy's head. Costumes and ornaments of hair, fur, shells, cane, ivory, carved and polished wood, and monkeys' skulls are not only for aesthetic effect but possess power and each ornament is restricted to certain groups. The same object can be used on different occasions depending on the tribe, particularly male status insignia. After head-hunting ceased in the late 19th or early 20th century, wood-carving of heads (or brass versions from Hindus) was important to males, symbolising their bravery and status. Such carvings are on drinking mugs, smoking pipes, and morung pillars, and are often decorated with cloth, hair, or beads and painted black or red. They are formal in expression with faces like the dead. Carvings on the morung are for prestige and power, and include warriors, dancing couples, powerful animals, and fantastic creatures such as a tiger with two heads. Erotic motifs among the Konyak are based on the mithuna (Sanskrit: loving couple) or buffalo, symbolising wealth or fertility. The hornbill is only carved on the chief's morung. Carved effigies of the dead were formerly placed before the tomb.

Among the tribes of eastern and central India, body tatooing and painting is important. Elaborate female hair combs also appear as love-tokens for the Juang and symbols of married status among the Muduva and others. Certain ornamental materials have magical significance, such as iron and cowries as a cure for headaches and to protect from lightning. Iron objects are associated with itinerant ironworkers and cowries with Lambadi nomads, who have special power due to their marginal status. Ritual significance of animals or birds is symbolised by horned headdresses worn at festivals and dances by the Maria, and the Khondh use the beak of a hornbill. Masks of wood and terracotta can be used to ensure success in hunting or may relate to former human sacrifice. Masks are offered to Dharni Pinnu, the earth mother, by the Kuttia Kondh of Orissa, and stones symbolise her. Hinduism is lampooned by tribes in the Mandla area at the Laru Kaj ritual when someone acts as a Hindu ascetic who is offered pork and alcohol.

The Bhil offer terracotta model horses as spirit riders at small shrines on hills and under trees. Uncarved symbolic stones in the central sanctuary represent Bhagavan. From the 6th century the influence of the Rajputs has brought the image of the mounted horseman. Gothriz Purvez, the collective ancestor, is shown as a small equestrian figure made of brass with copper from the anklets of the dead man's widow. The anklets symbolise the marriage and the clan. Together with a small figure of a cow, the spirit rider is central to Nukto ritual.

Until fairly recently Toda women were tatooed in patterns of dots and circles as a sign of adulthood. A small scar or scars on a boy's wrist, elbow or under the shoulder showed that he had the status for milking buffalo. Before British rule, most jewellery was made by metalsmiths of the Kota tribe for the Todas.

Gold pendants adorned sacrificial buffalo, one being in the form of a stylized buffalo mask with plant motif at the back. This had magical power. Another elaborate buffalo adornment is of three large rosettes of hundreds of cowries sewn on black cotton cloth with gold and silver beads and silver pendants at the edges of the rosettes. This ornament is triangular and hung between the forelegs of the buffalo with one rosette attached to each horn. The triangle symbolises Thekkis, the mother goddess. Large cloaks are worn by men and women. These are made by Hindus and then embroidered by Toda women in long stripes and zigzags as well as traditional motifs.

INTEGRATED TRIBAL DEVELOPMENT AGENCY

The geographical area of ITDA, Parlakhemundi extends over an area of 3574.41 Sq. Km covering 5 Blocks namely Gumma, Rayagada, Nuagada, R.Udayagiri and Mohana of Gajapati District. The total population of the ITDA area is 288468. Of this, 196068 belongs to ST, 12589 SC and 79811 OC. Among tribals, the Saora community constitutes memorically the largest group in this ITDA area and Lanjia Saora are considered most primitive in this area.

The British Government followed a policy of Laissez faire in matter of tribal development. At first the tribal areas were administered according to the special laws such as the Ganjam and Vizagapatnam Act, 1839. Later all these areas were declared as "Scheduled Districts" and their administration was conducted in accordance with scheduled district Act, 1874. In the Govt. of India Act, 1919 these areas were removed with different degrees of exclusion such as "wholly excluded Areas" and "Areas of Modified Exclusion" which were changed in the Govt. of India Act, 1935 as "Excluded areas" and "Partially excluded areas". The tribal tracts of Orissa were declared as "Partially excluded".

The philosophy of welfare state which emerged with independence has cast a heavy responsibility on Govt. with regard to protection and advancement of scheduled tribes. The first phase of development with a specially evolved strategy was the introduction of Multipuopose Tribal Development projects in selected areas of tribal concentration in the Second Year Plan. Encouraged by the response from tribals, the tribal development was taken up by carving out of T.D Blocks in the 3rd plan, which also continued in the 4th plan period. The programme of development of T.D Block was basically the same as that of the C.D Blocks. But the schematic provision was more than double in the T.D Blocks vis-a-vis C.D Blocks. These development efforts through Blocks resulted in diffusion of activities and in increasing the gulf between tribals and non-tribals, indicating the need for more concerted and concentrated efforts. The experience thus gained resulted in starting of Tribal Development Agencies in areas of more backwardness during the 5th plan period. A serious effort was made at the commencement of the 5th plan for an integrated development approach in planning for tribals in Blocks with tribal concentration of 50 % and more which was naked as tribal sub-plan. They were constituted into viable ITDPs. Accordingly, the ITDA, Parlakhemundi was constituted.

During Medium Term Plan starting from 1978 pockets with minimum population of 10,000 having more than 50 % tribals living in contiguous areas were taken up for intensive development under "Modified Area Development Approach". Similarly, micro-projects were formed in isolated pockets for development of primitive tribes. Accordingly, the LSDA at Seranga and SDA, at Chandragiri were constituted.

The 6th paln document envisaged a major break through in the field of tribal development. The strategy for tribal development as evolved during the 5th plan had two objectives, i.e area development and economic upliftment of individual tribal beneficiaries as against the main thrust on area development till launching of the 5th plan. These 2 objectives were further revolutionized during the 6th plan in favour of development of crtical infrastructure and bringing out 50% of tribal families above the poverty line through family oriented income generating schemes. The dispute as to whether a policy of isolation or a policy of assimilation should be followed in matter or tribal development has been shelved for ever with the 5th and 6th plan objectives to bring these people on par with general population and to induct them into the National main stream in a given time.

INTEGRATED TRIBAL DEVELOPMENT AGENCY, PARALKHEMUNDI

The ITDP, Paralakhemundi was grounded on 30.06.79 as per resolution no.19149 dt.28.06.79 of erstwhile H&TW Department, Govt. of Orissa. The ITDP, Paralakhemundi was converted into ITDA in pursuance of resolution No.19155 dt. 28.06.79 of Govt. in erstwhile H&TW Department, Orissa.The ITDA, Paralakhemundi was registered as society on 30.08.79 under the Societies Registration Act of 1860 bearing registration No.15998/832 of 1979-80.

Among tribals, the Saora (Saura) community constitutes numerically the largest group in this ITDA area and Lanjia Saora is considered most primitive in this area.

ASPECTS OF SAORA CULTURE

The saoras are one of the oldest known tribes of India. They are called by various terms such as Savaras, Sabaras, Saura, Saora etc.But here the term, Saora is used uniformly as it closely approximates their language. They are widely distributed from Bundelkhand in the west to Orissa in the east. But, they are found in great compactness on the edges of the Eastern ghats in Ganjam, Gajapati and undivided Koraput districts of Orissa and Srikakulam district of Andhra Pradesh. The saoras show their racial affinity to the proto Australoid physical characters which are dominant among the aborigines of central and Southern India.

Their language is akin to the Kolarian stock which has close resemblance to the forms of speech of wild tribes of Malayan peninsula and Nicobar. Their linguistic affinity with tribes of south east suggests their migration from the islands of India Archipelago and Malayan peninsula, unless contrary is proved that India was the cradle land of the Kolana speaking tribes and south eastern countries were colonized by them.

The term 'Saora' appears to have two connotations – one derived from 'Sagoriss', the Scythian word for axe and the other from 'Saba roye', the Sanskrit term for carrying a dead body. Both of them fit well with their habits of carrying on axe always on their shoulders with their primitive occupation of hunting.

The epics and puranas refer to their devotion to the Hindu religious heroes like Rama and the Jaganath cult. The legend of Viswabasu, a Saora king who worshiped the image of Vishnu in the term of Lord Jaganath indicates the impact of Vaishnavism on the Saoras.

It is well known that, like other tribal communities, the Saoras are the indigenous, autochthons of India in the sense that they had been long settled in different parts of the country particularly on the plains and river valleys and other fertile areas. Many of the Saoras were in a food gathering economy and a few were perhaps on the threshold of a real food producing economy. On the whole, they were in all respects primitive, wild and under developed.

The hill Saoras build their small huts at the foot of the hills or on the hill slopes, where suitable plain land is available in the proximity of a hill stream. A typical Saora house is rectangular in ground plan having mainly three portions – the open front verandah, the closed back porch and in between the bedroom-cum-kitchen. The fowl pen is provided either in one of the corners of bedroom or in the back verandah and the pigsty is in the front of the house attached to the front verandah. The mud walled and grass thatched huts give a feeling of warmth and comfort. It is dark inside because no window is provided in the house. For the Saoras who spend most of their time outside in the field, ventilation is not important as the darkness is not because of privacy but because of the need for keeping the inside of the house out of sight of Ghosts and spirits and safeguarding against the evil eye.

Saora village broadly conform to a linear pattern. Each village consists of two rows of houses facing each other and separated by a long and narrow village street road. The individual houses in each row are built adjacent to one another thus forming the front verandah of all houses – continuous one from one end of the row to other.

Among the hill Saoras, the villages are situated in the most inaccessible areas that can be imagined and in most cases lie hidden in the thick forests making it most difficult to reach them except through Zig-Zag foot paths. Their settlements are not shifting. There is nothing nomadic nature in their settlement pattern. The size of the Saora village is mainly governed by the extent of hill slopes and forest land available for shifting cultivation.

The Saoras can be divided broadly into two economic classes. (1) The Saoras of the plains depending on either wet cultivation or wage earning and selling fire wood and (2) The hill Saoras practicing shifting cultivation and terraced cultivation on the hill slopes. In most cases the Saoras of the plains are subservient to the advanced section of the neighbouring non-tribal communities. They provide labour to the non-tribal land owners at the time of weeding, transplanting, harvesting and other agricultural operations and sell fire wood and leaf plates in the local markets. In all theses works women rather than men take active part and earn the major part of the family income.

The Saoras live in a world of spirits and their culture is marked with elaborate ceremonialism and ritualism. The spirits control the course of nature and human life and the need to keep them under control has given rise to numerous religious practices, magical spells and incantations, sorcery and witch crafts. Religious specialists, magicians, sorcers and shamans are there in the saora society to cater to their religious and magical needs.

A number of sketches are seen both outside and inside (which is absolutely dark the house of a Saora. These drawings are symbolic and rarely, if at all, have anthropomorphic form. Family deity (Idai soom), Sun (Eoog soom) and Moon (Angei soom) are commonly represented in these symbols. After marriage, the bride and groom sit under these ikons.Agricultural produces after first harvest of the season are also placed before these deities as offerings. The drawing of designs on walls as representatives of deities and their worship is common throughout Orissa including in Laxmipuja and undoubtedly is of pre-historic origin. The Saoras keep a record of the departing souls by placing a long sharply outlined stone at a community place near the village on 1st death anniversary. The anniversary may not fall as per calendar. On the same day the village may have a common anniversary. Big stones are used in memory of adult (Souls) and Small stones for children. The place and the custom is known as 'Guara'.

The Saoras dance during the ceremonies and marriages. men, women and children crowd over each other and dance. The dance consists of rhythmic forward and backward rockings tuned to musical beats. Musical instruments are invariably played by men. Sometimes the musician may make the dancers travel up and down a slope. The men carry sticks, arrows and bow, swords, etc. and blow whistles and make peculiar sound. The religious dances are rarely accompanied by songs except during marriage ceremony. Ofcourse, songs go a begging during leisure hours, during work or from work.

All this has generated the necessity of musical instruments. The tribal economy, fairly self context, had to make its own instruments. Some of the instruments,the Saoras make are 'Dollun' (Hemispherical drum,'Tudumn', Dagadan (Kettle drum), 'Kadigan' and 'Jaltarang' made from reeds and played with bare fingers. There are three types of string instruments called 'Gogerajan', 'Mamerajan' 'Kuranrajan' of Lanjia Saoras of serango. One stringed instrument in Mahendragiri area is made as follows: "A hemispherical copra is sliced off at the narrow end and a thin animal skin is tightly tied up. Two holes are made on the diameter side and a bamboo rod (seasoned with fire) is inserted. Pegs are fixed at both end of the rod and metallic wires are tied. The bow is made from the dried tender of salpa vine, tied to a thin lamina of bamboo. An accompanying beat instrument is made from bamboo as follows:

A hallow green bamboo about 1feet long, with two joints at both ends intact is taken and a narrow strip along the length of breadth about 3cms is removed with sharp knife. The bamboo is seasoned with fire, so that it gives a clear resonant distinct beat, when beaten with a solid thin seasoned bamboo stick along the slit. Brass instruments like horn,gong,cymbal,trumpet played by tribals are purchased from outside." The dress of Saora is simple and supplied by a person of "Damba " caste (who is also his money lender). The dress of lady consists of a waist cloth with grey borders hardly reaching the knee. Only in chilly weather, the upper portion of the body is covered. The man's dress consists of a loin cloth. A few necklaces of glass, clay, Kaincha or Gunja laced with threads or wire plastic or horn beads, wooden or metal ear rings, brass hair pins, brass rings, little rings of alae of nose, metal bangles and anklets constitute the jewellery of saoras.

Archery continues to be important for hunting, fishing, and self protection. The bow string like bow of string instruments is made from tenders of salapa vine. Most of the fishing of saoras is still done with bow and arrow, this in turn depending on keen eyesight and sharp reflexes. Craftsmanship, as the outsider understands it, is not exactly the field of excellence of saora. But, some traditional designs deserves mention (i) the oil extraction unit which is fitted to a tree and oil is extracted by the sheer weight of man sitting on it. (ii) the distillery of portable type. (iii) containers-cum- tumblers for drinks from dried gourd for salapa and from bamboo for Mahuli. (iv) A brass tumbler for drinks made with extra finishing. This one, of course, like all other brass items is made by non-tribals.

EVOLUTION OF SUITABLE STRATEGY FOR DEVELOPMENT

The British government followed a policy of Laissez- faire keeping in view the strategy of isolating the tribals from the main stream. At first the tribal areas were administered according to the special laws such as the Ganjam and Vizagpatnam Act, 1839. Later all these areas were declared as "Scheduled Districts" and their administration was conducted in accordance with scheduled District Act, 1874. In the Government of India Act, 1919 these area were removed with different degrees of exclusion such as "wholly excluded Areas" and "Area of Modified Exclusion" which were changed in the Government of India Act, 1935 as "Excluded Areas" and "Partially Excluded Areas". The tribal tracts of Orissa were declared as "partially excluded".

The policy of welfare state changed after independence has cast a heavy responsibility on the Government with regard to protection and advancement of scheduled tribes. The first phase of development with a specially evolved strategy was the introduction of multipurpose tribal development blocks in select areas of tribal concentration in the second Five Year Plan. Encouraged by the response from tribals, the tribal development was taken up by carving out of TD blocks during 3rd Five Year Plan which also continued in the 4th Five year Plan period also. The programmes of development of Tribal Development Blocks were basically the same as that of C.D. Blocks. But, the schematic provision was more than double in TD Blocks vis-a-vis C.D.Blocks. These development efforts through Blocks resulted in diffusion of activities and increased the gulf between tribals and non-tribals which high lighted the need for more concerted and concentrated effort which resulted in launching of TDAs and ITDPs in the areas of more backwardness during 5th Plan period.

A serious effort was made at the commencement of the 5th Plan for an integrated development approach in planning for tribals in Blocks with tribal concentration of 50 percent and more which was named as tribal Sub-Plan. They were constituted into viable ITDPs.During Medium Term Plan starting from 1978, pockets with minimum population of 10000 having 50 percent tribal tribals living in contiguous areas were taken up for intensive development under "Modified Area Development Approach". Similarly, micro projects were formed in isolated pockets for development of primitive tribes.

The 6th Plan document envisaged a major break-through in the field of tribal development. The strategy for tribal development as evolved during the 5th Plan had two objectives i.e. area development and economic upliftment of individual tribal beneficiaries as against the main thrust on area development till launching of the 5th Plan. These two objectives were

further revolutionalised during 6th Plan period in favour of development of critical infrastructure and bringing out 50% of tribal families above poverty line through family oriented Income Generating Schemes and raising the level of productivity in core economic sectors like Agriculture, horticulture and animal husbandry etc. The dispute as to whether a policy of isolation or a policy of assimilation should be followed in matter of tribal development has been shelved for ever with the 5th and 6th plan objectives to bring these people on par with general population and to induct them into the national main stream in a given time span. As it involve massive investment of human and natural resources, the main thrust of development would come from general sectoral programmes. As it has been decided to bring the tribal population on par with general population in a given time span, the Sub-Plan approach envisages quantification of pooled resources under various sectoral programmes for speedy development of tribal people and tribal areas.

Prior to formation of ITDA, Paralakhemundi in 1979, the TDA, Paralakhemundi was functioning since March 1972 covering 7 blocks of Paralakhemundi Sub-Division (now Gajapati District) and Tumba Agency area of Berhmpur Sub-Division (now in Ganjam District). The TDA was constituted with the assistance from Govt. of India, Ministry of Agriculture to serve as a catalyst for stimulating, fostering and promoting the developmental activities in the project area for the tribals only. The TDA programme was only additive or supplemental in nature and is not intended to replace or substitute the normal flow of funds from the State Government source for execution of various developmental schemes in the project area. The programmes implemented during TDA period were mainly related to agriculture, Irrigation and rural communication programmes. Since TDA was functioning in this area, ITDP/ITDA was not constituted, although ITDPs were formed since 1974-75 in other tribal areas of State.

At the instance of Govt. of India, it has been decided that after 30.06.79, the uniform pattern of ITDP/ITDA should be extended to the entire Sub-Plan area.

Bibliography

Bhargava B. S. : *The Criminal Tribes: A Socio-economic Study of the Principle Criminal Tribes and Castes in Northern India,* Lucknow : Universal Publishers, 1949.

Bhaumik Subir : *Insurgent Cross Fire: North-East India,* New Delhi: Lancer Publishers, 1996.

Chandra, Prakash : *Rural Development of Indian Tribes*, Discovery, Delhi, 2006.

Chowdhury S. : *Ethno Medico Botany of Arunachal Pradesh Nishi and Apatani Tribes*, BSMPS, Delhi, 1998.

Fuchs, Stephen : *The Aboriginal Tribes of India,* New York: St. Martin's Press, 1973.

Fürer-Haimendorf : *Tribes of India: The Struggle for Survival,* Berkeley: University of California Press, 1982.

Goswami B. : *Constitutional Safeguards for Scheduled Castes and Scheduled Tribes*, Rawat, Delhi, 2003.

Gupta L.P. : *Administration for Educational Development of Tribes*, Classical, Delhi, 2004.

Karma Oraon : *Dimension of Religion, Magic and Festivals of Indian Tribe : The Munda*, Kanishka, 2002.

Kishore, Kamal : *Development of Gond Tribes in Modern Perspective : A Sociological Study*, Classical Pub, Delhi, 2005.

Lal Hira : *The Tribes and Castes of the Central Provinces of India*, Low Price, Delhi, 1997.

Maharatna Arup : *Demographic Perspectives on India's Tribes*, Oxford University Press, Delhi, 2005.

Mamoria C.B. : *Tribal Demography in India*, Allahabad: Kitab Mahal, 1958.

Manilei, Serto : *Education and Social Change Among Indian Tribes : The Koms of Manipur*, Akansha Pub, Delhi, 2007.

Mehta Sonu : *Cultural Heritage of Indian Tribes*, Discovery, Delhi, 2007.

Mohanty R.P. : *Gender, Land and Land Rights: Tribes and Caste Hindus*, Abhijeet Pub, Delhi, 2010.

Mohanty, P.K. : *Encyclopaedia of Castes and Tribes in India*, Indian Pub, Delhi, 2000.

Nongbri Tiplut : *Development, Ethnicity and Gender : Select Essays on Tribes in India*, Rawat, Delhi, 2003.

Parajuli, Pramod : *Grassroots Movements and Popular Education in Jharkhand, India*, Stanford University, 1990.

Purohit Mona : *Wild Life Laws and Its Impact on Tribes*, Deep and Deep, Delhi, 2007.

Sarkar, Benoy : *Economic and Social Aspects of Crime in India*, London : George Allen and Unwin, 1934.

Sharma S.R. : *Social Change Among Tribes in India*, Manak, Delhi, 2000.

Singh S.N. : *Caste, Tribe and Religion in Indian Politics*, Shri Sai Printographers, Delhi, 2005.

Singh, K. S. : *Rural Tribal Movements in India*, New Delhi: Manohar, 1983.

Thurston Edgar : *Castes and Tribes of Southern India*, New Delhi : Cosmo Publications, 1975.

Unnithan, Benoy : *Identity Gender and Poverty : New Perspectives on Caste and Tribe*, Rawat, Delhi, 2001.

Index

R

S

T

U

V

W

❑❑❑